Command Name	Function
bg [*jobIDs*]	Puts current job or specified jobIDs in the background. Korn shell only.
cal *month year*	Displays a calendar on the standard output. *month* can be a number between 1 and 12 or enough letters to represent a unique month. *year* can be any number between 1 and 9999 (you have to include all 4 digits).
cancel *requestIDs* or cancel *printer*	Cancels a print request generated by the lp spooler.
cd *directoryname*	Changes the current working directory.
chmod *mode files*	Changes the mode of files. A file's mode controls the permissions for access associated with that file. Only the owner of a file (or the Superuser) can change its mode. See the Command Reference in Appendix A for complete details on *mode*.
cp *file1 file2*	Copies *file1* (the file to copy) to *file2* (the destination name).
date *MMDDhhmmyy*	Displays the system date and time. *MM*=the month (01-12); *DD*=the day (01-31); *hh*=the hour (00-23); *mm*=the minute (00-59); *YY*=the year (00-99), optional.
fg [*jobIDs*]	Puts current job or specified jobIDs in the foreground.
finger *users*	Displays information about users on the system. *users* can specify either an exact login name or a first or last name.
head [-*lines files*]	Prints the first few lines of a file. -*lines* specifies the number of lines to print (default=10). *files* should be a list (separated by spaces) of the files you want printed.
jobs [*jobIDs*]	Lists running or stopped jobs. Include *jobIDs* to check on specific jobs. Korn shell only.

Command Name	Function
lp [*files*]	Sends *files* to the printer.
lprint -*file*	Sends a *file* to the printer attached to the terminal.
ls [*directories*]	Lists contents of directories. If no directories are given, lists the files in the current directory.
man *command*	Displays information from the online reference manuals about *command*.
mkdir *dirname*	Creates a new directory named *dirname*.
more [*files*]	Displays the named file(s) one screen at a time. Press RETURN to get the next line or press the SPACEBAR to get the next screen.
mv *source target*	Moves or renames files or directories.
passwd	Lets you change your password.
pwd	Prints the full path name of the current working directory.
rm *files*	Removes one or more files. To remove a file, you must have write permission for the directory that contains the file. If you don't have write permission for the file itself, you'll be prompted to confirm the deletion. This can be a very dangerous command. Be careful!
rmdir *directoryname*	Removes directories. The directory has to be empty first.
sleep *seconds*	Suspends execution of a process for the number of *seconds* specified.
tail [*file*]	Lets you view the last lines of a text file. The default is the last 10 lines.
time *command*	Prints the amount of execution time, process execution time, and system time for a process. *command* is the command you want to time.

UNIX & Linux

Answers!
Certified Tech Support

Charlie Russel & Sharon Crawford

Osborne **McGraw-Hill**

Berkeley • New York • St. Louis • San Francisco
Auckland • Bogotá • Hamburg • London
Madrid • Mexico City • Milan • Montreal
New Delhi • Panama City • Paris • São Paulo
Singapore • Sydney • Tokyo • Toronto

Osborne **McGraw-Hill**
2600 Tenth Street
Berkeley, California 94710
U.S.A.

For information on translations or book distributors outside the U.S.A., or to arrange bulk purchase discounts for sales promotions, premiums, or fund-raisers, please contact Osborne/**McGraw-Hill** at the above address.

UNIX & Linux Answers!
Certified Tech Support

1234567890 AGM AGM 901987654321098

ISBN 0-07-882446-X

Publisher		**Technical Editor**	
Brandon A. Nordin		Maggie Verdier	
Editor-in-Chief		**Copy Editor**	
Scott Rogers		Gary Morris	
Acquisitions Editor		**Proofreader**	
Joanne Cutbertson		Pat Mannion	
Project Editor		**Indexer**	
Claire Splan		Rebecca Plunkett	
Editorial Assistant		**Computer Designer**	
Stephane Thomas		Jani Beckwith	

Contents @ a Glance

About the Authors

Charlie Russel is the manager of information systems at an independent software company in the health care field. Before that, he spent nearly a decade administering a UNIX and Windows NT network at a car manufacturing plant. He is the author of *ABCs of Windows NT Workstation 4* (Sybex) and co-author with Linda Gaus of *SCO OpenServer: The Windows Network Solution* (Prentice-Hall).

Sharon Crawford has been hanging around the computer publishing business for more than seven years. After stints as a technical editor and development editor, she took up writing full-time in 1993. She is the co-author of *Windows NT 4 for Dummies* (with Andy Rathbone) and has written numerous books and articles on Windows 95, OS/2, UNIX, and Windows 3.1.

Together, Sharon and Charlie have written more than a dozen books about Windows NT, Windows 95, UNIX, OS/2, Windows 3.1, and DOS. Their titles include *Running Microsoft Windows NT Server 4* (Microsoft Press), *Windows NT and UNIX Intranet Secrets* (IDG), *Upgrading to Windows 95* (Sybex), *Voodoo UNIX* (Ventana), and *OS/2 for Windows Users* (Sybex).

Contents

Acknowledgments

This book, like all good books, is a work of collaboration. Many, many people are involved in the entire process—from the original idea for the book all the way through to the actual production. Most of them never get any recognition and, sadly, that's because we never meet them or even get to know their names. They're frequently relegated to the tail end of a list of acknowledgments, if they get mentioned at all, but without them, this book would never have seen the light of day, and we're deeply grateful for their efforts. Thank you:

To Linda Gaus, a long-time friend and frequent co-conspirator who deserves our thanks and appreciation for all her help in this project. It would have never been possible without you.

To Gary L. Foster, of Sun Corp., who was instrumental in the creation of the Linux chapter, and is both a friend and valued resource for all things UNIX.

To Yasmin Kureshi—our primary support contact at The Santa Cruz Operation (SCO), who once again was simply wonderful. You *are* the best, Yasmin.

To Dion Johnson—Czar of Free Stuff at SCO—personally, for the encouragement and support, and, as a user, for all the great goodies that you've made available to the us over the years. The world is a better place for your being here.

To Brian Ziel, our primary contact into the media relations group at SCO for this project, who was extremely helpful at all times and continues to be a pleasure to work with.

To the denizens and Sysops of the SCO Forum on CompuServe—you provide a service and an environment that helps all of us enjoy UNIX more. And you have the answers to far more questions than we could begin to deal with in this book.

To Jean-Pierre Radley, one of those Sysops on CompuServe, source of many tips and much help over the years who never fails to come through. Thanks, J-P.

To Bill Campbell—one of the many folks in the UNIX and Linux communities that we first met on CompuServe, and the maintainer of an excellent source of SCO binary and source files available for anonymous ftp at ftp.celestial.com.

To David Rogelberg, our agent, who proved once again that he's someone special.

To Maggie Verdier, our tech editor, for doing an outstanding, meticulous job and being a great person to work with.

At Osborne/McGraw-Hill, several people stand out for special mention:

● Joanne Cuthbertson, the Acquisitions Editor, who convinced us to do this book and was outstanding throughout.

● Claire Splan, the Project Editor, who managed to keep all of us on our toes and who was patient, thoughtful, a pleasure to work with.

● Stephane Thomas, Editorial Assistant, who kept everything sorted out and in its place.

● Gary Morris, our Copyeditor, who was both accurate and tolerant, a rare combination.

● Pat Mannion, the Proofreader, who did an excellent job.

● And the Production staff, including Marcela Hancik, Jani Beckwith, Roberta Steele, Lance Ravella, and Mickey Galicia, without whom this book would never have made it to your hands.

Introduction

The title of this book, *UNIX & Linux Answers!*, describes what anyone who uses UNIX or Linux can really use. Despite its power and flexibility, UNIX has a reputation for being cryptic (deserved) and hard to use (mostly undeserved). So here are the answers to the questions you'll find yourself asking whether you've been using UNIX ever since you can remember or you've just started.

WHO NEEDS THIS BOOK?

This is a book for the UNIX user who wants to work better, faster, and more efficiently. We've aimed our text at both experienced and novice users. Entries are short and to the point—no throat-clearing, no filler, just substance. You can pick up the book, read a paragraph, try it out, and come away with something helpful. We've collected tips and tricks of the trade that UNIX gurus use all the time—but you don't have to be a guru to master them.

Whether you're using UNIX because you love it or because it's your company's idea, you know that the UNIX universe is a vast one—bigger than any one person can ever master. But even if complete mastery is not your aim (at least not right now), you'll find a lot in this book to like.

WHAT THIS BOOK COVERS

What we want to do in this book is to help you "grow" your UNIX knowledge. We try to show new ways to use some commands you probably already use, and add some new commands to your everyday repertoire. We hope you'll take what's here and use it as the kernel for stretching your skills. Because that's what UNIX is really all about. The more you use UNIX, the more skills you'll develop and discover.

We've tried to organize this book in a reasonable way—sort of in the order you'd be learning UNIX if you were a newcomer. But you can use it in any order you like.

Chapter 1 presents the top ten FAQs (frequently asked questions) about UNIX. Here you'll learn the answers to the UNIX questions that everyone (whether newcomer or expert) is asking.

Chapter 2 gives you an introduction to and overview of UNIX, as well as all-important procedures for logging on and getting going. You'll find out about ways to set up your terminal and map keys to suit the way you work. You'll also find smart ways to pick a secure password and keep it private.

Chapter 3 shares shortcuts for navigating the UNIX filesystem and directory structures—how to name files, find strays, and move around your directories with maximum efficiency.

Chapter 4 concentrates on **vi**, the fabulous, flexible (though just a bit intimidating) text editor that comes with virtually all versions of UNIX. You'll find lots of clever ways to make your text editing go faster.

Chapter 5 gives you good ideas for customizing your work environment. Because UNIX, in general, is a rather drab-looking environment, this chapter takes on the tasks of beautifying your computer while making it more efficient. Prompts and colors and other decorative arts are covered with handy shortcuts. If you have to switch from DOS to UNIX and back again, you'll particularly appreciate the section on making painless transitions.

Chapter 6 is all about printing. Printing can present a complex series of problems in a UNIX environment. This chapter gives you the information you need to produce your print jobs expeditiously. Because you're likely to be on a network, you'll also learn how to share a printer and not step on toes.

Chapter 7 is full of tips on running your programs in the most efficient manner. There are shortcuts and insights that can help you every day—such as how to run foreground and background operations and when to use both.

Chapter 8 has all the cool stuff about the graphical user interface X Windows. You'll learn about fonts, training your mouse, and how to configure the X Windows environment to suit the way you work. This chapter also includes descriptions of many of the handy little (and not so little) programs that come with X Windows, and tips on which ones to ignore.

Chapter 9 takes you through the tools of your trade—tools that will make your life easier. You can turn to any page in this chapter and find secrets of the UNIX gurus that you can put to use at once. There are tools to help you navigate as well as manipulate files with ease. This chapter alone can double your arsenal of UNIX shortcuts and tricks.

Chapter 10 focuses on connecting to other computers. UNIX is the language of connectivity, and to get connected you need to know the magic words to send out in order to get replies. Chapter 10 also gives you useful information on network etiquette (or netiquette, as it's known).

Chapter 11 fills you in on the details of how to integrate UNIX and NT seamlessly on your network. You'll learn how to make UNIX and NT machines "talk" to each other, how to make your UNIX server function as part of an NT domain or workgroup, and much more.

Chapter 12 will show you how to avoid the UNIX mine fields that are waiting for the uninitiated. You'll see why UNIX can be not only a stimulating place to work but a dangerous one as well because it has no built-in security devices. This chapter gives you information that's hard to find anywhere else on keeping your UNIX environment safe. Included are ingenious and, best of all, *easy* ways to keep your work secure.

Chapter 13 shares some secrets of the Korn shell with you. You'll learn about variables and parameters, how the Korn shell does math, how it handles string operators, what predefined variables it offers you, and, last but not least, the ins and outs of flow control in Korn shell programs.

Chapter 14 introduces you to Linux, perhaps the most popular low-cost version of UNIX available today. This chapter includes Linux basics, as well as information about keyboard and password security issues and the availability of shells, text editors, and X Windows for Linux users.

Chapter 15 moves you forward to a more advanced level. Here we take you into some of the structure and programming constructs of the Korn shell—including tidbits about awk, perl, and sed—that can make you look like an expert, streamline your tasks, and impress others.

This book also has appendixes that include a glossary, command reference, and resource guide, which should help you if (or, more likely, when) you get stuck. Don't forget about the appendixes because you never know when they might come in handy!

STANDARD CONVENTIONS

It's probably helpful if you know exactly what the conventions that we've used in the book are, so here goes:

- **boldface** is used for UNIX terms and commands, as well as for user input.
- *italics* provide emphasis and highlight important terms.
- SMALL CAPS indicate keypresses.
- `Courier font` is used to separate lines of code from plain old text.

SPECIAL FEATURES

This book also includes some special features that you should know about, namely the @ a Glance sections, which provide an overview of each chapter; sidebars, which contain in-depth answers to questions raised elsewhere in a given chapter; and notes, tips, and warnings, which present brief asides and opinions relevant to the question at hand.

YOUR FAVORITE TRICK

Most of the tricks, tips, and warnings used in this book came out of experience and luck (both good and bad). But because UNIX is made up of hundreds of commands that can be combined in millions of ways, we're sure there are some truly cool tips we don't know about. You can imagine how annoying *that* thought can be! So if you have a trick— whether it's neat and clean, down and dirty, or sneaky and underhanded, we'd love to hear about it.

You can snail mail to Osborne/McGraw-Hill, 2600 Tenth Street, Berkeley, CA 94710. Or better yet, send e-mail to us at this address: UnixAnswers@scribes.com. Actually we'd love to get mail from you even if you don't have a tip, just to hear how you like the book.

Chapter 1

Top 10 Frequently Asked Questions

Answer Topics!

Top 10 FAQS @ a Glance

This chapter covers the ten most frequently asked questions about UNIX and Linux, including such crucial topics as:

- Logging on
- Cancelling a print job
- Protecting yourself from disaster, including a slick way to rename the **remove** command
- Understanding the rules for valid filenames
- And more

1. How do I log on and get going?

When you look at your UNIX terminal, you're presented with the login screen. This can be a cute graphical box with places for you to type in your username and password, or a simple

```
login:
```

In either case, type in your username and press the ENTER or RETURN key, whichever your system has. Next, enter your password, and we can get down to business.

Just a short aside here. Why, you might ask, should I have to go through this every single time I want to use the computer? Well, since UNIX is designed to be a multiuser operating system, it imposes certain security restrictions to protect you and your work from inadvertent or deliberate mischief. One of these security restrictions is that you have to have an "account" on the system before you can use it. And, so that only you can use your account, you have to have a password as well.

When you first log into a UNIX system, you will see a variety of miscellaneous stuff, most of which you don't care about at all. If you are at a text terminal, you will probably see a lengthy copyright notice go scrolling by, and a bunch of other things. Pay no attention. Finally, you may be asked what kind of terminal you're on. Chances are good you can just take whatever the default is and get down to your business. But if you see a bunch of funny stuff on your screen, or the keyboard seems to be behaving peculiarly, it's a good bet that something went wrong somewhere and the default is not going to be good enough.

2. How long can a UNIX filename be and what characters can it include?

UNIX filenames are much more flexible than, say, DOS filenames. At the very least, they can be 14 characters long on even the oldest systems, and these days most UNIX systems will support a file called **reallyridiculouslylong-andcomplex.filename**. But that is probably not a particularly useful filename. The only hard and fast rule for filenames is that they can include any character except a slash (/).

3. What is a good UNIX filename?

Realistically, you should probably limit your filenames to the following:

- alphanumeric characters
- underscores
- periods

Other characters may work on your version of UNIX, but may not translate very well to other systems.

4. How can I change a file's mode or permissions?

Use **chmod**. This command, which is short for "change mode," lets you easily change any file you own so that only those people you authorize can read it, change it, or execute it. There are three basic levels of users, as we saw above: the owner (user) of the file, the owner's group, and everyone else (others). And there are three levels of permissions: read, write, and execute. The types of users are abbreviated "u" for user, "g" for the owner's group, and "o" for all those other people out there, and "a" for everyone. The permissions are abbreviated the same as in the long listing above: "r" for read, "w" for write, and "x" for execute. So, to change the permission of the file **harold.cat** to allow users outside the in-group to read it, type in

```
chmod o+r harold.cat
```

The **chmod** command will let you make multiple changes to several files at once, so it is pretty easy to remove write permission from everyone and remove all permissions from those not in your group for all the **.cat** files:

```
chmod a-w,o-rx *.cat
```

5. How can I move quickly between frequently used directories?

If you have a directory you're using all the time, assign the path to that directory to a variable, and then export the variable so that it's always available. Make a simple alias to take advantage of the variable to move to it. For example, let's say you're working on a project with the new model group and you need to quickly move to the project's working directory, /users/shared/projects/newmodel/colormatch. That's a real handful, and not something you want to type every time! So, try this:

```
PHOME=/users/shared/projects/newmodel/colormatch
export PHOME
alias goproj=cd $PHOME
```

Include this in your **.kshrc** file, and it will be available whenever you need it. The best part is, if you change to a different project, all you do is change the variable. Your fingers can continue to use the same command.

6. Is there a command I can use to return quickly to my home directory?

Yes; try **cd** all by itself. This little trick will get you back to your home directory quickly, no matter how far away you have managed to stray.

? 7. Is there a way I can cancel a print job?

Quick! Use the **cancel** command to halt the print job you just sent. This command has the form

```
cancel [request-id|printer]
```

which means that you can cancel a job by specifying either the requestid or the printer; in the latter case this will cancel the job on that printer. Note that you can only cancel a print job that you created. To cancel someone else's print job requires (ta-da!) the superuser.

? 8. What can the more command do for me?

The **more** command lets you look through a file a page at a time. You can use **/regexp** to jump ahead in the file by searching for the regular expression, but you can't search backwards. There are other, more flexible, paging programs around, however, so if you find yourself frustrated by the limitation of **more,** ask your system administrator to get a copy of **less** for your system. This little program lets you page back and forth through the file, and is quite a bit handier than **more.** Or get in the habit of using **vi** in its read-only form, **view,** as a substitute.

? 9. Is it wise to create an alias for the rm command?

This is a touchy one. Some purists feel strongly that you shouldn't alias any of UNIX's built-in commands, while others do it all the time. We tend to think it's a bad practice if carried to the extreme, but in some cases it can be a lifesaver. For example, if you want to add an additional layer of protection, this is one way to do it. Try adding the following to your **.kshrc** file:

```
alias rm='rm -i'
```

Now, whenever you go to remove a file, you will be prompted for confirmation. The problem with this approach is that it can get pretty annoying if you have a bunch of files to remove and you're really sure you want to remove them. Under those conditions, you can get careless about the

removal, answering "y" to the prompt without really reading it. A better solution is to move the files out of the way temporarily, and only remove them when they are old enough that you are sure that you want to get rid of them.

10. What's the best way to protect my data against accidental erasure?

Backup, backup, backup. Absolutely nothing beats a *verified* backup when disaster strikes. The person with the primary responsibility for backups is the system administrator, but everyone who works with computers needs to take responsibility for backups of his or her own critical files. This isn't hard, it need not be onerous, and it can be a lifesaver. Read about the various UNIX backup options and how to take advantage of them in Chapter 12.

Chapter 2

Getting a Grip on UNIX

Answer Topics!

Getting a Grip on UNIX @ a Glance

To get a grip on UNIX, you might think the right place to start would be at the beginning with installation instructions. However, installing UNIX is an arcane art form—best left to those who do it for a living. Each version of UNIX (and there are zillions of them) has its own peculiarities and quirks, and each version requires an intimate knowledge of the hardware and software of both the actual machine it's being installed on and any other machines that it may be connected to. In other words, it's the special job of that most holy of holies, the "superuser" or system administrator. This book is not written for them, but for you, a person who works on a UNIX computer and wants to be better, faster, and more efficient. But even if you're a beginner, you'll still find plenty of useful information here.

What makes a UNIX computer unique? Most of us know pretty much what to expect from a DOS computer. It'll have one or two floppy drives, a keyboard, a monitor, an actual computer box, and maybe a few other things. You sit down at it and start working. You can usually figure that you're the only person working on it while you're sitting there, even if you're connected to a network. Not so with UNIX.

With UNIX, you may be sitting at a simple terminal, not much more than a screen and a keyboard, nothing but ugly text on the screen and no apparent computer anywhere around. Or you could be sitting in front of a beautiful, high resolution graphics screen with a powerful workstation standing alongside your desk. Or it could be some combination in between. And in virtually all cases, there's a very good likelihood that you're sharing the computer with other users. They may be in the same room, or on the other side of the world.

So, with all those differences, how can you reasonably expect this, or any other book, to apply to you? Not to worry! Even though there are lots of differences in the different flavors of UNIX, and the different machinery that it runs on, there are even more similarities. This book will focus on those similarities—where almost all the work is done anyway.

FIRST THINGS FIRST

? **Why does UNIX have a reputation as being an enigmatic, difficult and thoroughly nerdish operating system, and is this reputation justified?**

UNIX's reputation is based on the perception that, in order to use it, one must spend hours staring at a bare and unforgiving command line, typing cryptic sequences that only a computer could love. While this was once the case, UNIX has come a long way in recent years. There are now versions of UNIX that feature GUIs (Graphical User Interfaces) and even that bare command line is becoming more forgiving. These days, it's safe to say that the reports of UNIX's difficulty are greatly exaggerated.

? **Even if its reputation is often overstated, why would anyone in his or her right mind want to use UNIX?**

Because it's a powerful, stable and remarkably flexible operating system that, once you know some of its magic, can be a productive and even friendly environment. The goal here is to give you the tools and tricks to set your UNIX environment up the way you want it.

This book is not really designed for the rank beginner with UNIX. In most places, we assume at least a minimal familiarity with UNIX and with computers. We will deviate from that just a bit in this chapter, to make sure we are all on the same wavelength, so if this is all boring stuff, just bear with us a bit, or simply skip over what you already know.

? **Who developed UNIX and when?**

UNIX was developed at the Bell Labs, starting in the late 1960s, by many of the same people who created the C programming language (so now you know who to blame). In fact, they helped to drive and shape each other's design and implementation.

The idea was to create an operating system whose *kernel* (or core part) was as tiny as possible. The main driving force behind the small UNIX kernel was the fact that the developers were doing their work on what were, even by the standards of those days, tiny computers. The first kernel was implemented on a tiny DEC PDP-7. Eventually, they were able to obtain a new PDP-11 that had a total of 24K of RAM, of which the kernel took only 11K. This severe limitation on the amount of RAM resulted in a small, tight kernel with all the utilities implemented as separate, stand-alone programs. Each was itself tiny, and designed to accept input from the preceding program as well as provide output to succeeding programs. A setup like this, where the standard output from one program is accepted as the standard input for another, is called *piping*. It's a powerful concept and is central to UNIX today. It's also influenced all the operating systems that have followed it.

How do I log on and get going?

When you look at your UNIX terminal, you're presented with the login screen. This can be a cute graphical box with places for you to type in your user name and password, or a simple

```
login:
```

In either case, type in your user name and press the ENTER or RETURN key, whichever your system has. Next enter your password, and we can get down to business.

Just a short aside here. Why, you might ask, should I have to go through this every single time I want to use the computer? Well, since UNIX is designed to be a multiuser operating system, it imposes certain security restrictions to protect you and your work from inadvertent or deliberate mischief. One of these security restrictions is that you have to have an "account" on the system before you can use it. And, so that only you can use your account, you have to have a password as well.

When you first log in to a UNIX system, you will see a variety of miscellaneous stuff, most of which you don't care about at all. If you are at a text terminal, you will probably see a lengthy copyright notice go scrolling by, and a bunch of other stuff. Pay no attention. Finally, you may be asked what kind of terminal you're on. Chances are good you can just take whatever the default is and get down to your business. But if you see a bunch of funny stuff on your screen, or the keyboard seems to be behaving peculiarly, it's a good bet that something went wrong somewhere and the default is not going to be good enough.

TERMINAL SETTINGS

? How can I set the terminal type at login?

The first thing you need to know is what kind of terminal you have. Sometimes this is easy—if you're at a Hewlett-Packard workstation, for example, chances are pretty good you have a "hp" terminal type. If you're using a personal computer and SCO UNIX, "ansi" is a good bet, and on a PC with a communications program to log into a remote system, your best bet is probably a "vt100". Almost every communications program will be able to emulate that. So, how to set it up? Easy. Just add the following line to your **.profile** file (if you're running the Korn or Bourne shell):

```
eval `tset -m hp:\?hp -s -e -k -Q`
```

In a nutshell, this line uses the UNIX terminal setup command (**tset**) to select the appropriate terminal type and set the erase and kill characters for your terminal.

For those of you running the C shell, this operation is a little trickier. Add the following to your **.login** file:

```
set noglob
set term=(`tset -m hp:\?hp -s -e -k -Q`)
unset noglob term
```

The extra commands in this version just ensure that the **tset** command will be read correctly. All of the above, of course, assumes a default terminal type of "hp", which is nice if that's what you have. If your usual terminal type is something else, just substitute it for the "hp" accordingly.

? How can I check my terminal settings?

To find out what your current terminal settings are, type this:

```
stty -a
```

As you can see in Figure 2-1, this will give you more information about your current terminal settings than you are likely to ever want or need.

```
                                     xterm
$ stty -a
speed 9600 baud;    ispeed 9600 baud;    ospeed 9600 baud;    line = 0(tty);
rows = 24; columns = 80; ypixels = 364; xpixels = 724;
intr = DEL; quit = ^\; erase = ^H; kill = ^U; eof = ^D; eol = ^@;
swtch = ^@; susp = <undef>; start = ^Q; stop = ^S;
parenb -parodd cs5 -cstopb hupcl -cread -clocal -loblk
-ortsfl -ctsflow -rtsflow
-ignbrk -brkint -ignpar -parmrk -inpck -istrip -inlcr -igncr icrnl -iuclc
ixon -ixany -ixoff
isig icanon -xcase echo echoe echok -echonl -noflsh
-iexten -tostop -xclude
opost -olcuc onlcr -ocrnl -onocr -onlret -ofill -ofdel
-isscancode
$ ▆
```

Figure 2-1   The impressive output from using the **stty -a** command

How can I set terminal control characters?

Terminal control characters determine which special keys do what. You probably want to set these automatically every time you log on to the system using the **stty** command since this will ensure that they will mean what you think they mean. Table 2-1 shows you some of the standard control characters and what they mean. You can change these to other characters if you want. Many people, for example, map the kill key to CTRL-X.

To set these, use the **stty** command. Set just the ones you want to change or want to make absolutely sure are what you expect them to be. Then include the line in your **.profile** or **.login** file. I use the following:

```
stty erase "^H" intr "^C" kill "^U"
```

Name	Character	Function
erase	CTRL-H	Erases the previous character (Backspace)
kill	CTRL-U	Erases or discards the current line
eof	CTRL-D	End of File—ends the program or shell
swtch	CTRL-Z	Suspends the current program
intr	CTRL-C	Interrupts the current program or operation
quit	CTRL-\	Kills the current program, writing a core file

Table 2-1   Special Terminal Control Characters

Can I set the erase function to the DEL key instead of CTRL-H?

Yes. To do this, type **stty**, then a space, then **erase**, then a space, then CTRL-V, then the DEL key. However, the key combinations in Table 2-1 are by far the most common.

How can I fix my keyboard when I log in from a PC?

When you log in to your UNIX network from a PC, sometimes the version of telnet that's running on your PC doesn't re-map the BACKSPACE key properly. You'll think you have backspaced over a command, but when you press ENTER, you will find there are a bunch of control characters embedded in your command. So, change the setting yourself by typing in the following: **stty erase** followed by a space, then CTRL-V, then the BACKSPACE key, then the ENTER key. The result on screen will probably look like this:

```
stty erase ^?
```

Now the BACKSPACE key will behave normally. The CTRL-V key combination causes UNIX to read the next keystroke without performing the action.

How can I put a little sanity back into my terminal when things go haywire?

What if you got a little carried away with the **stty** command, or worse, your terminal settings got seriously messed up by a *program* that got carried away? To get back to reality, try the following:

```
stty sane
```

If your keystrokes are getting really wild try entering the command bracketed by **<ctrl+j>**. Enter the **<ctrl+j>** sequence by holding down the CTRL key and pressing the J key.

```
<ctrl+j>stty sane<ctrl+j>
```

This command won't get your preferred settings back, but it will get rid of any truly bizarre settings. Exactly what settings appear will vary depending on the system you're on, but it'll be cleaned up enough so you can at least type characters into the terminal and see the results. From here, you can reset things to the key combinations you prefer.

SHELLS, PASSWORDS, AND HELP

? What is a shell?

Many users think that what they see at the bare UNIX command line is the actual operating system, but it's really a command interpreter, called a *shell*. This shell is a program that sits between the user and the underlying kernel of the operating system. Its purpose is to protect the user from the kernel and, perhaps even more importantly, to protect the kernel from the user. In the MS-DOS world, this shell is called COMMAND.COM, which is, in turn, often surrounded by other shells such as DOSSHELL or the ultimate DOS shell, Microsoft Windows.

In the UNIX world, you have a choice of shells. The oldest of the shells currently in use is **sh** and is called the Bourne shell. The Bourne shell is available on all UNIX systems. For the interactive user, it lacks some critical features, like job control, but it provides a good base for writing most shell programs.

Until recently, the most popular shell for the interactive user was **csh**, the C shell. Originally developed at the University of California at Berkeley as part of their UNIX implementation, it has many features for the interactive user, including the ability to recall commands previously used, as well as the ability to move jobs from the foreground to the background and back again (job control). As the name implies, it has a syntax and command structure that's modeled after the C programming language, making it particularly popular with programmers. Most versions of UNIX will have the C shell available.

A more recent addition to the shell game, and possibly the most popular today is **ksh**, the Korn shell. Named for its creator, David Korn, this shell is fully compatible with the Bourne shell but adds most of the features that made the C shell so popular, plus some completely new goodies. One of the most important of these is the ability to not merely recall an old command, but to actually edit it. While the Korn shell is not available on some older versions of UNIX, it's becoming a standard part of most newer versions. In this book, we'll mostly be using the Korn shell, unless the C shell or Bourne shell is specified. The Posix shell, a close relative of the Korn shell, is rapidly becoming an important and widely available shell on many platforms. Since it behaves very much like the Korn shell, you should be able to use anything we suggest in this book on either.

❓ How can I tell which shell I'm using?

If your command line begins with % you're using the C shell. The more worldly $ indicates the Posix, Korn, or Bourne shell.

❓ How can I find out which shell is my default shell?

From the command line, type:

```
grep yourloginname /etc/passwd
```

If that comes back with nothing, you are probably on a system that uses Sun's Network Information Service (NIS) to manage network-wide files. If so, try this:

```
ypcat passwd | grep yourloginname
```

By one method or the other, you'll see the line in the system password file that controls your account. It will look something like the following illustration. The various fields are separated by colons, with the last field showing the shell.

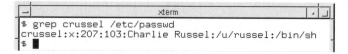

The rest of the fields from the left are the login name, your password (this will either be encrypted or, as on Sun, show an "x" or, as on AIX, show a "!", indicating that the password is stored in a separate file), your userid, your group id, a comment field which may contain such information as your real name and phone number, your home directory, and finally your default shell.

❓ Why does UNIX bother with passwords?

When you login, UNIX needs a way to know that you really are who you say you are. So, besides your login name, your account has a unique password associated with it. Your password is the most important protection you have against inadvertent or deliberate mischief that could cause you to lose files, or worse. Don't give your password to anyone, don't write it on your terminal or desk, and don't use anything obvious.

Of course by now you've heard all this before, but you should protect your password at *least* as well as you would your VISA card. An unscrupulous person who learns your password can cause you an incredible amount of grief.

+ ***Tip:*** *If you really need to write down your password, use some common sense. Don't put it anywhere near your terminal or on your desk. Keep it in your wallet. Write it down somewhere you can find it, but where it won't mean anything to someone who gets hold of it. And don't write the name of the computer or your login name in the same place as the password.*

? What are some examples of bad passwords?

Bad passwords are anything that could easily be guessed, such as the following:

- your login name
- your name or nickname
- your spouse's, child's, or parent's name
- your pet's name
- your license plate
- your social security number
- any of the above, reversed
- common swear words or combinations of them
- "wizard," "guru," or any similar sort of description

? Are there rules for good passwords?

In general, good passwords are those that can be easily remembered, but that don't lend themselves to being easily guessed. They should:

- be mixed uppercase and lowercase
- be pronounceable
- contain both alphabetic and non-alphabetic characters
- be six to eight characters long
- be easily typed

An example might be something like "Moon4you". It uses two short words, with a number separating them. Another good example might be an acronym that is special to you, if it isn't something easily guessed. Something like "OhiHacp" (Oh, how I hate all computer programmers).

How can I change my password?

You can easily change your own password at any time, and you should always do this immediately if you suspect that someone may know your old one. It's probably a good idea to change your password periodically, regardless. To change it, simply type:

```
passwd
```

You will be prompted first to enter your old password, then to type your new one. Finally you will be prompted to re-type your new password. If the two don't match, you will need to start over. *Remember your new password.* If you forget it, you will have to get your system administrator to give you a new one. The first time this happens, s/he will probably be fairly understanding. After the first time, the system administrator will either be seriously annoyed with you or, worse, make fun of you unmercifully and publicly.

 Tip: *Check your new password immediately after you change it. If you wait, and somehow mistype it twice, you won't be able to log in to your account. Inevitably, you will discover this only when you are in the midst of a crisis. So check it now, while you're logged in and have the chance to get it sorted out.*

? What can I do if I need help with UNIX?

UNIX comes with its own help system, and it is a good one. The entire UNIX manual set that takes up about a foot of your system administrator's bookshelf is available online. For example, to get help on the **cp** (copy) command, simply type:

```
man cp
```

which will give you several pages of information about the **cp** command. One of those pages is shown in Figure 2-2.

There are a couple of things to be aware of with the **man** command. It'll return the first entry in the online manual that matches the request, so if the command is one of those that appears in more than one of the manual volumes (usually numbered from one to eight), then you may not get quite the answer you are looking for. Usually this isn't a problem, since all the "normal" user commands are in the

```
─                                    xterm                              · ⌐
$ man cp
 cp(C)
 *****

 _____
 cp -- copy files

 Syntax
 ======

 cp [ -fip ] source_file target_file

 cp [ -fip ] source_file1 source_file2 ... target

 cp -R [ -fip ] source_file1 source_file2 ... target

 cp -r [ -fip ] source_file1 source_file2 ... target

 Description
 ===========

 cp copies files from a source to a destination.

 In the first form, when source_file and target_file are not directories, the
 :█
```

Figure 2-2   Help with the **cp** command

first volume of the manual set. If you know, however, that you need help from a particular volume, you can specify the volume on the command line. For example, a system administrator might well want to know a bit more about the **passwd** command than an ordinary user would. But the extra information is in Volume 1A of most manuals. So, to get that information, s/he would type:

```
man 1A passwd
```

which would skip over the more limited help for the **passwd** command, which is in Section 1 of the manuals, and go directly to the manual entry in Section 1A, which is for system administrators.

Tip: *Some versions of UNIX let you get all the manual pages with a single command. In SCO UNIX, for example, you can type:*

```
man -a passwd
```

*and get information on both the standard **passwd** command, and the extra help that's available to system administrators. So check your system to see what switches you can add to the **man** command to make it work better for you. To do this, use the **man** command on itself!*

```
man man
```

Note: *Manuals, even online manuals, will only get you so far. Sometimes they just aren't enough. When all else fails it's time to call your system administrator. This mighty and all-powerful person, who also goes by the names "superuser" and "root," is the one to go to when you have tried all other avenues of help and are desperate. S/he has the power to give you new passwords, or to log on to your account and fix things you have broken so totally that you can no longer log on to fix them yourself. S/he is generally the repository of a vast, though by no means limitless, storehouse of knowledge and tips about how your particular UNIX system works. For your own sake, be sure you always treat this person well!*

Chapter 3

Files and Directories

Answer Topics!

Files and Directories @ a Glance

UNIX **files and filenames** require some explanation, particularly for anyone who has never worked in a UNIX environment before. In order to work efficiently with UNIX, it's helpful to know how long UNIX filenames can be, what characters they can contain, and what the characteristics of a good filename are. You should know how to unhide hidden files, how to determine a file's type, and above all, the importance of case-sensitivity in the UNIX world.

Characters in UNIX sometimes seem to take on a life of their own. You'll want to know how to deal with embedded spaces or weird characters in filenames, and how a shell script can save you a lot of time by automating the renaming of multiple files.

Another UNIX time-saver is **wildcards**. Using multiple wildcards within a single command or using a wildcard set description to make the command line more intelligent will increase your productivity.

It's crucial to understand UNIX **file permissions and protection** if you're working in the UNIX world, since the way a file's permissions are set determines who may have what kind of access to that file. Especially if you're sharing a file or directory with a group of people, there are some timesaving tips that can save you considerable frustration.

You don't have to comprehend every facet of UNIX **filesystems and directory structures** unless you're the system administrator, but you'll be better off if you grasp at least a few basic concepts and if you know what's in your home directory and how to keep it lean and mean.

21

Finding lost files is something everyone has to do at some point. You can find files a number of different ways, depending on what you remember about them. Here you'll learn how to use everything you know about a file to find it as quickly as possible.

UNIX navigation can be clumsy unless you're aware of some clever **shortcuts** that can take you **to where you want to be**. Rather than typing in endless file, directory, and path names, you can use these tricks to get where you need to go as quickly as possible.

FILES AND FILENAMES

❓ How long can a UNIX filename be and what characters can it include?

UNIX filenames are much more flexible than, say, DOS filenames. At the very least, they can be 14 characters long on even the oldest systems, and these days most UNIX systems will support a file called **reallyridiculouslylongandcomplex.filename**. But that is probably not a really useful filename. The only hard and fast rule for filenames is that the filename can include any character except a slash (/).

❓ What is a good UNIX filename?

Realistically, you should probably limit your filenames to the following:

- alphanumeric characters
- underscores
- periods

Other characters may work on your version of UNIX, but may not translate very well to other systems.

❓ Can I unhide hidden files and directories?

Files that have names beginning with a period are called "dot files" and are hidden. Actually, they're not very well hidden, but an ordinary **ls** command will not show them. You can "hide" directories the same way. In fact, many programs will create a raft of hidden files and directories in the hope that you'll leave these files alone.

If you'd like to experiment with unhiding hidden files and directories, try the following, which works equally well with either the C shell or Korn shell.

```
alias la="ls -aF"
```

Then use **la** instead of **ls**, and you will see all the files, including the hidden ones. The difference is shown here:

```
$ ls
Charlies
Main.dt
Personal.dt
tmp
trash.dt
$ alias la="ls -aF"
$ la
./
../
.lastlogin
.odtpref/
.profile
.scoadmin.pref
.sh
.sh_history
.xdt_dir/
Charlies/
Main.dt
Personal.dt
tmp/
trash.dt
$ ▮
```

As you can see, there's a lot more useful information shown by the **la** command we just created than by the ordinary **ls** command. If your system supports it (and most do), you can change the **-aF** to a **-AF** and get rid of the dot and dot-dot ("**.**" and "**..**") from the listing.

❓ What if I'd like to know a file's type in addition to its name?

That's actually a little trick I snuck in above just to see if you're paying attention. The **-F** option to the **ls** command tells UNIX that you want to know the file type as well as the filename. If the file is executable, it gets a * after the name; if it's a symbolic link to another file, it gets a @ after the filename; and if it's a directory, it gets the slash after it.

? Are all UNIX filenames and commands case-sensitive?

Yes. You've probably already found out that **Charlie.txt** and **charlie.txt** are not the same file at all. So you can guess that it's not a good idea to get in the habit of distinguishing two files solely by a difference in capitalization. For one thing, if you regularly copy files from your UNIX system to other systems, like DOS or VMS machines, these two files will end up having the same name on the other system. For another thing, what makes you so sure *you'll* be able to remember which **Charlie.txt** is which? You can waste a lot of time opening the wrong files.

CHARACTERS

? Does UNIX let me do things I really shouldn't do?

Yes. This is but one more example of its essentially programmer-oriented roots. The assumption is that you know what you're doing, and really *mean* to do what you just did. Which is all well and good, but of course there's a potential for serious problems when you don't understand all the possible consequences.

For example, DOS is pretty restrictive about what it will let you include as an acceptable character in a filename. You're not allowed to create a filename with embedded spaces, or weird unprintable characters. (Well, actually you can, but it's tricky and difficult, to say the least, and there isn't any ordinary way to do it.) UNIX, on the other hand, makes it all too easy to do this trick. But do you really *want* to have embedded spaces and weird characters in your filenames? Probably not. It just makes it a pain to copy, move, delete, or otherwise do much with files that include such stuff, and it's by no means a foolproof way to protect them. So all it really does is make it a nuisance for you, while not providing any real security.

❓ How can I remove embedded spaces from a filename?

Just enclose the filename in quotes, and replace the blank space with an underscore. For this we will use the **mv** command, which is UNIX for both move and rename.

```
mv "file name" file_name
```

This will handle simple embedded spaces.

❓ But what if someone has managed to insert a weird character into a filename that *isn't* a space but looks like one to me?

Well, here's where we can use a wildcard to substitute for that weird character. I'll talk more about wildcards shortly, but for now you can use a question mark (?) to substitute for any single character in a UNIX filename. So we could solve the problem above, a filename with an embedded space, but this solution goes beyond the quote trick, since it works even if we don't know what character is buried in the filename.

```
mv file?name file_name
```

Well, that looks pretty good. But what happens if there are a whole bunch of them?

❓ Is there a way I can change the names of a series of filenames?

As most everyone who has used UNIX for any length of time has discovered, you can't use wildcards to **mv** a set of files to new names. Frustrating, isn't it? Heck, even lowly DOS lets you do *that*. Well, there are lots of ways to get there, including some really slick perl scripts. We'll touch on perl at the end of the book, in Chapter 15. But here's a simple little shell script that will automate the process of renaming a bunch of files, prompting you for a new name for each matching file:

```
# !bin/sh
#    Bourne shell script to rename files, interactively
for fname
do
        echo -n "Enter new name for '$fname':    "
        read newfname
        mv "$fname" "$newfname"
done
```

A couple of notes here. The **-n** in the **echo** command line causes most versions of **echo** to suppress the new line that they would normally put at the end of the prompt. Putting single quotes around the original filename makes it clearer what filename you're talking about, especially when you expect to use this on filenames that have embedded spaces. And, finally, you could just as easily use this script to *create* a filename with spaces in it, since the output filename is enclosed in quotes. So be careful.

WILDCARDS

? What are the basic UNIX wildcards?

Before you try your hand at wildcard tricks, let's review the rules. There are three basic wildcards in UNIX:

● the ? character substitutes for any single character

● the * character substitutes for zero or more characters

● the notation [*charset*] substitutes for any single character in the set *charset*

This last one takes a bit more explanation. An example of a *charset* is **[cChH]**, which matches the characters "c" and "h" whether uppercase or lowercase. A charset can also describe all the characters between two character pairs, such as **[a-z]**, which would match any single lowercase letter in the alphabet. Or there's **[a-zA-Z]**, which would match any single character in the alphabet. Note that the character pairs match all the ASCII values between the two characters, inclusive.

As you can see, UNIX supports a much richer and more flexible use of wildcards than DOS, which is why it's so particularly frustrating that some commands such as **cp** and **mv** don't support wildcards at all well for the target.

But in most ways, UNIX is far better with wildcards than DOS. In DOS, everything after the * is ignored up to the period, so that the result of the following command might well *not* be exactly what you had in mind:

```
del *bak.*
```

Oops, you just deleted all the files in the current directory unless you were paying attention when DOS asked you to confirm it. Not so with UNIX, where the * character substitutes for any number of characters, *including none*, but the rest of the pattern matching in the line is respected. So ***bak.*** would match **newbak.save, oldbak.new,** and even **bak.temp**, but would not match **newbak** because the trailing dot (**.**) is missing. Well, that's pretty slick, and it does make life lots easier. The phrase ***bak*** would match all of the above, including **newbak**.

? Can I use multiple wildcards within a single command?

Yes. Consider the following:

```
rm a*out*tmp?
```

to get rid of a bunch of temporary output files that looked something like **ab.out.tmp1, ac.out.tmp2**, and so forth. You can see how you can use multiple wildcards to simplify your work. But UNIX gives you another, even more useful option.

? How can I use wildcards to make my command line more intelligent?

UNIX understands certain groups as being part of a set, and lets you use pattern matching with that set. So, if you have a series of files, **file1.tmp, file2.tmp, file3.tmp, .. file9.tmp**, you can delete (remove) them with

```
rm file[0-9].tmp
```

The best part of this trick is that you can remove only the ones you want. Let's say you make a "dump" (an export) of a highly important database every morning. You save the file to **dump.`date%h%d`** , which yields a bunch of files called

```
dump.Jun23
dump.Jun24
dump.Jun25
dump.Jun26
```

and so forth. Let's also say the disk fills up pretty fast because each file is 100MB or so. So what you do is go in every few days and delete the old ones, leaving the most recent two. In the example above, you'd type

```
rm -i du*[34]
```

This will remove all the files that start with *du* and also have either a *3* or *4* at the end.

❓ How can I protect myself when I'm using the rm command around crucial files?

The **rm** command is irrevocable and permanent. If you have critical, irreplaceable files that you need to protect, use **rm -I,** which is the *interactive* remove command. This will prompt you for confirmation before any file is deleted. In fact, make it an alias, and use it whenever you want to be sure:

```
alias del="rm -i"
```

You can even make this option the "normal" way **rm** is used, but you may quickly get tired of being prompted every time you remove a file.

FILE PERMISSIONS AND PROTECTION

❓ What can you tell me about UNIX file permissions?

Since UNIX is a multiuser operating system, it assumes that you might not be the only person who uses the computer. That's nice, and it makes some things, like sharing files with your coworkers, much easier. But it also means that there are certain protections built into the system that allow you to control who sees, uses, and manipulates the files you "own." Each user on a UNIX system has a unique user name and id. Any files that the user creates are owned by that user and can only be read, used, or changed with the permission of the owner. If you get a "long listing" of a file, you can see this set of permissions. For example, a long listing of the file **harold.cat** might look like this:

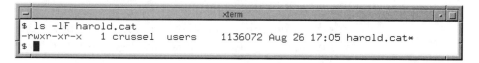

```
$ ls -1F harold.cat
-rwxr-xr-x   1 crussel   users     1136072 Aug 26 17:05 harold.cat*
$
```

This says that the file is owned by crussel, who has permission to read, write, and execute the file—the first **rwx** in the file listing. Further, users of the same group ("users") have permission to read the file and execute it, but may not change or write to it—the second **r-x** in the file listing. And finally the world at large may execute the file, but not read it or write to it—the third **--x** in the listing.

How can I change a file's mode or permissions?

Use **chmod**. This command, which is short for "change mode," lets you easily change any file you own so that only those people you want can read it, change it, or execute it. There are three basic levels of users, as we saw above—the owner (user) of the file, the owner's group, and everyone else (others)—and three levels of permissions—read, write, and execute. The three types of users are abbreviated "u" for user, "g" for owner's group, "a" for everyone, and "o" or all those other people out there.

The permissions are abbreviated the same as in the long listing above—"r" for read, "w" for write, and "x" for execute. So, to change the permission of the file **harold.cat** to allow users outside the in-group to read it, type in

```
chmod o+r harold.cat
```

The **chmod** command will let you make multiple changes to several files at once, so it is pretty easy to remove write permission from everyone and remove all permissions from those not in your group for all the **.cat** files:

```
chmod a-w,o-rx *.cat
```

❓ How can I protect my files from accidental changes?

Add the following to your **.profile** (or **.login** if using C shell) file.

```
umask 022
```

Obviously, some explanation is in order. There are three sets of permissions for any given file. These are read, write, and execute permissions for the owner, the owner's group, and the world. We can think of these as three octal numbers, where full read/write/execute permission has a value of "7" ("111" in binary). To figure out what the **umask** command does, subtract the number for each set of **umask** permissions ("0" for user, "2" for group, and "2" for world) from the default of "666" and you get "644," which means that the owner (that's you) can do what you want with the file but that others, whether in your group or the world at large, can read the file but not change it.

If the file is one that would normally be executable, such as the result of a compilation, the same mask of "022" will be subtracted from "777," leaving "755"—readable and executable by the others in your group and the world as a whole, but changeable only by you. Only the permissions of files created *after* adding **umask** to your **.profile** or **.login** must be changed manually.

❓ Is there a way I can make life easier in a shared directory?

If you share files in a common directory, say on a project, you can make everyone's life easier by changing your **umask** setting to **002** whenever you are working in that directory. This way, new files created for the project can be shared and used by the others in your group. A sample alias for this would be

```
alias project="cd /users/common/newmodel;umask 002"
```

Then, whenever you want to work on the new model project, you simply type **project** and you're on your way.

? Can I use aliases to make setting permissions easier?

Yes. Here's a quick trick to modify the permissions of a file, adding or subtracting write permission from the file. Add these aliases to your **.kshrc** or **.cshrc** file, and they will always be there.

```
alias w-="chmod a-w $@"
alias w+="chmod u+w $@"
```

If you're a C shell user, this looks a little different, since the **alias** command has a slightly different syntax:

```
alias w- chmod a-w
alias w+ chmod u+w
```

In either case, the first line removes write permissions from everyone and the second line adds write permissions back for the owner of a file. This is just good conservative practice. It's generally a bad idea to make global, irrevocable, or far-reaching commands too easy to execute. Before you let everyone, even your boss, read your résumé, you want to make sure it is on purpose. Which leads to another tip!

? Can I hide my files and directories from the superuser?

Nothing is secure from the superuser. It's important to understand this subtle but important point. You can set permissions such that no one but you can even read your secret file by setting it to a permission of **600** with the **chmod** command:

```
chmod 600 resume.doc
```

But this will only go so far. Even if we haven't accidentally left a back door open into this file, by not setting the directory permissions correctly, *the superuser can always read (and change) your files*. So think long and hard about what you leave on the hard disk. If something is really secret, a floppy is a far better place for it. Also, remember that anyone who has your password has access to your files, just as if they were you.

❓ So what do I need to know about UNIX directory protections?

There's more about directory structures later (see "UNIX File Systems and Directory Structures" below), but it's important here in the security section to mention how permissions work for directories. A directory in UNIX is simply another filename for most purposes. It has the exact same set of permissions attached to it, except for the first column, which for most regular files is shown as a "-" in the first column:

```
-rwxr-x--x  1 crussel users 76884 Jan 30 14:47
alfie.cat
```

However, when the listing is a directory, the first column of a long listing will have the letter "d" in it, and the meaning of the permissions will be subtly different, as shown here:

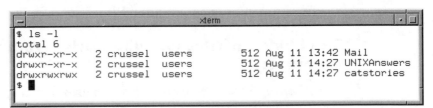

```
$ ls -l
total 6
drwxr-xr-x   2 crussel   users        512 Aug 11 13:42 Mail
drwxr-xr-x   2 crussel   users        512 Aug 11 14:27 UNIXAnswers
drwxrwxrwx   2 crussel   users        512 Aug 11 14:27 catstories
$
```

The permissions on a directory break down as follows:

- *read* permission to list the files in the directory
- *write* permission to create, rename, or delete files in the directory
- *execute* permission to use the files in the directory

This means that even if you don't have permission to read a file, if you have permission to write to the directory in which the file resides, you can make a copy of it (which you will now own!), delete it, move it, or rename it. And even if you can't read the contents of a directory or write to it, if you have execute permission you can still execute programs within the directory as long as you know (or can guess) the exact name of the program.

UNIX FILESYSTEMS AND DIRECTORY STRUCTURES

? What is a UNIX directory and how does it relate to other (sub)directories?

UNIX, like virtually all major operating systems, uses what is known as a *hierarchical* directory structure. This is sometimes also called a *tree* structure, but under either name, it is the same basic structure as most operating systems these days. There's a "root" directory and under it a series of subdirectories. Each subdirectory can in turn have multiple subdirectories under it, which in turn can have multiple subdirectories under them, and so on. How deep this structure can go depends on the particular flavor of UNIX, but in virtually all cases, it goes far enough that you never need to worry about running out of levels.

So what *is* a directory? Well, actually, it's really just a file that holds the names of the files and subdirectories that lie within it, along with the inode number for each file or directory. (Wonder what an inode is? See "Do I really need to understand inodes?" below.)

? What are . (dot) and .. (dot-dot)?

These are two special directory names that make moving around easier. The dot directory is your current directory, while the dot-dot directory is the one above where you are. So, if you are working on a project with a group of people, and you have your documentation files stored in one directory, your source code files in another, header files in a third, and so on, it can be a pain to move to the documentation directory using an absolute path name. Do you really want to type **cd /usr/projects/newmodel/docs** every time you want to update the documentation on the change you just made to the header file, which is in **/usr/projects/newmodel/headers**? Hardly. So, to change to the documentation directory, just type: **cd .. /docs**. There, isn't that easier?

? Do I really need to understand inodes?

Thankfully, no. The *inode* (pronounced "EYE-node") is the data structure that UNIX uses to keep track of where each file is in the system, as well as other important information such as its permissions, ownership, timestamp, and so forth. In this sense, it's a little (but not very much) like the FAT table on a DOS disk. You can see the inode number associated with a file by using the **ls** command with the **-i** switch:

```
$ ls -il
total 4
441315 -rwxr-xr-x  1 crussel  users  884 Jan 30 14:47
stanley.cat
```

What does this mean to you as a user? Not much. After all, we *did* imply that you could ignore this section. This is the province of those shadowy figures known as system administrators—the ones with pocket protectors and a persecuted expression.

? How does the UNIX filesystem work?

Feel free to skip this section if the subject doesn't interest you, but for those of you who are curious, here goes. The UNIX concept of filesystems is somewhat different from what a typical DOS or even Macintosh user has come to expect. There's a "root" filesystem that every UNIX machine must have, which resembles the "C:" drive on a DOS machine, but there the similarity between UNIX and other filesystems ends. Instead of additional drive letters for each additional hard disk you add, the hard disks each get their own filesystem, which then "mounts" on the root filesystem. So, on a large system with many users and a substantial number of commercial programs, you might well have, for example, the root filesystem and a "**/u**" filesystem that contains the home directories for all the users, and another "**/usr**" filesystem that contains most of the commercial programs. And it's very possible if you are working in a distributed workstation environment (as opposed to one with a large, central server) that the **/u** filesystem is actually the same regardless of which machine you happen to log in on. On one of the machines, it's physically in that box, but on all the rest, it's remotely mounted. This sort of setup allows you to use any available workstation without worrying about which one it happens to be. Your home directory is exactly the same, regardless.

? What is a home directory?

This is the directory that every user on a UNIX computer has that is his or her very own. For the user "charlie", this directory may be **/u/charlie**, or **/users/charlie**, or **/home/charlie,** or any one of several other places in the filesystem, depending on the flavor of UNIX and the biases of the superuser on your system. But the result's the same— it's *yours*. Files and directories that you create in it are owned by you, and changed and used by others only with your permission. With, as always, the proviso that nothing is hidden from the superuser.

? What subdirectories does a typical user's home directory contain, and what files are in these subdirectories?

Your home directory is where you'll store the files that control your environment, your start-up files, and it will also usually include a hopeless jumble of miscellaneous other files you've created over time. In this sense, it's sort of like the closet you throw everything into when company is coming. This makes it hard to figure out which file is which, or to find the one file you absolutely have to have right now. So do a little organizing. Every user should have a couple of subdirectories to sort particular kinds of files into, and then use them. For example, my home directory has the following subdirectories:

- *bin* Executable programs and scripts go here
- *docs* General purpose WordPerfect files go here
- *notes* A place for quick notes to myself
- *wrksheet* Spreadsheet files go here
- *source* Source files for various executable programs that are in bin
- *tmp* A place for temporary files

● *Mail* Required storage spot for elm, my mail reader

● *arc* A place to store compressed versions of things I don't often need, but don't want to erase

● *junk* Stuff that doesn't fit anywhere else

Other subdirectories come and go, depending on what projects are being worked on. For example, I currently have a UNIXanswers directory in the docs directory. When this book is finished, the entire directory will get compressed into a single file and stuck into the arc directory.

So what actually gets left in the root level of your home directory? The absolute minimum possible. Everything that doesn't *have* to be in your home directory should be in a subdirectory. UNIX will run faster because it has a positive dislike of directories with too many files in them. And you'll spend less time floundering around looking for files.

❓ How can I keep my home directory clean?

Basically, the only files in your home directory should be the "dot" files that control your start-up, shutdown, and environment. Files like **.profile, .kshrc, .login, .cshrc, .logout, .exrc,** and **.xsession**. We'll examine most of these files in much greater detail in Chapter 5, because they're essential to automating and controlling your setup. Since they begin with a dot, these files aren't normally seen because they're hidden from a simple **ls** command.

FINDING LOST FILES

❓ How can I find a file I've changed recently?

Try **ls -t**. This little trick by itself will find 85 percent of the files you're looking for. The **-t** (for time, one assumes) will give you a listing of files sorted by the time they were last changed, with the most recent first. Add the **-u** switch to this, and the sort is by the time they were last accessed, whether they were changed or not. Combine this with **more** to prevent the listing from scrolling off your screen, and you have a useful alias:

```
alias lt="ls -laFtu | more"
```

This will give you a long listing of all the files in the current directory that have been accessed recently.

? Can I find a file when I know what kind it is but not where it is?

Now it's time to call in the heavy hitter—the UNIX **find** command. This powerful utility will search your entire filesystem looking for a file or files that match a set of criteria, or any subset of the entire filesystem. This command syntax is

```
find <pathname-list> <operator>
```

where **pathname-list** can be one or more directories and their subdirectories and **operator** can be any of the following:

- **-name <filename pattern>**
- **-perm <file mode>**
- **-type <filetype>**
- **-user <username>**
- **-size <# blocks>** (+# blocks means larger than)
- **-atime <#days>** (accessed time)
- **-mtime <#days>** (modified time)
- **-ctime <#days>** (changed time)
- **-newer <file>** (newer than the designated file)

Of these options, the most useful is probably the "**-name**" option. This will take wildcards and perform the usual sort of pattern matching, so it can be pretty flexible.

For example, you know you have a file that you used for your monthly progress report last month, and you want to use it as a template, but you can't find it. You do remember, however, that it had a filename with "Aug" in the name somewhere. No problem. Just use the command

```
find ~/. -name "*Aug*" -print
```

In other words, find all the files with "Aug" in their name, starting from the top of the home directory tree, and print the result out to the screen. Note the use of quotes around the name. This prevents the shell from interpreting the wildcards before **find** has a chance to. This is the most basic of **find** commands, and all other **find** commands come from this one.

? Can I find a file even if I don't know whether its name begins with an upper- or lowercase letter?

If you aren't sure whether the above-mentioned report was "Aug" or "aug", you can easily add a second argument to the operator portion of the above command:

```
find ~/. -name "*Aug*" -o -name "*aug*" -print
```

In this expression, we've used the "**-o**", which says use a logical OR to do the search. Any file with either "Aug" OR "aug" in the name will satisfy the condition.

You could also use regular expression matching to perform the above search in a way that's a bit cleaner:

```
find ~/. -name "*[Aa]ug*" -print
```

Here we've said to find all files whose names include the string "ug" preceded by either an "A" or "a"—the [Aa] syntax says either letter will satisfy the regular expression.

? Why does find keep complaining about a missing conjunction?

One of the problems with **find** is that it tries to expand the entire command line to figure out what you want. But you need to hide special characters ("metacharacters") from the **find** command until it's ready for them. So we either enclose the special characters quotes or use the backslash character to escape the meaning of the next character. Thus:

```
find ~/. -name [Aa]ug* -print
```

will return the error message: "find: missing conjuction", but if we use

```
find ~/. -name \[Aa\]ug\* -print
```

we'll be searching for any filename that begins with Aug or aug, which is probably what we intended.

❓ Is there any common wisdom about how best to find a lost file?

Yes—use everything you know. Sometimes you know several things about a file (except what you really what to know, namely, where it is). Let's say you worked on a file a couple of days ago, and that there are several other files on the system with similar names. In this case, you know two things about the file. To use both bits of information (part of the name and the fact that it was worked on recently), type in

```
find ~/. -mtime -4 \(-name "*Aug*" -o -name "*aug*" \) -print
```

Here's the same logical OR expression, but it's evaluated with the **-mtime** operator, now in a logical AND operation. So the whole expression means, "Find all the files that have been modified in the last three days *and* that have either "aug" or "Aug" in the name."

The combinations are virtually endless and the more you use **find**, the more skillful you'll get with it. It doesn't always behave quite as you expect, however, so if you try something and it doesn't work, try breaking the command down piece by piece, and see where *you* broke down. In the process, you will learn more and more tricks.

SHORTCUTS TO WHERE YOU WANT TO BE

❓ How can I move quickly between frequently used directories?

If you have a directory you're using all the time, assign the path to that directory to a variable, and then export that variable so that it's always available. Make a simple alias to take advantage of the variable to move to it. For example, let's say you're working on a project with the new model group and you need to quickly move to the project's working directory—**/users/shared/projects/newmodel/colormatch**. That's a real handful, and not something you want to type every time! So try this:

```
PHOME=/users/shared/projects/newmodel/colormatch
export PHOME
alias goproj=cd $PHOME
```

Include this in your **.kshrc** file, and it will be available whenever you need it. The best part is, if you change to a different project, all you do is change the variable. Your fingers get to continue to use the same command.

? Is there a command I can use to return quickly to my home directory?

Yes; try **cd** all by itself. This little trick will get you back to your home directory quickly, no matter how far away you have managed to stray.

? Can I use ~ as a shortcut to my home directory?

Yes. When you want to describe a directory or file that can be found below your home directory, save yourself some typing by using "~" as a shorthand for your home directory. For example, to get to your personal **bin** directory from anywhere, type **cd ~/bin**.

? Can I use ~ as a shortcut to someone else's home directory?

Yes. When you want to describe a directory or file that can be found below someone else's home directory, save yourself some typing and figuring out exactly where their home directory is by using "~" plus their user name as a shortcut to their home directory. For example, if you know that Gladys Meep has a useful set of utilities stashed in her home **bin** directory, you could get to it, assuming she has her permissions set to allow this, by typing **cd ~gmeep/bin**.

❓ Can I define a variable to describe any directory or filename I use a lot?

Yes! Shorten the long path name to any file or directory you use a lot simply by substituting the variable in the command. Make sure you remember to **export**—or setenv in csh—the variable, however, and include it in your **.kshrc** or **.cshrc** file. This way, it'll always be available.

Chapter 4

vi

Answer Topics!

vi @ a Glance

Whatever your interaction with UNIX, sooner or later you'll need to edit a text file. And then you're faced with that most wonderful of text editors—**vi**. Before you start using **vi**, however, it's best if you understand its **modes**, for it works quite differently than the text editors you're probably used to.

Once you've learned **the basics of using vi**, you'll be able to open a file or files for editing, and manipulate these files as you wish.

The **vi** commands for **moving around** within a file are not difficult to learn, but they're not exactly intuitive either. In order to work efficiently, it's helpful to know the quickest way to get where you want to go.

Inserting and replacing text are the two most basic functions of any text editor. Whether you want to change a character, word, or entire line, here are the commands that will make **vi** do your bidding.

What text editor would be complete without the ability to **search for and replace text**? **vi** offers you many search-and-replace options, so read on to find out what you'll need to know.

Cutting and pasting are two more crucial text editor functions. With just a few hints, you'll learn how to cut and paste text exactly as you want it, and how to give your text just the right look.

Another of **vi**'s timesaving features is the ability to create **macros** that allow you to automate the typing of frequently used words and phrases or sequences of commands. You'll find that by cutting down the number of keystrokes you have to enter, you'll greatly reduce the time and effort it takes to get your work done.

Other essential vi commands include how to save your work and quit **vi**, how to include another file in the current file, how to find out how many words or lines are in a file, and more.

But what if you're using a UNIX system and you'd like to find an alternative to **vi**? Well, there's always **the other editor—emacs**. While we won't teach you how to use **emacs**, we will compare and contrast its features with those of **vi** so you'll be able to make an informed decision about which editor is right for you.

THE MANY MODES OF VI

What is a modal editor, and what are the modes of vi?

When you're working with a modal editor, what you type is interpreted differently depending on which mode you're currently in. **vi** has three basic modes: *command mode, insert mode,* and *external mode*. In command mode, you give commands to the editor, such as "cut this line out of the text." or "save my work," or "move to line 37, and replace every occurrence of xxx with Osborne up to line 459." In insert mode, you simply type in text and it's inserted into your file. (Well, actually, into the buffer, but let's not be picky at this point.) Finally, in external mode you are actually issuing commands to the **ex** editor or the shell directly. In command mode, you can't just type text into the file; and in insert mode, you can't just move down a page or over a word. And in external mode, you aren't really working with **vi** at all, but with **ex**. All this is just a bit different from most editors or word processors, and can take some getting used to. OK, a lot of getting used to.

How do I move between modes in vi?

When you start **vi**, you're always in command mode. Where you go from there depends on the commands you issue. In order to switch to insert mode, type a command that expects text input (see "Inserting and Replacing Text" below). Similarly, to switch to external mode, type a command that begins with : since that's what precedes an **ex** command (see "Searching for (and Replacing) Text" below). To return to command mode, ESC is always the best bet.

What do I do if I find myself suddenly in ex instead of vi?

Simply type **vi** to bring things back to normal. Chances are you accidentally pressed **Q** (that's the shifted "Q" key), which is the shortcut to **ex**.

THE BASICS OF USING VI

What is vi, and are there different versions of it available to me?

Short for "visual interface," **vi** is actually an extension of the **ex** editor, which is itself an extended version of the **ed** editor. Almost no one uses **ed** anymore, so we can forget that, and the only people who use **ex** are generally those stuck on some sort of terminal that won't support **vi**.

There are actually three versions of **vi** included in most implementations of UNIX—the standard one, which is mostly what we will talk about here, and the one that you start with the **vi** command. The second is a read-only version, useful for viewing files, that won't allow you to change files—either accidentally or on purpose. You run this version by typing **view** from the command line. And, finally, there is a brain-dead version for neophytes that you start by typing

vedit at the command line. This last one you can safely ignore. Some of the options included in the **vedit** version are pretty useful, but in this chapter, we show you how to add those to your standard **vi**.

? Can I edit a series of files when I'm using vi?

Yes. Just include all the files you want to work with in the command line when you start **vi**. You can use wildcards here, so it's simple to edit all your "dot cat" files by typing

```
vi *.cat
```

You can get much more sophisticated, of course, using the pattern matching built into the shell to load your files, but you get the idea. Once you have them all included on the command line, it's really easy to move between them in **vi**.

? How can I finish editing the current file, save my changes, and move to the next file in the file list?

Use **:n** from command mode. This little trick saves you lots of time, and makes it easy to edit a bunch of files. Just remember if you want to cut and paste between files, you will need to use named buffers. See below under "Searching for (and Replacing) Text" and "Cutting and Pasting" for more on named buffers.

+   ***Tip:*** *Some versions of **vi** don't support the automatic save and edit of the next file shown above. For those, you'll need to do two separate steps—save the file and then move to the next one—if you've made any changes to the current one. Use **:w** followed by **:n** in command mode if you're stuck with one of those versions.*

? Is there a way I can back up and edit the previous file in the file list?

Yes. Use **:e #** from the command mode. The pound sign is shorthand for "the previous file I had open."

? **Can I reload the current file and start again from scratch?**

Use **:e!** % from the command line. Here we are using external mode again, telling **vi** to edit a file without saving the current file (the ":e!" part), and the file we want to edit is the current file (the "%" part).

? **How is the ! pronounced?**

It is pronounced "bang," as in "e-bang."

? **Is there a way I can see what files are left to edit?**

Yes; try **:args**. Loading a bunch of files on the command line is nice, but if you lose track of what's still lined up and waiting, this external command will show you what remains.

? **If I discover I've made a terrible mistake, can I start over on the same list of files?**

Yes; just rewind them. To accomplish this, use the **:rewind** command to save any changes to the current file, and start back at the beginning of the list, or use rewind-bang (**:rewind!**) to abandon any changes to the current file.

MOVING AROUND

? **What are the basic cursor movement keys in** vi**?**

The basic cursor movement keys in command mode are the "j," "k," "l," and "h" keys. They move you down a line, up a line, right one character, and left one character, respectively. Add a number in front of them and you move that many lines or characters. So, to move 25 lines down in the current file, issue the command **25j**. However, if there are fewer than 25 lines below the current cursor position, all **vi** will do is beep at you. The same applies if you're moving up and there are fewer lines than you specify. You won't get any movement until you supply a command that's possible.

? ### How can I page through a document one screen at a time?

Use CTRL-F to move forward a screen or CTRL-B to move backwards (up) a screen. If you have a standard display with 24 lines per screen, this should be pretty good as is. However, if your display is some other number of lines, you can modify the behavior for an individual **vi** session by preceding either of these with a number telling the command how many lines to scroll. So, if you type in 15 followed by CTRL-B, your display will move up 15 lines.

? ### Can I move the cursor a half page at a time?

Yes; use CTRL-D to go down and CTRL-U to go up. Like the CTRL-F/CTRL-B pair, this can be preceded by a number to tell **vi** how many lines to move at a time.

? ### Is there a quick way to move to the top or bottom of a file?

To move to the top of a file, press **1G**. This is a specific version of the general command **G** for Go, which will move to the beginning of any line number in the file, if the command is preceded by the appropriate number. To move to the bottom of a file, press G.

? ### How can I move to the beginning of the current line? How about the end?

To move to the beginning of the current line, press **0** or **|**. Zero is the shortcut. To move to another column other than the first one, use **n|** where **n** is the column you want to move to. To move to the end of the current line, press **$**. This one's worth remembering. You'll use it as you build some of the more interesting external commands.

? ### Is there an easy way to set things right if my screen gets seriously garbled?

Yes; press CTRL-L to force a redraw. This will usually fix the problem. But if this doesn't work or it seems to be happening a lot, you may need to ask your system administrator to sort out the problem. It may have to do with a slightly off terminal emulation.

❓ Are there other movement commands in vi?

There are lots of other movement commands, such as **M** to move to the line at the middle of the screen, **H** to move to the line at the top of the screen, and **L** to move to the line at the bottom of the screen. Don't try to remember them all. Just get used to using a couple of them that you can combine to get where you need to be, and you'll be fine. Don't forget that all of these commands are case-sensitive. Type in a lowercase letter instead of a capital and the results will be unexpected.

❓ Is it safe to depend on the "cursor" keys on my keyboard in vi?

No! Learn the basic movement keys, and use them. If you get in the habit of always using the cursor keys, sooner or later you will end up in trouble. You'll have to work on a different keyboard or you'll log into a remote machine that uses a different keyboard. The command keys are independent of the keyboard you're on, but that's not true of the keyboard's cursor keys, which may or may not be correctly mapped.

❓ Can I see where I am in the current file?

Yes; press CTRL-G. This will also give you a few other pieces of information, like whether the file has been modified since the last time you saved it. Another way to get this same information is the **:f** external mode command sequence.

❓ How can I swap two characters?

Put the cursor on the second character, and type **xp** while in command mode. This deletes the second character and then puts it in front of the first, which moved under the cursor.

❓ Can I change the case of a character I've typed?

Yes; use the ~ (tilde) command. Like most **vi** commands, you can place a number, n, in front of this command to make it change the case of the next n characters.

INSERTING AND REPLACING TEXT

*   *Note:*   *These are two of the most important capabilities of any text editor. Issuing any of the commands discussed below will automatically move* ***vi*** *into insert mode and cause it to add or alter text according to your specific instructions.*

?   **What are the basic text insertion commands in** vi**?**

Here is a short list of the essentials:

- *i*   Insert text starting from in front of the current cursor until ESC is pressed
- *I*   Insert text starting at the beginning of the current line until ESC is pressed
- *a*   Insert text starting after the current cursor until ESC is pressed
- *A*   Insert text starting at the end of the current line until ESC is pressed
- *r*   Replace the character at the current cursor position
- *R*   Replace text starting from the current cursor position until ESC is pressed
- *o*   Open a new line below the current line. ENTER will open another line, ESC returns to command mode
- *O*   Open a new line above the current line. ENTER will open another line, ESC returns to command mode

Almost all these text insertion commands work the same way. When you're in command mode, they'll switch you to text insertion mode and allow you to start entering text. The only difference among them is where the text will actually get entered. There is one command on the list that's slightly different: the **r** (lowercase "r") command, which will replace a single character and return immediately to command mode.

? ## Is there something I can do if I don't like the word I just entered?

Yes; press CTRL-W to retype it. This is one of the few ways you can move the cursor position while staying in insertion mode.

? ## What if I want to start my text insertion all over?

Press CTRL-U. The other way to do this is to ESC back to command mode and press **u** for undo. The undo command is only a single level deep, though, so undo immediately, or you will have to fix it the hard way.

? ## How can I undo all the changes I've made to the current line?

Try pressing **U** from command mode. This gets around the single-level undo limitation, but only for the current line. Once you move your cursor off the line, you can't undo the changes on that line, unless they're still in the single-level undo buffer.

? ## Can I replace the current character and then insert more text without overwriting what's there?

Yes; use the **s** command. We know we can replace a single character with **r**, and we can insert text with **i** or **a**, but by using **s** we get around the limitations of **r** without having to worry about overwriting something we don't want to. If you want to replace the next ten characters, and then start inserting text, just type **10s** and start making your change.

? ## How about replacing the entire current line?

Use **S**. This will delete the current line, move the cursor to the first column, and change to insert mode.

? What exactly can the c command do for me?

It can change a word, a line, or a sentence. Actually, this command can do even more. Combine a simple **c** with a more complicated cursor movement command, and you can get really slick. First, the simple ones, and a table is probably the easiest way to list them all, so take a look at Table 4-1.

On most versions of **vi**, the text you are about to change will be delimited by a $ at the last character of the change. And in all cases, when you reach that last character, you'll change from writing over the existing text to pushing the existing text to the right in front of your cursor. This provides a powerful way to quickly fix a word, phrase, or sentence, and then move on about your business.

Command	Result
cw	Change text from current cursor to end of current word.
c*n*w	Change text from current cursor to end of *n*th word.
cb	Change text from beginning of current word to character in front of cursor.
c*n*b	Change text from beginning of *n*th previous word to character in front of cursor.
c)	Change text from current cursor to end of sentence.
c(	Change text from preceding start of sentence to character in front of cursor.
cc	Change entire line.
c}	Change text from current cursor to end of paragraph.
c{	Change text from preceding start of paragraph to character in front of cursor.
c*f*c	Change text from current cursor through first occurrence of character *c*.
c*n*fc	Change text from current cursor through *n*th occurrence of character *c*.
cF*c*	Change text from previous occurrence of character *c* through current cursor position.
c*n*Fc	Change text from *n*th previous occurrence of character *c* through current cursor position.

Table 4-1 The Change Command

? Is there a way I can repeat my last text change?

Yes; use the dot command (.). This little trick saves loads of time. Need to add a couple of spaces at the beginning of the next several lines? Well, you could figure out the exact command sequence and write a macro to do it (see "Macros" later in this chapter), or just do an **I Escape** ("I", space, space, ESC) on the current line, press **j** to move down to the next one, and press . (dot). Do this for as many lines as you need to indent.

SEARCHING FOR (AND REPLACING) TEXT

? What's the easiest way to find some text?

Ah, now we get into external mode. Here we use the **ex** command set. So, to search from the current cursor position for something we use

```
/searchpattern
```

To search backwards, use

```
?searchpattern
```

The search pattern can be a simple bit of text, like searching for the word "Priscilla" in a file, or a more complicated pattern-matching string. Let's save the pattern-matching discussion for just a moment.

? Can I search for and replace text?

Certainly. Search for one pattern and replace it with another, using the external mode substitute command. The syntax is

```
x,ys/searchpattern/replace/options
```

where *x,y* are the beginning and end of the search and replace zone, and *options* include **g** for "globally do it and don't bother asking mc," and **c** for "ask me to confirm each change."

So, to find a series of unflattering references to your boss and replace them with "Priscilla," the following will work:

```
1,$s/catbrain/Priscilla/g
```

As a substitute for the **1,$** of this command, you can use % if saving the two keystrokes is important enough to you to bother remembering it.

❓ Do I have to know what line I'm on to run substitute on the next ten lines?

No. Use the . (dot) to represent the current line, and then tell **vi** to do the substitution for the next ten lines:

```
.,+10s/fishbreath/Alfie/g
```

To make sure you don't accidentally change something you didn't mean to, use the **c** option after the final slash. This will print the string to be substituted with "^" characters highlighting it. Press **Y** to make the change, and anything else to leave it as is.

❓ How can I execute a command on an entire file?

Use the global command. This lets you search through a file and execute the **yank** command, for example, to append the lines that match a particular pattern to a buffer. Thus:

```
:g/Priscilla/y A
```

will grab all those lines with "Priscilla" in them, place them in buffer a, appending them after anything that is already there. This command lets you do some fairly tricky things, like search for all lines that begin with a number, and indent them five spaces:

```
:g/^[0-9]/s/^/     /g
```

Using this command, the text in Figure 4-1 becomes lined up like the text in Figure 4-2.

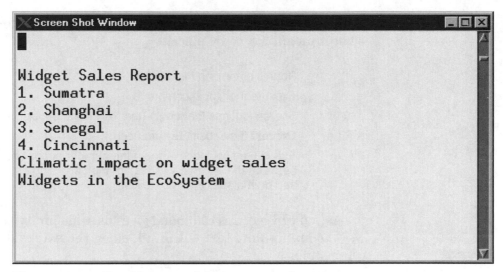

Figure 4-1 Text before a global command to rearrange

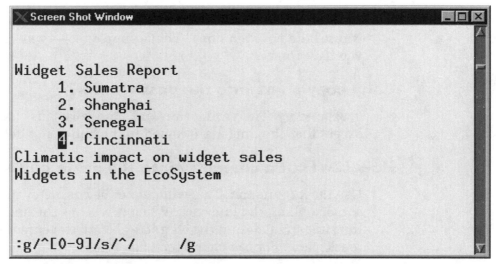

Figure 4-2 After the global command, the numbered lines are indented

Let's examine this command a bit more closely. Here's what it means, piece by piece:

:	Do this command in ex mode.
g	Execute the global command.
/^[0-9]/	Search for lines that begin (the ^) with a number.
s	Execute the substitute command.
/^/ /g	Substitute five spaces (or put the number of spaces you want between the last two slashes) for the beginning of the line, and do it globally without asking.

As you can see, this command gives us some pretty powerful ways to manipulate text within **vi**, using the external mode commands.

CUTTING AND PASTING

What's the command for cutting a line into the paste buffer?

Simple—**dd**. This will cut a single line of text. Oh, you wanted the next ten lines? That's simple too—type **10dd** and you have them.

Can I copy a line into the paste buffer?

Yes; press **yy**. The **yank** command, this works just like **dd** except that the line(s) are copied to the buffer, not deleted.

How can I cut a character into the paste buffer?

Use the **x** command. This will delete the character under the cursor, pulling the line back. When it reaches the end of the line, it starts deleting the character before the cursor (backspace). For ten characters, use **10x**.

Tip: *Text in the paste buffer is only a single level. As soon as you make a deletion or "yank" (copy) to the paste buffer, you lose what was in there before. So think before you yank or delete something. Have you finished with the current buffer's contents?*

? I've heard that using the dd command is better than yanking. Is this true, and if so, why?

If you yank text, it doesn't go into the stack, so you can only get at the last text you yanked. But if you delete it, it goes into a nine-level "stack" (last in, first out). So, to add a line to the stack without actually deleting it, do a **dd** followed by an immediate **P**. Your file hasn't changed, but you have added the current line to the buffer. Now, go ahead and delete something else. Want that first line back? It has now been pushed one up on the stack by the second deletion, so to get it back, do a **"2p** and you will insert it after the current line. Pretty slick. The only problem with this, however, is keeping track of what's in which buffer. Using named buffers is better, because they don't change unless you overwrite them, but if you get in the habit of using the **ddP** combination instead of **yy**, you will save yourself some grief often enough to make the extra keystroke worth it.

? Can I use the named buffers to make editing easier?

Absolutely. All that deleting and yanking is nice, but what if you need to grab a piece from here, a piece from there, and another piece from somewhere else? Hmmm, that single-level buffer isn't going to get it done, is it? No sweat— **vi** provides for a total of 26 "named buffers." That should be enough for almost anyone. The buffers are named a–z, and you cut or copy text into them in exactly the same way you would into the regular cut/copy/paste buffer. Except you precede the cut or copy command (**dd** or **yy**) with "a for the a buffer, "b for the b buffer, and so on.

? What's the smartest way to use named buffers for my paste operation?

Try preceding the paste command with **"a** where a is the named buffer. If the text you want is in the b buffer, use **"b**, and so forth.

? **Is there a way I can put the contents of the paste buffer after the current line?**

Yes; use the **p** command. If you have cut or yanked only a partial line, the text in the buffer will be placed in the current line, after the current cursor position. Use **P** to place the text before the current line or position.

? **How can I cut a word into the buffer?**

Use **dw**. Actually, this is the simplest example of the more general rule. Use **d***cursormovement* or **y***cursormovement* to cut or copy text into the buffer. The cursor movement keys are the same as for the **change** command of Table 4.1.

? **How can I give my text the right look?**

Editors are very personal things. What works for some people may not work for others. So, a good editor lets you change the way it behaves and looks to the point where you can be comfortable with it. In **vi**, there are three basic commands to change the look and feel of your editor, and all are external mode commands. The first is the **:set** command. Use this to set all sorts of options. The list may vary slightly, depending on your particular implementation of **vi**, but Table 4-2 shows some of the most common.

Option	Description
ai	Autoindent—new lines start lined up with the indent from the previous line.
noai	Autoindent off (the default).
aw	Autowrite—current buffer contents are written when escaping to the shell, or using :n to go to the next file.
noaw	Autowrite off (the default).
flash	Flash screen on an error instead of beeping (the default).
noflash	Use a beep instead of a flash.
ic	Ignore case on searches or pattern matching.

Table 4-2 **vi** options

Option	Description
noic	Don't ignore case (the default).
lisp	Set autoindent to line up better when editing lisp programs.
nolist	Autoindent lines up with the beginning of previous line (the default).
magic	Use the full set of metacharacters when doing pattern matching (the default).
nomagic	Limits metacharacters to only ^ and $.
mesg	Allows other users to write to your terminal (the default).
nomesg	Disables write permission to your screen.
nu	Display line numbers along the left edge of the screen.
nonu	No line numbers displayed (the default).
ro	Read only; prevents the file from being changed without explicitly overriding the setting with :w!.
noro	Normal read/write mode (the default).
remap	Allows macro definitions to link directly to already mapped commands (the default).
noremap	Causes macro definitions to be explicit.
showmatch	Highlight matching { or [briefly when a closing] or } is typed.
noshowmatch	No highlighting of matching delimiters (the default).
showmode	Show a highlighted mode indicator on bottom line when in text entry mode.
noshowmode	Don't indicate the current mode (the default).
ts=n	Set tab spacing to n characters. Default is 8.
warn	Warn before a shell escape when text has been modified since last write command (the default).
nowarn	Don't warn before shell escapes, just do it.
ws	Searches wrap around to the beginning of the file and keep going (the default).
nows	Don't wrap when the end of the file is reached in a search.
wm=n	Wrapmargin—when set to other than zero, automatically insert a new line when the current word would exceed the margin. The number of characters from the right-hand edge of the display for the margin, i.e., wm=8 sets the right margin on an 80-column display at column 72.

Table 4-2 **vi** options (*continued*)

Now that you know what your options are in **vi**, here's some free advice:

● *Set showmode to on.* It's a nuisance to suddenly find you are inserting text just because you accidentally hit the wrong key. This simple little change gets over that, giving you a gentle reminder whenever you are in text insertion mode. Just type **:set showmode** to turn this on.

● *Use autoindent when you are writing shell scripts or program code to make your files easier to read.* This way, when you write if or case statements, or other programming structures, it's easier to set them off so that they are clear.

● *Use showmatch to help find matching braces when you are writing programming code.* This can make it much easier to tell which brace or bracket you are closing, since the cursor will jump to the corresponding opening brace or bracket for a second, and then back. When you aren't writing code, just typing a letter or simple text file, this can be a minor annoyance, so turn it back off with **:set noshowmode**.

● *Put all your "normal" settings in the file **.exrc** in your home directory.* This file is automatically loaded every time you start **vi** unless there is a file of the same name in your current directory.

● *If you have different settings for different tasks in **vi**, create directory-specific **.exrc** files for each task.* If you use **vi** to write notes as you work on things, keep all these notes in the same directory. It's easy to set up a special **.exrc** file for a directory that's more appropriate for note taking. You might want to set **wrapmargin=72** for this directory, for example, while your shell script directory gets an **.exrc** with wrapmargin off and autoindent on.

● *Use comments in your **.exrc** file to make it easier to understand.* Any line that begins with a double quote mark (") is ignored by **vi** when it starts. It may take a moment longer to start up, but it's a lot easier to remember why you have a certain option set if you put a comment in the file. And as we will see with mappings in the section about macros below, this really becomes important there.

The **.exrc** file has a format exactly as if you were entering the commands inside **vi** while in command mode, so it might look something like Figure 4-3.

MACROS

What are macros?

Macros are a way to automate frequently used command sequences and shorten the number of keystrokes it takes to do the things you do all the time. Plus it's a lot easier to remember that you use CTRL-F1 to run UNIX's spell checker and put a list of the misspelled words at the bottom of the current file than to remember and type in the command every time. **vi** has three different kinds of macros: the **:map** command, which runs a series of keystrokes from the command mode; the **:map!** command, which does the same thing when you start in text insertion mode; and the **:abbr** command, which lets you abbreviate frequently used words or expressions, and have them automatically expanded by **vi**

```
:set ai
:set ts=5
:set wm=5
:set showmode
:set showmatch
:set nonu
"Now some simple mappings to make the book easier.
:map ; :
"Map F7 to search for uans and substitute the book title
:map #A ^[1,$s/uans/UnixAnswers UNIX/g ^M
"Map! F7 in insert mode to place " uans " in the text at the
"current cursor position.  The extra spaces have to be escaped
"with ^V to enter them, or vi ignores them.
:map! #A uans
"And an abbreviation, cause I'm lazy
:abbr ux UNIX
```

Figure 4-3   Using comments as reminders in your **.exrc** file

as you type them in text insertion mode. You can enter these commands directly in **vi** when you are in command mode, or include them in your **.exrc** file. We find it helps to have different sets of these for each project, and include them in a separate **.exrc** file in each project's main directory.

? How can I automate frequently used sequences that start in command mode?

Use the **:map** command. The syntax is

```
:map key replacement
```

The key can be almost any key on the keyboard, but if it's a function key or control key, you will have to "escape" its meaning by first entering a CTRL-V. So, for example, to map CTRL-F1 to run UNIX's spell checker, and put the results at the bottom of the current buffer (file), the command is

```
:map #^ G:w!^M:r !spell %^M
```

The ENTER keys in this sequence would cause the map to terminate, so you must use the key sequence "CTRL-V, CTRL-F1, space, G:w!, CTRL-V, ENTER, :r, space, !spell, space, %, CTRL-V, ENTER". The ENTER keys have to be "escaped" with CTRL-V first. They appear in the command as ^M or CTRL-M, which is what the ENTER key actually is, of course. So what does this command do? First it moves to the bottom of the buffer, the "G"; then it writes out the current contents of the buffer to the disk file unconditionally, the ":w! Enter". Then it reads *into* the buffer the result of running the spell command on the current file, the ":r !spell %Enter".

The total number of **:map** and **:map!** commands you can define at any one time is 32 for most versions of **vi**, and they can be no more than 512 characters total. This should be more than enough for almost all purposes, especially if you split them into separate **.exrc** files for each task, which makes the most sense.

? Is there a way to automate frequent tasks that start while in text insertion mode?

Yes; try using the "map-bang" macros. For example, if you are the sort of person who likes to save your current work frequently (not a bad idea, though **vi** will usually be able to recover even if you do crash or have a power failure), here's a simple macro to save your current work and continue without losing your place in the file.

```
:map! #= ^[:w!^Ma
```

This command, which is mapped on the F3 key, begins with an escape to take you to command mode, then the ":w!Enter" sequence to write the current file out to disk, and finally an "a" to take you back into text insertion mode right where you left off. Note that both the "ESC" key and the "ENTER" key must be escaped with CTRL-V or they will be misinterpreted.

❓ Can I use the map! command to make a text insertion mode command that behaves like the CTRL-G of command mode to see where I am in the current file?

This one is handy if you just want to know where you are in the file without having to go out to command mode and come back. Well, actually you do have to go out and back, but it's all automatic.

```
:map! ^G ^[^V^Ga
```

This one's a little tricky. Because CTRL-G has a special meaning, you can't just enter it, and if you enter a single CTRL-V, it will escape what you are trying to do. So the trick to this one is that the first CTRL-G must be entered with a CTRL-V,CTRL-G sequence, then CTRL-V, ESCAPE,CTRL-V,CTRL-V,CTRL-G, and a final "a" to go back into text insertion mode.

❓ How can I reduce the number of keystrokes I need to enter for common phrases?

Use **:abbr**. This one is so simple you should do it on the fly whenever you find yourself repeatedly using the same sequence. And it's handy for creating standard phrases so that an entire workgroup uses the same wording for critical phrases. For example, while writing this chapter we must have used the sequence "**.pgvi.pgx**" a zillion times, since we wanted it to appear in "program text," not in regular text, and the publisher wanted a ".pg" at the start of inline program text, and ".pgx" for when it was done. Well, that got awfully old real quick. So, we added the following abbreviation to my **.exrc** file:

```
:abbr vvi .pgvi.pgx
```

As you type along, abbreviations are automatically expanded to their full meaning as you go, unlike some word processors that wait until you explicitly tell them to expand the abbreviations.

OTHER ESSENTIAL COMMANDS

? How can I save my changes and quit vi?

To save your work and quit, you can use the command mode sequence **ZZ** or the external mode sequence **:wq**. We find the **:wq** more intuitive and easier to type, but to each her own. And if you want to create a series of function key mappings to do this, feel free. We have spent so much time with WordPerfect that we have my F7 key mapped to do this: **map ^[[S :wq!^M**. Other people we know have theirs mapped to ALT-F4.

? Can I include another file in my current file?

Yes; use the **:r** (read) command. This is handy if you want to include some standard header text, for example, that's too big a block to put in a map or abbreviation.

? Is it possible to write out part of my current file to a "scratch" file?

Sure, you'll just need to tell the **write** command how much and where. To write the whole current file back out, we use the short form of the write command **:w**. But to write out the next ten lines, including the current one to a file called "junk," use the longer form of write:

```
:.,+10w junk
```

This will write out the current line and the next ten lines to the file named "junk."

? Help! What can I do if I'm sure I have done something horrible to my file?

Use "quit-bang" to quit without saving. That's **:q!** and it always gets you out.

? What's the "smart" exit command?

Use **:x** if you want to save the current file if it has changed, or leave it unchanged if you haven't modified it, and either way, exit back to your shell. This should probably be your "normal" exit command, unless you want the file's date and time to be updated when you exit, even if you haven't made any changes.

? How can I find out how many words or lines are in my file?

You can send your file through the UNIX **wc** word count utility to find out how many words or lines are in your file. It will even give you a total for all the files in the list you give it. To get a total word, line, and byte count for the seven dot-cat files in our /save directory, we get

```
$ wc -lwc *.cat
      14        84       573 alfie.cat
     140       790      6346 guz.cat
     280      1580     12692 harold.cat
      56       311      2600 meep.cat
      70       395      3173 possm.cat
     266      1496     12119 pris.cat
     560      3160     25384 stanley.cat
    1386      7816     62887 total
```

Which shows us that we have a total of 1,386 lines, 7,816 words, and some 62,887 bytes of text in the seven files. And almost enough cats in our life.

The Other Editor—emacs

Well, there are other editors out there in the UNIX world if you just can't stand the thought of **vi**. Personally, we think you're making a mistake, but it's your call. Of the generally available ones, the most common is certainly **emacs**, which is short for "editor macros." Unlike **vi**, it's not a modal editor, but a more traditional editor. What you type generally goes into the file, and when you want to do something other than just enter text, you use a CTRL key or keys to tell **emacs** you want it to do something special. And **emacs** can do a lot of special things. It's a powerful package, and can do all the things that **vi** can do and lots more, if you care to teach it those extra things. To extend **emacs**, you really need to be a lisp programmer, since **emacs** is a lisp-based program. But don't let that frighten you. You can make a very good start indeed by just borrowing some of the things your friends have done, and tweaking them for yourself. Plus, some things, like building macros and abbreviations, are already there and ready to go. So, if you want to give **emacs** a try, and you don't have a copy on your system, ask your system administrator to see about getting a copy. There are also other editors to be found, and many of them are available for the price of a download. In addition, there are now commercial, graphical-based editors for those of you running under XWindows. These are generally friendly and easy to use. But you won't find many, if any, that are as powerful as either **vi** or **emacs**. The current version of **gnu emacs** has a graphical mode that even supports rodents, for those who simply can't live without a mouse. To each his own. We'll stick with our old standby, **vi**, however. Especially since it's almost always available, and we even have versions running happily in Windows 95 and Windows NT for those times we're stuck working on a regular PC.

? What happens if my system crashes before I've written my changes?

Quick! Use the recover command. If you end up exiting from **vi** because something causes your system to crash, you can almost always recover what you were working on by using the special **vi -r** *filename* command. Then save the file back out, just in case.

Chapter 5

Customizations and Profiles

Answer Topics!

Customizations and Profiles @ a Glance

Start-up script basics are where you'll need to begin if you want to make your UNIX desktop your very own. Decisions about your workspace can be as simple as changing the color of your screen and desktop in XWindows or as far-reaching as deciding on a particular shell to run. Only you can decide how many and what kind of changes you'd like to make.

- By **setting and using variables**, you can save yourself a lot of time. Here's what you'll need to know to use variables to travel quickly between directories, to spruce up your terminal's looks, and more.

- If you're a confirmed DOS user, you may want to know how to create a set of **UNIX commands that work like their DOS equivalents**. This may sound like an odd thing to do, but if you're sick of wasting time because your fingers are typing DOS commands while you're working in a UNIX environment, here's a solution.

- In the section about **shell script shortcuts**, you'll learn from other people's mistakes. These are the basic do's and don'ts of working with UNIX shell scripts.

START-UP SCRIPT BASICS

Start-up Scripts

The single most important change you'll make to your work environment is in your start-up scripts. Depending on the shell you use, this may involve only a single file or several.

For the most part, though, you'll have two very important files to worry about if you're in text mode, and one or more additional ones for those of you running in XWindows or some derivative of XWindows, such as HPVue, SCO Open Desktop, or CDE (short for "Common Desktop Environment," the new standard for XWindows desktops). The specifics of each XWindows shell are too individual for this book, but we'll deal with some of the more general things you can do and you can use the documentation you received with your system plus what you learn here to tweak HPVue or whatever to your heart's content. (There's lots more on XWindows in Chapter 8.)

? What are start-up scripts, and what can they do for me?

Start-up scripts are really just customized segments of code that live inside your UNIX start-up files. Their purpose is to tell UNIX exactly how you'd like your terminal and environment variables set, among other things. Once you understand how they work, start-up scripts can save you an enormous amount of time and frustration, so read on to learn more about them.

? How do I edit a start-up script?

Easy. Load the relevant file(s) into your favorite editor and go to it. To be safe and save yourself some grief, however, heed the following tips:

● Any time you make changes to start-up scripts, be sure you make a backup first. It's possible—in fact, easy—to do something that will prevent you from being able to log in. Your system administrator will be fairly forgiving the first time, but increasingly less so after that. So always back up originals of your scripts to a safe place before you start messing with them.

● Use **rlogin** to test your changes before you log all the way out. This little trick can save you all sorts of embarrassment. Whenever you make changes to any of your start-up files, try the following before you go any farther:

```
rlogin localhost
```

where **localhost** is replaced by the hostname of the machine you're currently on. The worst that can happen is you'll find out that what you just tried to do didn't work, and you can kill the **rlogin** and restore the saved version of
the file.

? How can I customize UNIX if I'm a Korn shell user?

The Korn shell uses two basic files to control its start-up. The first, **.profile**, is read only by the original login shell and resides in your home directory. This is the place to put terminal setting commands and environmental variables.

However, once this file is read the first time, it's not normally read again for that session, unless we explicitly call it or in some other way force it to be read. The second file, **.kshrc**, is read every time another shell is spawned, if we've set ourselves up to use it at all.

? How do I tell the Korn or Posix shell to check if there is a secondary start-up file, and use it?

The Korn and Posix shells check to see if there is a variable called "**ENV**" in your environment, and if there is, they look at its value to find out what the secondary start-up file is called. So add the following to your **.profile** and all will be well:

```
ENV=$HOME/.kshrc
export ENV
```

Some Advice for Korn Shell Users

OK, we know you didn't really ask me for any advice, but here are a few tips that may help you:

● Put the things that can be exported into **~/.profile** and save aliases and special settings for your secondary start-up script. The usual name for this second start-up script is **.kshrc**, and it should also reside in your home directory.

● We used **~/.profile** above, and then used **$HOME/.kshrc** right after. But there is, in fact, absolutely no difference when running Korn or Posix shell between **~** and **$HOME** when used this way. They both refer to your home directory, the place where you start out when you first log into the system. We'll use them interchangeably, and you'll see both in other books.

● If you're writing a shell script that must be interpreted by the Bourne shell, use the **$HOME** construct. This is necessary because the Bourne shell doesn't support the **~** version. In fact, it's probably a good idea to get in the habit of using **$HOME** in scripts as a matter of course. And it's easy enough to make that a **vi map!** command so you don't have to type it all out.

● Use different **.kshrc** files for different projects. I use this trick all the time. Instead of having **ENV** always refer to your home directory, have it point to the current directory first and then, only if it doesn't find a **.kshrc**, have it look at your home directory. This way, you can easily load a set of special aliases for each project and still have a default set for general use. Your initial login window, of course, will always see your default resource file, **$HOME/.kshrc**, since that will be the current directory when you log in. The following illustration shows how to do it.

```
if [[ -f ./.kshrc ]]
then ENV='./.kshrc'
else ENV='$HOME/.kshrc'
fi
export ENV
```

If you have a terminal with multiple windows available, or you're running XWindows and have multiple windows open, then each window you open will look in the directory that's current at the time you open the window to see if there is a **.kshrc** present. If there is, it'll load that **.kshrc**. Unfortunately, however, it *won't* load your general one if there isn't a **.kshrc** in your current directory.

+ ***Tip:*** *When running XWindows, your* first *window into a directory should be a login shell.*

* ***Note:*** *The login shell will look to see if the current directory contains the resource file. If it doesn't, then it will load your default resource file, - $HOME/.kshrc, as will all subsequent windows loaded from that window.*

? ## How can I customize UNIX if I'm a C shell user?

C shell users should use **.cshrc** to add customizations. This file, which should be in the home directory, performs the same functions for **csh** users that **.kshrc** does for Korn shell users. In the C shell, the login script is the ~/.login, which equates to the Korn shell users' ~/.profile. However, the C shell also lets its users set default actions when they log out.

These are stored in the ~/.logout script, so if you're feeling adventurous, you can experiment with this one, too.

? Can I get rid of that boring old $ prompt?

Yes! The Korn shell defines a variable, **PS1**, which is the normal prompt. So, if you change the value of **PS1**, you change your prompt. This prompt can include the values of other variables, or any text string. For example, if you like to think of yourself as the master of the computer, you might try this for a prompt:

```
PS1='How may I serve you, Master? '
```

Go ahead; try a few things. You can have some fun with this, but when you get done fooling around, you'll probably want something more useful, so keep reading.

Use the **$PWD** variable that is built into the Korn shell to track your current directory. Most of us are familiar with the DOS prompt that tracks our current directory. So, if you try to achieve the same thing in UNIX, you might try

```
PS1="$PWD \$ "
```

Looks good at first glance. If you are in your home directory, it might look something like this:

```
/users/harold $
```

But what happens when you change to harold's bin directory? You type in

```
/users/harold $ cd bin
```

then ask for the identity of the present working directory,

```
/users/harold $ pwd
```

and end up with the following:

```
/users/harold/bin
/users/harold $
```

Maybe this isn't quite what you had in mind. That's because the double quotes allow the Korn shell to "see" the **$PWD** variable and interpret it. Once that happens, it's converted into a string and becomes static. To prevent this, we enclose it in single quotes, which will stop the initial evaluation of the **$PWD** variable, and allow it to be passed to the command line, where it will then get interpreted. So now we type

```
$ PS1='$PWD \$ '
```

and when you change to harold's bin directory and ask for the present working directory, the prompt will show

```
/users/harold/bin $
```

Now the prompt will track the current directory as intended. The deep directory structures possible in UNIX can make for a pretty long prompt, however. For this reason, we like to use the following, a two-line prompt with the current directory on the first line, and then the "**$**" on the second line. Type in the following:

```
/users/harold $ PS1='$PWD ^J\$ '
```

to get a prompt that looks like this:

```
/users/harold
$
```

Now we have a nice two-line prompt that shows us the current directory.

Tip: *Include your "pseudo terminal" in your prompt. If you work on a machine that supports multiple pseudo terminals, keep track of which window you're working in by using this prompt:*

```
PS1="\[$(tty|cut -c9-11)\]"'$PWD ^J\$ '
```

The result will show

```
[p01]
```

followed by your directory name information.

Tip: *Include the hostname in your prompt, so you know where you are. If you work in a distributed environment, where you regularly log in to different machines from your "normal" machine, it can be a pain to keep track of which machine you're on. So include it in your prompt!*

```
PS1="$(hostname)":'$PWD ^J \$ '
```

But when I do that on my system, I get

```
rci1.rci.com:/users/charlie
$
```

So, use the %% trick to strip off the unwanted stuff from the right side of the hostname. If you're stripping something off the left side, you'd use ## instead.

```
host=`hostname`
PS1=${host%%.*}:'$PWD ^J \$ '
```

This puts the local hostname into the prompt, stripping out the domain name stuff that may be returned by running the **hostname** program.

❓ Which quote is which and why should I care?

Throughout this book, and in other UNIX books, you will see three different kinds of quote marks: single quotes ('), double quotes ("), and grave quotes (`). Each one has a very different meaning to the shell.

The single quote says to the shell—look, everything inside here is a plain, unadulterated string. Don't even *try* to check to see if you can interpret any of it. Just leave it alone and pass it on to the next process. Which means this is almost always the kind of quote you should use for an alias, because you want the first pass to simply ignore the inside of the quotes, and let it pass the contents to the second pass, which will then have the quotes stripped off, and will be able to actually interpret what you are trying to do. But if you do have variables inside the single quotes, they won't be expanded but simply passed on, complete with their dollar signs.

Double quotes, on the other hand, are still enclosing strings, but now the shell is allowed to look inside to see if there are any special characters it should interpret. This allows it to expand any variable that it finds, for example, so that **"$PWD"** gets expanded immediately to the full current working directory. However, once the shell has expanded the inside of the double quoted section, it passes the result to whatever follows as a literal, quoted string. This means that the inside of the double quotes will be evaluated when it is first seen, and not again, so you can't use it in things like prompts and aliases where you want a secondary evaluation.

Finally, the grave quotes (` ) are very special, since they tell the shell to actually *run* the program inside the grave quotes and replace the quoted section with the result of the quote. This means that `hostname` will be replaced in the command with the result of running the hostname program, which would be something like **rci1.scribes.com** on my machine. Again, however, this is evaluated immediately, which means that the result is static. Many modern versions of the Korn shell have replaced this usage with a completely different-looking—but essentially similar—working construct: **$(hostname)**.

 Tip: *PATH too long for a prompt? Strip off the extra. Use the # pattern-matching operator to strip out your home directory as shown here:*

```
$ pwd
$ /users/charlie
PS1='${PWD#$HOME*/}\$ '
/users/charlie $ cd /users/charlie/bin
bin $ cd
/users/charlie $ cd /bin
/bin $
```

This prompt tracks directories under your home directory nicely, but when you're in your home directory you see the full current directory as part of your prompt, and whenever you wander out into the general part of the filesystem, you see where you are. Use **##** in place of **#$HOME** in Figure 5-2 to see only the lowest directory in the prompt.

C shell users, don't despair. All this prompt stuff is nice if you are a Korn shell user, but what about the C shell users, you ask? Well, the good news is that these same tricks work pretty much in the same way for C shell users. The syntax is a bit different, of course, but the overall effect is pretty much the same. For example, suppose you want your basic prompt with the current directory in it:

```
set prompt="${cwd}% "
```

This should work on most systems where C shell supports the variable **cwd**. How about some of the other stuff? Well, you can easily set up an alias, just like with the Korn shell. Here's our alias to get a long listing of the files in the current directory:

```
alias ll ls -lAF
```

For start-up files, the C shell uses **$HOME/.login** and **$HOME/.cshrc**. The .login is only read by the initial login shell, while the **.cshrc** file is read by all shells. So put your aliases in the **.cshrc** just as you would put them in the **.kshrc** file with the Korn shell.

SETTING AND USING VARIABLES

+ ***Tip:*** *You can make your use and navigation of UNIX much easier by using variables. Try to keep the use of aliases to a minimum, since every time you start a subshell it must be evaluated. Reduce the number of aliases you need by creating variables and exporting them.*

? Can I use a variable to describe a frequently used working directory?

By all means. Then, when there's a change, you can simply change the directory that the variable points to, and all your other aliases and shell scripts that use this variable will now point to the new directory. For example, suppose you are working on a project with a group of coworkers. The files for the directory are stored in **/users/projects/newmodel/ network**. You're not going to want to type that too often. So create a variable that points to that directory—we'll call it **PROJHOME**—and include it in your **.profile**:

```
PROJHOME=/users/projects/newmodel/network
export PROJHOME
```

Now you can change to the proper directory with

```
cd $PROJHOME
```

+ ***Tip:*** *Add a variable to keep out prying eyes. Let's say we have a special group working on this project and because it's super-secret, we don't want anyone else looking at our plans. So let's add another variable, **PROJGRP**, that we can use.*

```
PROJGRP=netwrk
export PROJGRP
```

Now a simple shell script will get us where we want to be, change to the necessary group, and fire off a copy of WordPerfect to edit the functional specification for the project. The script is shown here, where we've also defined the variable **FSPEC** to point to that functional spec.

```
# Shell Script to edit the functional spec
# for the current project
# Script stays the same as the projects change.
sg -a $PROJGRP
cd $PROJHOME
/usr/wp/xwp $FSPEC
```

Now our shell script, which we called **proj**, will automatically handle the whole process of getting us to where we want to be, firing off WordPerfect, and loading the working file. Sure beats doing all that by hand, doesn't it?

? ## Is there a way I can spruce up a boring text terminal a little?

For those of you stuck at a boring text terminal, here are a couple of little tricks to try. If your terminal supports color but you've still got nothing more exciting than plain white text on a black background, try this to change the background color.

```
alias -x blue='^[[37\;44m'
alias -x black='^[[37\;40m'
alias -x revrs='^[[7m'
alias -x norm='^[[0m'
```

In the above aliases, the ^[is the escape character. You can enter this by pressing CTRL-V and then ESC. Now, if you want a little blue screen with white text, just type echo blue. You could have included the echo as part of the alias, of course, but this would make the alias less useful. By doing it this way, with the -x parameter to alias, the "blue" is available from within your scripts. This is especially useful for using the revrs and norm aliases for highlighting text.

Table 5-1 shows the colors and their corresponding numbers for sprucing up your terminal's looks.

Position	Value	Color
Overall	0	All attributes off
	1	Bold
	4	Underscore
	5	Blink
	7	Reverse video
	8	Concealed
Foreground	30	Black
	31	Red
	32	Green
	33	Yellow
	34	Blue
	35	Magenta
	36	Cyan
	37	White
Background	40	Black
	41	Red
	42	Green
	43	Yellow
	44	Blue
	45	Magenta
	46	Cyan
	47	White

Table 5-1 ANSI Escape Sequences for Changing Colors

* ***Note:*** *Values must be preceded by ^[[(**Escape[**) and be separated by an "escaped" semicolon (\;). The sequence is terminated by an **m**.*

? Do I need to export single-use variables?

No. Reduce clutter in your environment. If you're going to use a variable only as a "local variable" inside a script, don't bother to export it in the script and especially not in your dot-profile. Just create it in the script and use it there. When the script terminates, the variable will be unset once again.

? But should I export variables that I expect to use repeatedly?

Yes. Put them in your **.profile** file (**.login** for the C shell) and they will be available throughout the entire session, and in all your subshells or scripts or whatever.

? Should I remove variables?

No. They generally won't hurt anything, but if you're incurably fussy about such things, go ahead, knock yourself out! The command to remove a variable is **unset variable**.

? How can I see the value of a variable?

Use the **print** command. You can see what a variable is set to by using **print "$variable"**. The **echo** command will also work for this, but it's better to use **print** since **echo** may behave differently on different systems. Also notice that we enclosed the variable name in double quotes. The shell will still see the $ inside the double quotes and expand the variable to its value.

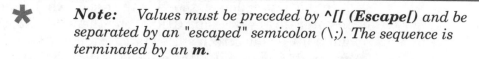

DOS Commands in UNIX

Those of us who must constantly switch back and forth between UNIX and DOS or Windows machines are always having problems with the differences. The commands in the two operating systems are enough alike that our fingers are constantly confused. The answer is to create a set of UNIX commands that work like their DOS equivalents, and then do the same in DOS (or Windows 95/NT) so that our fingers won't get confused when we're there, either. Here's a set of useful aliases. You'll probably find other situations that you want to alias. Just add them to the list, and then put them in your **.kshrc** file.

```
# DOS aliases, only available from an interactive shell so we
# don't slow down scripts.
case $- in
*i*)    # If $- matches *i*, this is a shell, not a script
        alias copy='cp'
        alias move='mv'
        alias rd='rmdir'
        alias deltree='rm -r'
        alias cls='clear'
        alias dir='ls -l'
        alias type='cat'
        ;;
esac
```

We have a similar set I use from within Windows NT and Windows 95 to handle that side of the problem. Create a file called **unix.bat** and stick it somewhere in your path. Then call the file from within your **autoexec.bat** file. Here's my set of UNIX in DOS commands.

```
REM Only need to load DOSKEY inside here if you aren't using
REM it already. To load it from within here, unREM the next
REM line. Note the fairly large buffer size. You may need it.
REM doskey /bufsize=2048
doskey mv=move $*
doskey cp=copy $*
doskey ll=dir $* /p
doskey pwd=cd
doskey more=type $1 $b more
doskey cat=type $*
doskey man=help $1
doskey rm=del $*
doskey env=set | more
doskey grep=find $*
```

Finally, you may find that the single most annoying difference between the two environments is the difference in text editors.

Tip: *If you have to work in DOS or Windows much, you'll miss your* **vi***. There are good replacements that run in the DOS world, however. One is Oak Hill Vi, from Oak Hill Software, Inc. in Scottsdale, AZ. The MKS Toolkit has an excellent vi and a graphical vi for windows as well as a complete replacement for DOS' (and Windows 95's) COMMAND.COM (or Windows NT's CMD.EXE) shell that looks very much like UNIX. As we discuss in Chapter 11, a copy of the MKS Toolkit can make all the difference for those who have to live in both the UNIX and NT environments.*

Shell Script Shortcuts

The more you use UNIX, the more you'll find yourself writing shell scripts. Most will be short little things that serve a simple purpose. Some may be long, complicated scripts that have all sorts of error checking in them. But whatever scripts you write, there are certain things they *should* have in common. Probably the easiest to forget, but the most important, is to always document your scripts. Yeah, right. Everyone always says that. But we really mean it. In fact, let's repeat it for emphasis.

- *Always document your shell scripts.* No matter how simple they are, it costs almost nothing to insert a simple little header in them that includes key information like the name of the file, the date it was created, and the task it was supposed to perform. Sure, you know what it does now. But you won't remember in two weeks, much less two years.

- *Make a standard header file for every script.* Every script should have a header that you automatically include in each and every shell script that will be around long enough to get out of your **~/tmp** directory. You can include whatever you want in yours, but we strongly recommend that you add comments throughout the script as well. You'll thank yourself later.

- *Let the system create unique filenames for you.* If you run a script every day—for example, a backup of a set of important files onto a different filesystem—let UNIX do some of the work for you. If you need a filename generated every day, let the date command do the work for you. The following illustration shows a script that runs every day to make an export of a critical database. We use the **date** command to generate a filename. This makes it easy to keep track of which file is the most current, and at the same time lets us take this entire command and stick it into a **crontab** to make it happen automatically. For more on **crontabs** and running jobs automatically at specified times, see Chapter 7.

```
==============================================================================
#
#Filename: db_exp.ksh
#
#Author: Charlie Russel
#
#Description: Script to create an automatic export of the database.
#
#Last Modification: 8/15/97-Modified to compress file on creation - cpr
#Prev. Modification: Added absolute path to exp - 7/14/97
#
#
==============================================================================
#
#
./scripts/oracle_setup DUMMY
#
# Run Script
print \n
print 'Executing script db_exp.ksh'
ORACLE_SID=rci; export ORACLE_SID
file=/safety/`date +%b%d`.dmp # Create unique filename with today's date
#
# Put command into variable
oracmd="/oracle/bin/exp system/rcipw file=$file grants=y indexes=y full=y"
#
print "Executing command..."
print \"$oracmd \"
$oracmd
# Execute the compression on the created file to reduce space.
# This could simply be piped from the export, but is separate for historical reasons.
compress $file
exit
```

If you only need a file as a temporary storage place, let the system do the work. Let UNIX worry about cleaning up after you and keeping track of the filename. Some commands need a file as an intermediate storage spot, so use UNIX's built-in functions to create and delete the temporary filename. The **mktemp** command exists in many implementations of UNIX, but if it doesn't exist in yours, you can let the shell generate a name. If **mktemp** exists, try this:

```
filename=`mktemp`
```

Then, when the script is finished, just add a final line to clean up after yourself:

```
rm $filename
```

If your version of UNIX doesn't support **mktemp**, use the built-in functionality of the shell to do the work:

```
filename="/tmp/$LOGNAME.$SECONDS"
```

This will generate a filename based on your login name, and the number of seconds since you started this shell. Just remember to remove the file when you're done with it. Otherwise, your system administrator is likely to become grumpy about cleaning up after you.

Chapter 6

Printing

Answer Topics!

Printing @ a Glance

Printing is another operation that almost every computer user will want to perform at some time. In UNIX, you have a couple of options: printing now or printing later. But even once you've decided that you'll be **printing now**, you have some decisions to make, so read on for tips on determining which printer you'll be sending your job to, how to print multiple copies of a document, and controlling how a printed job looks.

Printing later is quite similar to printing now, except that you need to know how to schedule your print job. For your convenience, you may also want to check the status of a particular job (or jobs) to see where it is in the print queue.

Formatting your print job is important since it determines how your finished document will look. Here you'll learn how to double-space or add a left margin to a document, how to remove hard tabs and realign tabstops, and how to put a file into multicolumn format, among other things.

Last but not least come some **other useful printing tricks**, including how to stop a print job, getting the status of a print request, and how to tell where your job is printing.

PRINTING NOW

What is the standard UNIX command to print a file?

On System V UNIX systems, this standard printing command will be

```
lp notes
```

If you're on a Berkeley UNIX system, the standard command to print a file is

```
lpr notes
```

We'll be showing the System V version of the commands first, and the Berkeley system versions second. You'll see that they're very similar.

? How can I change the default printer destination?

Use the **LPDEST** environment variable. Your system administrator (or on some systems, the lp administrator) can set an overall default printer for each machine on the network, but if you usually want your output to go a different printer, add the different destination to your **.profile** file:

```
LPDEST=laser ; export LPDEST
```

This will set your default printer to "laser" instead of the machine's normal default. This can be useful for using different printers for different projects, as well. In Berkeley systems, you usually substitute **PRINTER** for **LPDEST** above.

? Can I override the default printer destination for a particular print job?

Yes. Use the **-ddest** option. You can easily override your default destination for any particular print job. If you knew you had a memo that you wanted to print on the laser printer next to the department secretary's desk, for example, you could use this command.

```
lp -dsec_laser mymemo
```

Berkeley systems use the **-Pdest** option to accomplish the same thing.

? Is there a way I can eliminate that silly banner page?

Try using the **nobanner** option. This isn't such a hot idea, by the way, if you work with a shared printer on a network that gets a lot of different print requests, because there'll be no way to know whose print job just came out of the printer. But on small networks, or where the printer is physically fairly close to you, by all means, dump that banner.

```
lp -onobanner notes
```

Different systems have a different shortcut for this, usually **-onb** or **-ob**, but the long form is usually the same on all systems. For Berkeley systems, the option is **-h** for no header.

? **How can I control the number of copies of a file that I want printed?**

Use the **-n** option. When you need more than one copy, just put the number on the command line:

```
lp -n 3 notes
```

The above command will give you three copies of the notes. Berkeley uses **#n** where **n** is the number you want.

UNIX Printing Idiosyncrasies

Because UNIX was designed to be a multiuser and multitasking environment, the early designers realized that they needed to have a way for people to continue to work on the system while printing was going on. Printing is a slow process, even on the fastest printers, and it doesn't require very much in the way of raw processing power. To make everyone wait while the printer was doing its thing would be a serious waste of time and resources. So UNIX borrows from the mainframe world and sends all printing tasks, or "jobs," to a spooler. The printing spooler is a background task, known as a *daemon*, that's always there, waiting for something to do. When you send a job to the printer, what you're actually doing is sending it to the printer daemon, which first stores it on the hard disk in a temporary file, and then sends it to the printer, a little piece at a time. This way, you (and the rest of the users on the system) can go on about your business, and the print spooler prints your job without tying up the main processor, since the spooler needs only a tiny portion of the available processor time to get its job done.

If everything goes well, you click on the Print button in WordPerfect, select the printer you want your updated résumé to go to, and send it off. By the time you walk over to the printer, the job is coming out, and you grab it before anyone else has a chance to see it. No problem.

But wait, someone else has started a print job on that printer that will take an hour to complete and your print job is stuck behind it! Hmmm. Think your boss will mind if you just sort of hang around the printer? It's time to figure out how to handle this, and lots of other little problems that crop up in a shared printing environment.

❓ Is there a way I can have UNIX tell me when my print job is done?

Certainly. Let the print spooler send you a message when the job is finished. Use the following command:

```
lp -m notes
```

This will send you a mail message when the job is done. Use **-w** to have it write the message directly to your terminal upon job completion. Use this option with caution. Lots of programs don't like having messages dumped to the terminal while they're running. If you aren't logged in when the job finishes, the message is mailed instead. For Berkeley users, the option is the same: **-m**.

❓ Can I control the way my printed job looks?

Of course. Each printer type or model will have a list of possible options that it will support. These range from the fairly simple ones available for dot matrix printers, to the more complicated ones for a typical laser printer. You can add as many options as you want to the command line; just remember that each option requires a preceding **-o**. The printing on a UNIX system is controlled by a script that knows the options that the particular printer will support, and which escape sequences it requires to set each option. This script file, which can be modified by the system administrator to add special characteristics for an individual printer, usually resides in the **/usr/spool/lp/model** directory. To see what options are supported for your printer, you can print this file out. But in general, these include options to control the character spacing and font type, and the quality and orientation of the printout. On typical dot matrix printers, for example, the options may include such things as using elite or compressed type, and whether to print in draft mode or in near letter quality. On a typical laser printer these options are likely to include the ability to change fonts, and even settings for using different font cartridges or paper trays. The quality of the printer support will depend on a variety of factors, including how recent the revision of UNIX is.

Printing Now vs. Printing Later

Most printing you do will be like this: You finish editing a document, you want to print it. If you're working inside an application program, like WordPerfect or IslandCalc or whatever, just follow the commands appropriate to that program to print your document. Give it the destination you want, and go pick up the output when it's done.

One of the problems with working in a shared printer environment is that you can't always use the printer as you might want to because it would be too disruptive to others on the system. An example of this is large print jobs that could tie the printer up for long periods. How long is a long period? This is really subjective and depends on your environment. If you share a printer with a small group of three or four other people, and you ask first, you can probably get away with a print job that takes a half hour or even an hour. But try that on a centralized printer shared by 25 or 30 users and listen to the screams. There are a couple of ways to handle this problem, depending on how your system is set up. Probably the easiest one is to simply fire off the print job on your way out the door as the last thing at night. If that's not an option, here are some ideas to keep the peace.

PRINTING LATER

? **Is there a command I can use to hold my print job for later?**

Yes. Use the **hold** option to get your file ready for printing but not actually start it until later. If you use the **hold** option when printing that big job, it'll be held until you tell it to actually go to the printer. Meanwhile, however, it's been fed to the spooler and is ready and waiting. Then, when the printer will be free for an extended period, you can start it up. To print the file bigdocument to the printer netlaser but hold it until you say, try this:

```
lp -dnetlaser -H hold -m bigdocument
```

Then, when you want to start the printing, use

```
lp -i requestid -H resume
```

This still requires some degree of planning and attention on your part, but at least you know everything's ready and waiting. There's a second problem with it as well: you need to know what the requestid is for the job you want to resume. As you can see in Figure 6-1, you'll be told the requestid when you first issue the print command, so write it down and hope that when it's time to resume the job, you'll be able to find where you wrote it.

? How can I find out the status of my print jobs?

Use **lpstat**. This command will tell you all sorts of information. In its simplest form, without options, it will tell you what jobs are in what printer queues. Use the **-u** option to display information about your jobs only. (In HPUX you need the **-t** option to show the status of printers and jobs.)

? Can I schedule a print job for later?

By all means. If your system administrator has given permission, you can use the **at** command to schedule a print job for later execution. We'll look at the **at** command in more detail in Chapter 7, but for the moment here's a simple example to run a series of print commands at 5:30 p.m.

```
at 05:30pm < commandfile
```

```
xterm
$ lp -dlaser /H hold /tmp/hugefile
request id is laser-7566 (1 file)
$ lpstat -u
laser-7566      charlie      5245111  August 15 16:20 being held
cprdot-7570     root         7126     August 15 16:21
cprdot-7571     stanley      23450    August 16 16:21
$ lp -i laser-7566 -H resume
$
```

Figure 6-1   The **lp** command will tell you what the **requestid** is for your print job

In this case *commandfile* is a file you have created that contains each of the commands you want executed at 5:30 p.m., one line to a command.

FORMATTING

? What are some of the basic formatting options that UNIX offers me?

The built-in **pr** utility manages all sorts of little formatting chores with ease. It can handle multicolumn output, set tabstops, double-space a file, add a left margin, expand tabs to spaces or convert spaces back to tabs, or add line numbers to a file. We're not talking desktop publishing here, but for simple tasks it's quick and easy.

Formatting with UNIX

If you want your print jobs from UNIX to be something other than plain old dull Courier, you're going to have to take some steps to make that happen. You *could* go out and buy a high-priced word processor or even higher-priced desktop publishing package and there certainly are some excellent ones that run on most UNIX platforms. If you intend to do a lot of heavy-duty formatting and want to see what your document looks like before you actually print it, you're probably going to need one of these programs. But if all you need to do is spiff up your output a bit, or include an equation or graphic, you don't really need to use anything but the tools you probably already have on your system. And if you're comfortable with simply entering in the commands to print in bold, double-spaced, and have faith that that is what will happen without actually being able to see the result until you print it, then you can publish whole books with the native UNIX tools.

How can I double-space my file?

Easy! Use the **-d** option with **pr**. UNIX editors like **vi** don't want to give you double-spaced text, so to get it you need to run the job through **pr** as you print it:

```
pr -d filename | lp -
```

This takes the input file and double-spaces it, sending the result straight to the default printer and leaving the original unchanged. This will also add a header that includes the date and time as well as the page and filename.

Can I add a left margin to my file?

Yes; use the **-on** option. Again, **vi** isn't going to give you a left margin, and it can be awkward to add it manually, so just run the file through **pr** to handle this little task.

```
pr -d -o10   filename | lp -
```

Now our document is double-spaced and has a left margin of ten characters added.

Figures 6-2 and 6-3 show the file before and after the above command line.

Is there a way I can remove hard tabs and realign my tabstops?

Try the **-eck** option. One very annoying trait of **vi** is that it uses "hard" tabs. You can change the amount of space each one represents with **:set ts=n**, where **n** is the spacing. But

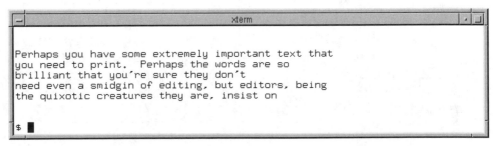

Figure 6-2 A simple little document before **pr** has done its job

```
        Perhaps you have some extremely important text that

        you need to print.  Perhaps the words are so brilliant

        that you're sure they don't

        need even a smidgin of editing, but editors, being

        the quixotic creatures they are, insist on

  I
```

Figure 6-3　The same document, with a left margin and double-spaced

when you go to print the document or view it without setting **ts** the same, everything gets jumbled up as in Figure 6-4.

　　Well, here's a simple little shell script to convert tabs to spaces, lined up with the tabstops every three spaces. You could spruce this one up to have a variable number of spaces for your tabstops, add error checking, whatever. It works and it's simple.

```
### File ~/bin/detab -- removes tabs from a file and
                          converts to spaces
### File name remains the same.
pr -t -e3 $1 > /tmp/tabtmp
cp /tmp/tabtmp $1
```

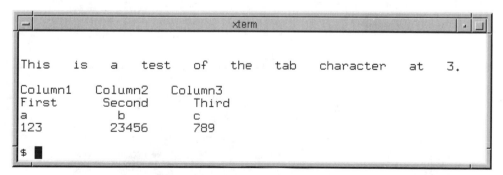

Figure 6-4　The hard tabs result when using **vi**

This little gem is something we added to my **~/.exrc** file as a **map** so we can run it from within **vi**. We have it mapped to CTRL-T for tabs:

```
map ^T ^[1G!G pr -te3^M
```

Voila! Just hit CTRL-T, and all your tabs are converted to spaces, with your columns still lined up nice and neat, with three space indents as shown in Figure 6-5.

? But what can I do if I need to put the spaces back?

Use the **-in** option to replace spaces with tabs. If you need to make sure you have tab characters in a file you put spaces into, use the **pr** command again, but this time use **-i** to insert tab characters. This is useful, for example, if you'll later be importing the text into a word processing program that uses a variable-spaced font, one that will correctly interpret the tab character.

? Can I turn a list into a multicolumn format?

Yes, a simple **-n** will tell **pr** to convert your list of names into an *n* column list. If you want it as columns ordered across the page, instead of down, add **-a** to the command.

```
pr -3a -t names > names.out
```

This will convert the list of names into a three-column list. Combine this with UNIX's built-in sorter and you have a sorted list in three-column format.

```
sort names | pr -3a -t > sorted.names
```

```
This      is       a        test     of       the      tab      character      at 3.

Column1            Column2           Column3
First              Second            Third
a                  b                 c
123                23456             789
```

Figure 6-5   The proper way to line things up

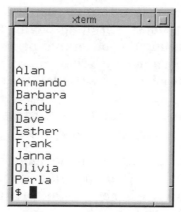

Figure 6-6 Our unsorted list of names

The before and after appear in Figures 6-6 and 6-7.

OTHER USEFUL PRINTING TRICKS

Is there a way I can cancel a print job?

Quick! Use the **cancel** command to halt the print job you just sent. This command has the form

```
cancel [request-id] [printer]
```

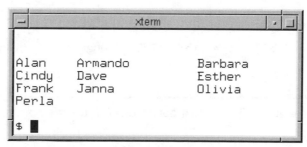

Figure 6-7 The list sorted into easy to read format

which means that you can cancel a job either by specifying the requestid or by specifying the printer and thereby canceling the job on that printer. Note that you can only cancel a print job that you created. To cancel someone else's print job requires (ta-da!) the superuser.

? Can I use the lpstat command to get the current status of my print request?

Yes. Use this command, along with **-u yourname**, to get a list of just your current print jobs. Jobs that are currently printing will show as **on printer** where *printer* is the name of the printer. Figure 6-8 shows that Charlie has two jobs queued up for the printer laser, and the first one has already started printing.

? How can I find out where my job is printing?

Again, the answer is **lpstat**. In an environment where you may have several essentially similar printers, often you will specify that your print job should go to a *class* of printers, rather than a particular one. In this case, use the **lpstat** command with the **-o -l** options to see not only which jobs you have queued, but which printers they are queued for. Where you have used a printer class instead of a specific printer as the destination, you will see something like Figure 6-9.

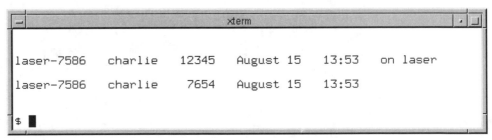

Figure 6-8   The report back from the **lpstat** command

```
┌────────────────────────────── xterm ──────────────────────────────┐
│                                                                    │
│ laser-7586    charlie     7654    August 15    13:53               │
│    on laser                                                        │
│                                                                    │
│ dotmatrix-7896    charlie    89987    August 15    14:04           │
│    assigned fastdot                                                │
│                                                                    │
│ $ █                                                                │
└────────────────────────────────────────────────────────────────────┘
```

Figure 6-9   A more detailed report from **lpstat**

Here, you have one job currently printing on printer *laser*
while a second job is assigned to *fastdot* but hasn't started
printing yet.

Chapter 7

Running Programs

Answer Topics!

Running Programs @ a Glance

Running a program is simple if you only know how. Here's what you need to know in order to launch various kinds of programs in UNIX.

Controlling flow and making sure data goes where you want it to be are the purpose of **piping and I/O redirection**. You'll need to know how to redirect output into a file and where you can find it if you need it; knowing how to get input from a file (rather than the keyboard) can be helpful too. Piping, the most important kind of redirection in UNIX, allows you to take the output of one program and redirect it to another program, which can save you an enormous amount of time and effort.

Even before there was MS Windows, UNIX was a fully functional multitasking operating system. The key to **multitasking** in UNIX is knowing how to manage all those programs or jobs you're running simultaneously.

It's extremely important to understand how to **set priorities** when you're working in a UNIX environment, since you're almost always sharing memory capacity and processor time with others. Here's how to be **nice**.

Scheduling jobs is another way to be courteous to your fellow users and to improve your own efficiency. You can put a job to sleep until later, schedule a job for a specific time in the future, or use a **crontab** to automate your tasks.

RUNNING A SINGLE PROGRAM

Executing a File

Actually, UNIX is always running several programs, so you can't ever just run a single program. But most of that happens in the background and behind the scenes, so we'll just let it stay there for the moment. You'll remember from Chapter 3 that each file on your machine has a set of permissions. These include the permission to read the file, write to the file, and to execute it. By "execute" we mean to make the file *run*, as in actually *do* something.

It's important to understand that very few programs, and probably none you will have to worry about unless you end up as a superuser, are actually executed directly by UNIX. This is done by the shell. Whether you are running Bourne, Korn, C, or one of the less common shells, it's actually the shell that interprets what you type at the prompt and issues the necessary commands to start up the program. It's also the responsibility of the shell to examine the permissions for the file and decide if you even have the right to run the program. So, if you don't first set the execute permission bit for your program, you aren't going to get very far with it.

❓ How can I make a program executable?

Use **chmod +x**. This seems pretty obvious, but if you have this nice little program that you wrote to say "Hello, World!" (OK, we know that's hardly original, but sometimes one must bow to tradition) and when you try to execute it, it looks something like Figure 7-1, you forgot to give your file permission to execute.

❓ Is there a way I can automatically make my shell scripts executable?

Yes, by creating a simple shell script. This is sort of a recursive fix. Use a shell script to make your shell scripts execute. You can get fancy about this, if you really want to, but we use just the simple little **vix** script shown in Figure 7-2.

❓ Can I control which shell my script is executed by without having to change scripts?

Figure 7-2 showed a little trick we were going to save for Chapter 13 when we talk about shell script secrets, but since it's in this figure, we'll talk about it here. Notice the first line of the script, which reads

```
#!/bin/ksh
```

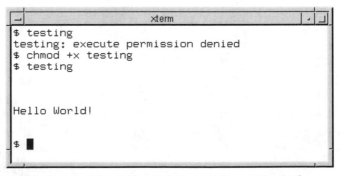

Figure 7-1 This is what happens when you forget to make a program executable—and how to fix it

```
 -                             xterm                              . _|
# !/bin/ksh
#     Filename: vix
#     Description: simple shell script to create and edit
#                 a file and make it executable all in one pass.
#     Last modified: 8/25/97 by cr
cd /u/russel/bin                    # Put all scripts in bin directory
vi
chmod +x


$ █
```

Figure 7-2   Use a shell script to call your editor and change the
permissions all in a single step

You would think that this is a comment, since it starts
with the **#** character, but what it really does is tell whatever
script is executing the file to execute **/bin/ksh** (the Korn
shell) and feed it the rest of the file. We'll use this trick later
in Chapter 15 when programming with **perl** in order to
actually have **perl** do the executing instead of a shell.

? How can I reissue commands?

Use the history list. One of the most useful features that the
C shell added to UNIX was the ability to reuse a command
rather than have to retype it. The Korn shell takes this even
farther. You can not only reuse your commands, but edit
them with your favorite editor, right there on the command
line. To reuse the most recent command that started with the
letter "v", for example, use **r v**, which will recycle the last
command you issued that begins with **v**. So if you are editing
a file, then executing it to see if you have it the way you want
it, and then going back in to try again, this trick makes it
easy to cycle back and forth between the two commands. The
more you include of the command, the more precise the
match. For example, if your last four commands had been

```
vi .kshrc
. .kshrc
vi .exrc
vi notes
```

then **r v** would recall the **vi notes** command, while **r vi .**
would recall the **vi .exrc** command, and **r vi .k** would recall
the **vi .kshrc** command.

? What's the easiest way to cycle through and edit my previous commands?

If you're using the Korn shell and include the following in your profile, you can actually use **vi** to edit your commands right at the command line, cycling through them and then modifying them as needed.

```
EDITOR=vi ; export EDITOR
```

This, plus the presence of a **~/.sh_history** file, tells the Korn shell to use the familiar **vi** editor commands to let you edit your command lines before you issue them. Just press the ESC key to enter **vi** mode, and then use the familiar cursor movement keys, "j", "k", "l", and "h" to move through the commands. Press the "k" to move up one line to the previous command, "j" to go down, and so forth. Once you find the command you want, just hit the ENTER key to reissue it, or use the familiar editor keys to modify it. This is harder to explain than it is to do. Just try it. This feature alone is reason enough to switch from the C shell to the Korn shell.

? Can I edit my previous commands even if I'm a confirmed emacs user?

Yes; don't despair. You don't have to know **vi** commands to use command line editing in the Korn shell. Just add this line to your **.profile** file, and you can now use your **emacs** keys to move through your command history and edit the commands.

```
VISUAL=emacs ; export VISUAL
```

Why the difference between the environment variables we set for the two modes? Actually, either one will work. Some sources seem to prefer setting **EDITOR**, while others seem to prefer setting **VISUAL**. But both appear to work the same. The one thing we wouldn't recommend, however, is setting them to different values. If you do, **VISUAL** will win.

Piping and I/O Redirection

Redirection and piping in UNIX are analogous to plumbing, in the sense that what's important is controlling a flow, making sure data goes where you want it to be. You can redirect the input so that instead of coming from the keyboard it comes from a file, or you can redirect the output so that instead of going to your monitor it goes into a file. And finally, you can take the output from one program and feed (pipe) it into another program.

Probably the first kind of redirection we all learn to do is *output* redirection. That means getting all that stuff that we usually don't want to see off the screen and into a file where we can find it if we need it but otherwise not be bothered. To redirect the output from a program to a file, use the greater than symbol, ">". For example, to sort a file of names:

```
sort names > names.sorted
```

The second kind of redirection is *input* redirection. This uses the less than symbol, "<". With this, instead of a program getting its input from the keyboard, it gets it from a file. So, for example, to mail a file that includes the text of a new proposal to Dale in Engineering, you'd use the command

```
mail dale < proposal.txt
```

The third and most important kind of redirection is *piping*. This uses the bar or pipe symbol, "|". A pipe takes the output of one program and feeds it into another program. Suppose, for example, you just got a really cool game from your favorite ftp site on the Internet. To expand it and un-tar it, all in one operation (more about tar format in Chapter 12, use the following code:

```
cat newgame.taz | zcat | tar xvf -
```

Piping is central to the way much of UNIX works. Because it was originally designed to run on very small machines with limited memory, UNIX is made up of literally hundreds of little programs. Each one doesn't do much by itself, but they're all designed to work together in the UNIX repertoire to create a powerful command set.

MULTITASKING

Running Multiple Programs in UNIX

Unlike DOS and Windows, UNIX is by its very nature a multitasking operating system, so you can take advantage of that multitasking to run multiple programs or jobs. If you are running the X Windows System, this is as simple as opening up another window and starting up the second program. But even on a simple character-based terminal you can take advantage of multitasking in most implementations of UNIX. At the very least, you should be able to send a job to the background to let it run while you start something else.

❓ How can I send a job to the background?

Use the **&** following a program's command line. Some jobs, like long **find** operations or program compilations, tend to take a while and don't really require any input from you. Send these jobs into the background by putting an ampersand (**&**) after the command line. This gives you your prompt right back while the job you have *spawned* goes on about its business. Figure 7-3 shows a simple example that a system administrator might run periodically to clean up some large files that were taking up disk space.

❓ Is there a command I can use to check on my background jobs?

Try **jobs**. As you can see in Figure 7-3, the **jobs** command will tell you what the status of your background job is. If the job has finished, you will see the job number and a "Done" after it. The other possibilities are "Running" and "Stopped". What about the "+" we see there? That indicates that this job was the most recently invoked job that is in the background. The next most recently invoked would be shown with a "-".

```
                              xterm
/# find / -name core -a -mtime +7 -exec rm -f {} \; &
[1] + Running find / -name core -a -mtime +7 -exec rm -f {} \; &
/#jobs
[1] + Done find / -name core -a -mtime +7 -exec rm -f {} \; &

$
```

Figure 7-3   Use the *&* operator to move big jobs into the background

? Can I bring a background job back into the foreground?

Yes, with the **fg** command. This command will bring the most recently invoked job back into the foreground. If the job has been stopped (suspended) for some reason, it will restart when it comes into the foreground. If you have several jobs running in the background and you need to bring one to the foreground and it's not the most recent, use one of the ways in Table 7-1 to refer to the job. Thus, to bring the **grep** operation you started several jobs ago back to the foreground, use

```
fg %grep
```

This will bring the **grep** job into the foreground. From there you can send it back into the background, suspend (stop) it, interrupt (kill) it, or simply wait for it to finish.

Reference	Background Job Referenced
%*n*	The job whose number is *n*
%*string*	The most recent job whose command line begins with *string*
%?*string*	The most recent job whose command line contains *string*
%+	The most recent job
%%	The most recent job
%-	The second most recent job

Table 7-1   Ways to Reference a Background Job

? Is there another way to send a job to the background?

Yes, with the **bg** command. Suppose you started a search for the changes in your doctoral thesis and you discover that it's going to take a lot longer than you expected. Fortunately, you had it set for all the output of the **diff** command to go into a log file, so just suspend the job and send it into the background. The usual command to suspend a job is CTRL-Z unless you have changed it with **stty**. So, simply press CTRL-Z and type **bg**, and the job will go into the background and restart. If you want to see how it's going, you can just **tail** the log file.

! *Warning:* *Don't send a job into the background that needs input from you or that will send lots of output to the screen. If a job is in the background and it needs some input from you, it will just sit there waiting. Not quite what you had in mind, one suspects. And if the job will produce a lot of messages that would normally go on your screen, unless you send these messages to some sort of log file, they will all end up on the screen anyway, right in the middle of what you're trying to do. Again, probably an annoyance at most. The best way to handle this is to redirect the output to a log file, with any errors sent to a separate error file. Here's an example of how to do that:*

```
diff thesis thesis.edited > /tmp/edit.log 2> /tmp/edit.err &
```

*Now the command will run in the background and not bother you with output you aren't ready to deal with anyway. The **2>** means to send standard errors to the file we have pointed to, in this case **/tmp/edit.err**.*

? Can I use redirection to send both normal program output and error messages to a file?

Yes. In fact, if you want to send them to the same file, you use a special combination. A typical example of this might be when running a backup or a long compilation. You aren't bothered with the output from it while you are doing other things, but when the compile or backup is done, you can quickly check to see where any problems were. Here we use a special way of describing the pipe of standard error.

```
make > /tmp/make.log 2>&1 &
```

This uses redirection to send normal messages from our **make** to a log file and any error messages will go to the same place. Here, **2>&1** means "take standard error and redirect it to standard output." But since we have already told standard output to go to a log file, both will go there.

? What can the tee command do for me?

Use **tee** to send output to both a log file and the screen. This lets you start a process, like a backup, where you want to be able to see if anything untoward happens but store all the messages from the command in a log file as well. This is particularly useful on a windowed system where you can continue to work and yet keep your eye on what's happening.

```
make 2>&1 | tee /tmp/make.log &
```

Now when your **make** hits a snag, you'll have the pleasure of watching all those lovely warning messages scroll by on the screen and you'll know they're saved to a log file. Later you can stare solemnly at them and pretend you actually know what they mean before you go twiddle with the **makefile** and try again.

! **Warning:** *Don't use **nice** on a foreground job. If your system gets bogged down anyway and you have given your foreground job a **nice** command, you may not be able get its attention long enough to suspend or kill it. You'll essentially be locked out until the job finishes.*

SCHEDULING JOBS

? How can I put a job to sleep?

The simplest of the time-related commands is **sleep**. This command does just what its name implies—it puts commands or script files to sleep for the number of seconds

Setting Priorities

When you work in a multitasking and multiuser environment, you can easily bring the entire system to a virtual halt by starting a job (or two) that's very memory and processor demanding. Even if you're the only person on the system, starting a big compile job in the background may slow your foreground task to an unacceptable pace. UNIX, naturally, has a solution. The **nice** command decreases the command's priority by increasing its *niceness*. Unfortunately, this particular command is different in virtually every version of UNIX, and even different depending on which shell you are using. But the general effect is the same—you can reduce the amount of CPU time that a particular process requires by starting it with **nice**. So, for specific details of how your version is implemented, check the man pages for **nice**.

```
man nice
```

Note that you can make a command be nicer, but, unless you are the superuser, you generally can't make a command have a higher priority (in other words, be *less* nice) than it would normally have. Also, it doesn't generally make sense to reduce the priority of jobs that are essentially I/O bound, since these jobs don't require much of the processor's resources anyway.

you specify. Why would you want to do this? Well, it can be useful to display a message on the screen in the midst of a shell script, for example, leaving it there long enough for you to see it. A good example of this is when you are going to do something irrevocable, like delete a file or set of files, and you want to give yourself a chance to back out if things don't look right; if you don't interrupt the process it will go through automatically. In this case, what you do is **print** or **echo** the command that is about to be executed to the screen and then let the script sleep for five or ten seconds. If things don't look right, you can break out of the script and fix it before it's too late. Or, if you need to fire off several processes, each of which grabs lots of resources when it first starts, but which then settles down, you can use **sleep** in the script that starts them to space them out a bit.

? Can I use sleep **as a simple alarm clock or reminder?**

Certainly. There are more complicated ways to do this, but if you tend to get involved in what you're doing and lose track of the time, here's a simple way to remind yourself that you have a meeting for which you need to leave in 15 minutes.

```
(sleep 900; print "Time for your meeting with Lance!")&
```

This will go happily and quietly to sleep in the background, eating almost no resources at all; in 15 minutes (900 seconds) it will wake up, print the message out to the screen, and terminate. The trick here is the use of the ( ) around the command. This groups the entire command together into a subshell, and allows you to send it together into the background.

? Is there a way to use the sleep **command to give myself a chance to back out of a command?**

We like to do this whenever we have either an irrevocable command or one that has automatically built a fairly complicated string that might have gotten garbled in transit. Just add a **sleep 5** to the command to allow yourself time to interrupt the script before it actually executes. Figure 7-4 shows how this works.

In this simple example, the variable **$tmpdir** will, of course, get expanded to whatever temporary directory you are clearing out. The result of the command will be to delete all the files in the temporary directory that have not been accessed in the last seven days.

? What can the at **command do for me and how do I go about using it?**

The **at** command lets you schedule an activity at a specific time. Unlike **sleep**, it lets you enter a clock time, not just x minutes in the future.

A good example of a common use of **at** is to schedule a big compile to occur when everyone's gone home for the night and the system won't get bogged down by it. The **at** command is pretty flexible about what it understands for time descriptions, but a bit unusual in other ways. The best way to handle it is to list the commands to be executed in a simple file, and then redirect that file into the **at** command,

```
-                                    xterm                              . _|
Print "Removing all old files in directory $tmpdir using command line..."
Print "\n\t find $tmpdir -atime +7 -exec rm {} \; \n"
Print "If this doesn't look right, press Ctrl-C to interrupt the script"
Print "within the next 5 seconds."
sleep 5
find $tmpdir -atime +7 -exec rm {} \;
```

Figure 7-4   Using the **sleep** command as a hedge against disaster

along with the time it is to be executed. Understand that all commands executed by the **at** command will be executed using the Bourne shell, not the C shell or Korn shell, so don't depend on any specific features of these more versatile shells. The **at** command will understand all of the following time parameters, as well as lots of others.

- **at 10:15am**—at 10:15 a.m. today (tomorrow if it is already after 10:15 a.m.)
- **at 1120pm Jun 17**—at 11:20 p.m., on June 17th
- **at 1 am Sunday**—at 1:00 a.m. next Sunday morning
- **at 18:00 Monday next week**—at 6:00 p.m., next Monday
- **at now +2 hours**—two hours from now

As you can see, this is pretty flexible. The syntax for running a backup routine of the **/users** filesystem to the DAT tape drive at 1:00 a.m. tomorrow morning would be

```
at 0100 tomorrow < backup.users
```

where **backup.users** contained the single line:

```
tar -cvf /dev/dat /users > /tmp/backup.users.log
```

which includes the **tar** command with the necessary options to write a new archive out to the DAT drive and keep a record of all the messages in a log file for later perusal.

? Can I use cron to automate tasks, and if so, how?

If your system administrator has given you permission, you may create a **crontab**. This is a file that describes one or more actions that you want to occur on a regular basis.

It's handy to know that you can use **crontab** to automatically run programs repeatedly. You can schedule jobs to run once a month, every night, or every Friday. There are lots of possibilities. The **crontab** file consists of six fields:

- *minute* a number from 0–59 indicating the minute the command will be run
- *hour* a number from 0–23 indicating the hour for the command to be run
- *day of month* a number from 1–31 indicating the day of the month to run the command
- *month* a number from 1–12 indicating the month to run the command
- *day of week* a number from 0–6 (Sunday to Saturday) for the command to be run
- the *command line* to be run

Fields that contain an asterisk (*) mean all possible values for that field. So, for example, to run a backup of your home directory to the floppy drive every night at 1:15 a.m., you might have the following as a **crontab**:

```
15 1 * * * /usr/bin/tar uvf /dev/rfd0 $HOME > /tmp/
$LOGNAME.bak.log 2>&1
```

One thing to note about this command is that we were careful to direct the output from the command to a log file, and we also made sure that any error messages went there as well. Otherwise, the output from the command will be sent to the console, which could cause other problems. Also, like the **at** command, all **crontab** jobs are executed using the default Bourne shell. Your **crontab** file is in **/usr/spool/ cron/crontabs/username**. But you should first create the file in your home directory, and then submit it to the **cron** process with

```
crontab cronfile
```

which will overwrite any existing **crontab** file with the new one.

!

Warning: Always make a copy of your old **crontab** file before you submit a new one. We find it's distressingly easy to forget that any new **crontab** will overwrite your old one. So, we have a little script that first saves a copy of the existing **crontab** and then submits the new one. That way, we automatically make a copy and submit the new one. The relevant lines from the script are:

```
cd $HOME
crontab -l > oldcron.$(date +%m%d%H%M)
crontab new.cron
```

*This saves a copy of the old **crontab** in a time- and datestamped file, and then submits the new **cronfile** which we always keep in **new.cron**. This makes it easy to keep a copy of your old **crontab** files.*

+

Tip: Use **crontab -l** to see your current automatically scheduled jobs. The **-l** switch to the **crontab** command is short for "list", and it tells you what work you have scheduled for the **cron** process to handle.

Chapter 8

X Windows

Answer Topics!

X Windows @ a Glance

So far we've talked about "conventional" UNIX, which is a text-based, command-line interface that only a nerd could love. But in this chapter we will explore the **X Window System**, which, thanks to the **display manager** and the **window manager**, has a pretty enough interface to cure you of lusting after Microsoft Windows. Here you'll learn the difference between the display and window managers, if only so you can use this information to impress your UNIX-savvy colleagues.

More important, X Windows takes advantage of the **mouse**, menu bars, and other features of a graphical user interface. With the mouse at your command, you'll find that you're happier and more productive than ever before.

If you're serious about using X Windows, it's probably a good idea to be familiar with **common X programs**. We'll introduce you to the standard ones and tell you about what they can do for you.

Using X Windows is pretty straightforward, but it's useful to know some **Xterm tricks** that can make your life easier. Changing the colors and font on your terminal will help you see better, and creating a larger scroll buffer will let you scroll back and forth with ease on even the longest of **man** pages.

Some **X Windows programs** are more impressive than others, but even the **less impressive** ones can be helpful sometimes. The latter group includes a calculator, system monitor, clock, and an easy-to-use front end for **man** pages.

The **less useful X programs** are ones such as **xeyes**, which will increase the cute value of your UNIX system immeasurably. We'll leave you to explore most of these programs for yourself, but we wouldn't feel right telling you how to make your X Windows system your own without mentioning their presence.

Customizing your X is a fine and highly idiosyncratic art. We won't tell you exactly how you should customize your system; instead, we'll show you how to customize the X server, your desktop, and Motif, and then leave you to your own devices.

Note: *A word of disclaimer is in order here. You will hear the X Window System referred to variously as "X," "X Windows," and "The X Window System." Well, the last of these three is the official way, but in normal conversation, most people will say "X" or "X Windows," as we will in this chapter.*

The X Window System was originally developed at MIT, and the principal developmental work on it is still carried out there. X has gone through many revisions over the years, and as of this writing is currently at a version known as "X11R6." Most of what we will discuss here, though, is equally true for at least X11R4, X11R5, and in some cases for X11R3 as well. So, even if you are still running on an older version you should be able to take advantage of many of the same tricks, though the syntax may be a bit different in some cases.

MOUSE COMMANDS

Can I use the mouse to copy text between windows?

Certainly. If you have two windows open, it's easy to copy text from one window to another. Select the text you want to copy from the first window by positioning the mouse cursor at the beginning of the text you want to copy, pressing down the first mouse button, and dragging the cursor over the text you will be copying. The text will now be shown in reverse, and is *highlighted*. Click on the second window to activate it, and click the second mouse button. This will insert the highlighted text at the current text cursor position.

Warning: *Whenever you're moving or copying text, remember that the mouse cursor and text cursor are not the same. When you click once, you simply move the mouse cursor to the point where you click.*

Display Manager vs. Window Manager

The X Window System is the display manager. By itself, it isn't a very pretty sight. It takes the addition of a window manager to give you the look and feel you expect. All those nice little borders, buttons, and mouse tricks are really part of the window manager's job, not that of the display manager. The two most common commercial window managers in the UNIX world are Motif and Open Look. Of the two, Motif seems to be winning the window manager wars, though Sun systems still used Open Look by default until very recently. However, even in the Sun world, Motif is available. It is the window manager that allows you to move a window, resize it or shrink it to an icon, drop down a menu, and so on. The display manager (or more properly the X server), on the other hand, interacts directly with the mouse, keyboard, and display. The display manager manages fonts, colors, and the background screen (the root window), and is responsible for opening and closing windows and generally managing the resources.

❓ How can I select an entire word?

Click twice. When you click twice in quick succession (called a *double-click*), you will both move the cursor and select or highlight the word at the cursor.

❓ Is there a way to select an entire line?

Yes, by triple-clicking. If you click the mouse three times in quick succession, you will get an entire line highlighted. This is a quick way to transfer a command to another window.

❗ *Warning:* *When you transfer text with the mouse, you transfer it as actual keystrokes. This means, for example, if you are in **vi**, you might actually be passing commands to **vi** if you're still in command mode instead of text insertion mode when you paste the text into the second window.*

X Programs You May Already Have

While every vendor's version of the X Window System is just a bit different, most come with a bunch of cool programs and some that are merely cute without being useful. The ones you are most likely to have, as a minimum, are:

- *Xterm* a terminal emulation program
- *xcalc* a calculator
- *xclock* yet another clock program
- *xman* a graphical front end to the **man** pages
- *xload* a graphical indicator of the system resource utilization over time
- *xeyes* a cute little program that features two eyes that follow your mouse pointer
- *xlogo* a totally useless program that displays the X logo
- *ico* another cute but useless little program that draws a bouncing icosohedron on your screen

In addition to these, there are several utilities for manipulating or displaying the properties of the X server. The essential one of these programs is, of course, **Xterm**, which provides the interface for you to access all of the rest of UNIX.

? How can I pop up a menu?

Click on the root window. This menu will let you do a variety of things like shuffle your windows up or down to find a window that is buried in a stack of others, open a new window, restart the Motif Window Manager, or just refresh your screen if the graphics have gone haywire. You can take this menu much farther by adding new stuff to it. We'll show you how below in the section called "Customizing X."

XTERM TRICKS THAT MAKE LIFE EASIER

Xterm Enhancements

Every version of the X Window System comes with at least the minimum version of Xterm. Plus, many vendors include their own custom terminal window that takes advantage of some of the specifics of their system. SCO, for example, includes **scoterm** with its Open Desktop package, and HP includes a couple of different versions of hpterm with its systems: one for VUE, their "Visual User Environment," an all encompassing desktop environment based on X; and another for those running just the X Window System. Each of these add specific features that enhance the overall look and feel of the basic Xterm, but we'll stick to just the basic Xterm here. Most of the third-party enhanced Xterms accept the same command-line parameters as the basic version, in addition to any that control the specifics of their own implementation. The basic result of typing **Xterm &** is pretty boring, so let's spruce it up. You can control the fonts, colors, and all sorts of other stuff.

? **Can I change the colors of** Xterm **to make it easier on the eyes?**

Absolutely. Colors are a very personal and individual thing, but here's a combination that works for us.

```
/usr/bin/X11/Xterm -fg white -bg MidnightBlue &
```

This gives you white text on a dark blue background. Of course, we know someone who finds this look far too middle class, and opts instead for

```
/usr/bin/X11/Xterm -fg yellow -bg purple &
```

But then he's just a bit on the outer edges on most questions.

? How can I get a list of color possibilities?

Use **showrgb**. This will print out a list of colors that are defined in your system. Even if your system doesn't have the **showgrb** program, you can still see this list. Just use **vi** (in its read-only mode, so you don't accidentally mess something up). Type in:

```
view /usr/lib/X11/rgb.txt
```

This will give you a look at the default color database that your system uses. Pick any colors you want from here for your Xterm colors. But don't forget to enclose the color name in quotes if the name includes any spaces.

! ***Warning:*** *When you type in your Xterm color selections, don't forget to enclose the color name in quotes if the name includes any spaces. A two-word color without quotes will confuse UNIX and cause the command to fail.*

? Is it possible to change the title on my Xterm?

Yes. You can even have your Xterm tell you where you are and who you are logged in as by adding this information to the title bar of the Xterm. The only catch is, this information is static, so if you use the window to log into another, remote machine, it won't be accurate. But we find it useful nonetheless, since it tells us where we started from. Use the **-T** option like this:

```
Xterm -T "$(hostname):$LOGNAME -- $(date +%X)" &
```

This will put your hostname, login name, and time the window was started all in the title bar.

? Is there a way I can change the font in my Xterm to make it easier to read?

Of course. The older we get, the bigger the fonts have to be. We know young programmers with six or eight Xterm windows open on their screen, each one with tiny little fonts. For them, this may be OK, but we like something just a bit larger and easier on the eyes. So we use one of the larger standard fonts for our Xterm:

```
/usr/bin/X11/Xterm -fn 10x20 &
```

This makes for a large enough window to actually see what you're doing. Of course, if you're running on a display with a lower resolution than our 1280 x 1024, or you have good enough eyes and want to squeeze the window size down a bit, try

```
/usr/bin/X11/Xterm -fn 8x13 &
```

This should give something small enough for most purposes. A good middle choice is the "9 x 15" font. But examine the other choices on your system. Each vendor's implementation of X includes different fonts, so you may have some additional choices.

? How can I see which fonts are available?

Use **xlsfonts**. This program, if run with no options, will send a complete list of all the fonts you have available on your system to standard output. To limit this list, you can add the **-fn pattern** option to the command line, or pipe the whole thing through **grep** to see a more limited list.

? Can I see ahead of time what a font will look like, and what characters are available for it?

Yes. **xfd -fn fontname** will show you all the characters for that font, as well as give you far more information about each individual character than you are likely to need.

? Is there a way I can add scrollbars to my Xterm to make it easy to scroll back through text?

Certainly. In fact, we're sure this will quickly become your standard Xterm. You can add scrollbars to the standard Xterm by using the command-line option **-sb**, which will put a simple scrollbar on the left side of the window like the one in Figure 8-1.

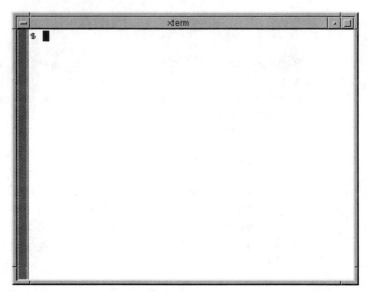

Figure 8-1 Adding scrollbars to your Xterm makes it more useful

> ✚ ***Tip:*** *Use the enhanced Xterm if your vendor supplies one.*
> *Most of the enhanced versions of Xterm provide useful*
> *additions as well as a slightly different look and feel, but take*
> *the same command-line arguments as the default Xterm.*
> *Figure 8-2 shows a typical example of an enhanced Xterm,*
> *complete with menus and a right-hand-side scrollbar.*

❓ Can I make a bigger scroll buffer to use for man **pages?**

Of course. This is one place where a scrollbar comes in very handy. But the normal wimpy little 64-line scrollbar isn't enough for a lot of **man** pages. So crank it up to a full 30 screens full—720 lines—with the **-sl nnn** option. This lets you scroll back and forth through even long **man** pages. Figure 8-3 shows an example from the Xterm manual.

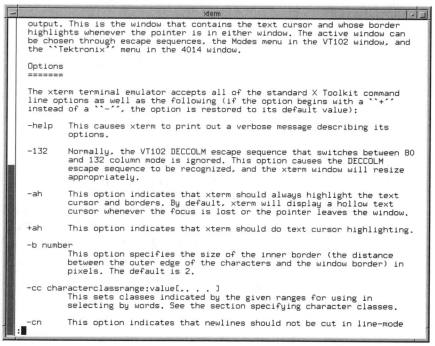

Figure 8-2   Use the improved Xterm if your vendor provides one

```
output. This is the window that contains the text cursor and whose border
highlights whenever the pointer is in either window. The active window can
be chosen through escape sequences, the Modes menu in the VT102 window, and
the ``Tektronix'' menu in the 4014 window.

Options
=======

The xterm terminal emulator accepts all of the standard X Toolkit command
line options as well as the following (if the option begins with a ``+''
instead of a ``-'', the option is restored to its default value):

-help     This causes xterm to print out a verbose message describing its
          options.

-132      Normally, the VT102 DECCOLM escape sequence that switches between 80
          and 132 column mode is ignored. This option causes the DECCOLM
          escape sequence to be recognized, and the xterm window will resize
          appropriately.

-ah       This option indicates that xterm should always highlight the text
          cursor and borders. By default, xterm will display a hollow text
          cursor whenever the focus is lost or the pointer leaves the window.

+ah       This option indicates that xterm should do text cursor highlighting.

-b number
          This option specifies the size of the inner border (the distance
          between the outer edge of the characters and the window border) in
          pixels. The default is 2.

-cc characterclassrange:value[,. . . ]
          This sets classes indicated by the given ranges for using in
          selecting by words. See the section specifying character classes.

-cn       This option indicates that newlines should not be cut in line-mode
```

Figure 8-3   Use a large scroll buffer to view manual pages

LESS IMPRESSIVE X PROGRAMS

xcalc

Along with the essential Xterm come several other useful but more limited X programs, and even some really useless ones. First, the X Calculator, **xcalc**. This is a handy little program that puts a calculator on your screen to let you figure out how you're going to spend your future lottery winnings. Obviously, it must be able to handle negative numbers. Like all the included X programs, it resides in the **/usr/bin/X11** directory. So if this isn't on your path, you are going to want to put it there.

? Can xcalc **handle scientific calculations?**

Yes. The Xcalc program has two basic modes: "normal," which emulates a TI-30 calculator, which is fine if you like a standard algebraic mode calculator; and the **-rpn** command-line option. If you want to use the more flexible Reverse Polish Notation that HP made popular, add **-rpn**. This result is shown in Figure 8-4.

? What can xload **do for me?**

Use it to monitor your system. This little program will give you a constantly updating display of the amount of system resources you are utilizing. While not directly a measure of

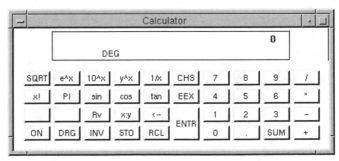

Figure 8-4   Xcalc can emulate an HP-10 calculator

CPU usage, once you get used to evaluating it you can get a pretty good idea of exactly how loaded down your system is. Each line of the graph will indicate approximately 10 percent usage. But if you find yourself consistently running over two or three lines in the graph, we suggest you find a way to distribute some of the load. Or perhaps a memory increase for the system will lower the number by reducing the amount of swapping that must occur. In any case, you might like to keep a little Xload graph open down on the corner of the screen. Over time, you'll get a feel for what's normal, and if you suddenly find that you are running higher than you would expect, chances are that you should ask your system administrator to look into the situation.

? Is there a way to control the size and placement of an X program?

Try the **-geometry** option. The xclock, for example, likes to pop up in the middle of the screen. To put a standard analog clock up in the upper right-hand corner of the screen, try this:

```
xclock -geometry -1+1 &
```

and you'll get a nice little clock like the one in Figure 8-5 in the upper right-hand corner of your screen.

? How can xman help me browse for help?

The Xman program provides an easy-to-use front end to the manual pages, letting you find what you need by searching

Figure 8-5   The Xclock makes a useful addition to your desktop

for the specific item, or by opening up a window and choosing which volume of the manuals to look for the **man** page in. Once you choose the volume, you can easily pick from the list of available commands to view.

The Xman program also makes it easy to browse through the manual page for the command you are interested in, providing a scroll bar on the side and formatting the page for your display. To find out more about Xman, just use the **xman** command and click on Help. You'll get a useful help screen and you can then choose other pages to get help on by clicking on the Manual Page button.

Tip: *Try* ***xeyes*** *to spice up your desktop. Stick it up in the upper-left corner of your screen, and give it some nice blue eyes. You can think of it as your boss, keeping his watchful eye on you, if you are the paranoid type, or as a favorite sweetie-pie gazing soulfully at you, if you are the more amorous type.*

```
xeyes -geometry 100x100+0+0 -fg steelblue -center white &
```

The result of this command is shown in Figure 8-6. Actually, the picture doesn't do it justice; it has to be seen.

Less Useful X Programs

But enough about useful programs. Let's talk for a minute about some of the less useful programs that come with the X Window System. Our favorite little useless program is **xeyes**. This does absolutely nothing useful. It puts two eyes on your screen, which calmly follow your mouse pointer wherever it goes. See, we told you it was useless. But it is kind of charming, and you might well like to have it open, if only to wow the rubes.

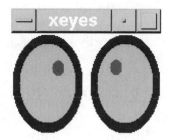

Figure 8-6 **xeyes** follow your mouse, wherever it goes

CUSTOMIZING X

? What are some of the things I can do to customize X Windows and what files do I need to change in order to do this?

Among other things, you can change the colors, fonts, appearance, and menus. There are two basic files that you have control of and they both reside in your $HOME directory—**.Xdefaults** and **.mwmrc**. The first controls the options and settings for the X server itself, while the second controls the behavior of the Motif Window Manager. You can also add other, task-specific files for a particular situation. And, finally, each application may have a special set of defaults that you can set. The default versions of these files, which should only be changed by your system administrator, are kept in the **/usr/lib/X11/app-defaults** directory. However, you can easily copy any of these files to your home directory to give you a baseline to work from. Some applications will read a "dotted" version of these files on start-up; others prefer that you include the settings in your **.Xdefaults** file. But in all cases, you can explicitly load these settings if you want. We strongly recommend that you do this when first making changes to a particular set of resources. Then and only then, if they really *are* what you want and expected, should you add them to the default files.

When you first log in to your workstation, these two files are read, and they are not read again unless you explicitly load them. So any changes you make will not be apparent until then.

? How can I customize the X Server?

The basic X server defaults are just that, pretty basic and bland. But you can easily make changes to the way your desktop looks and behaves by modifying the resource files for either the individual clients or for all clients. The basic syntax of a resource specification is

```
client*resource_name:      resource_value
```

? Is there a way I can change the default background color for all my Xterms?

Yes. To set it to LightSteelBlue, try the following:

```
Xterm*background:      LightSteelBlue
```

Now, whenever you start an Xterm, if you don't explicitly set the background color on the command line, you will get an Xterm window with a light steel-blue background. Well, almost. First you have to force your system to read this resource change. We recommend that you put any changes you are trying out into a separate file and that you *not* add them to your **.Xdefaults** file until you are sure they are what you want. We put our changes in a file called **.Xtest** until we're sure they are OK. The command to tell the X server to read this file and incorporate its settings into the X server's database is **xrdb** with the **-merge** option. So this gives us:

```
xrdb -merge ~/.Xtest
```

which will load the **.Xtest** file you just created into your X server's database. Now, try the change you made by starting an Xterm and see if the background changed. If you didn't muck up the syntax, all your Xterms should now have a light blue background.

!

Warning: The **xrdb** command gives you no error messages, but it is very fussy about exact syntax and even the presence of trailing white space. If your changes don't seem to be working, the two most common problems are leaving out the colon (:) between the resource and its value, and having a space or two after the value. This is especially true if you are converting from X11R4 or earlier to X11R5, since these older versions of the X server were less punctilious. The latest version has, for reasons that are clear only to the programmers who made the change, become intolerant of stray spaces and tabs.

How can I customize my desktop?

Your underlying desktop, or more properly your root window, is by default an annoying variegated grey color that we find really hard on the eyes. You can easily fix this, however, using the **xsetroot** program, which changes the defaults (or restores them). If you want a solid black background, for example, use

```
xsetroot -solid black
```

which will change the backdrop to solid black. If you want to try a graph paper look, use

```
xsetroot -mod 8 8
```

However, we don't think you'll stick with that for long. Frankly, there isn't much the plain old version of **xsetroot** that comes with X will do to perk up your background. You can add a bitmap with it, but these aren't nearly as cool as the backgrounds that you can do with Microsoft Windows. There are probably dozens of little utilities out there that will get around this limitation, but one we have used and like is the **xv** program, which is available as shareware from several different sources. The author is John Bradley, and his email address for more information about the program is bradley@cis.upenn.edu. We use it to add **.bmp** or **.gif** files into the root window, resulting in backgrounds that will banish Windows envy quite effectively. Figure 8-7 below is just one example of the sort of things you can do, but you are limited only by your imagination and your resourcefulness in finding images.

Tip: *Use the **xset** program to change font paths, screen saver, and so forth. Normally, you don't need or want to change this stuff, but sometimes you may add a program and it doesn't put its fonts where they belong, or there may be some other problem. Use **xset** to add the new font path to your existing one, and then **xset fp rehash** to make the change actually happen. You can also control the behavior of the built-in screen saver as well as the keyboard and mouse with the **xset** program. For a quick command-line help with the program, use **xset -help**; to see what the current settings are, use **xset -q**.*

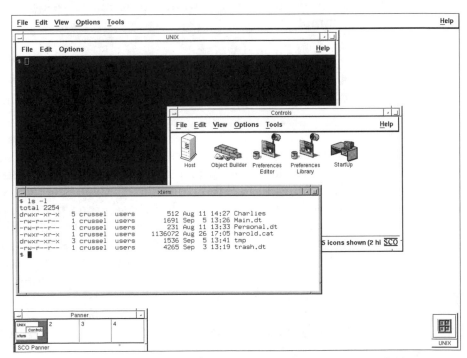

Figure 8-7   The **xv** program lets you customize your root window

? **Can I use the Motif resource file to add features to X?**

Yes. The Motif window manager allows you to add commands to its menus, and even change the behavior of the mouse buttons and keystrokes. We aren't going to go into all the different ways you can do this, or the many different things you can add with this file. But here are some suggestions that will give you some ideas of the kinds of things you can do. But first, a word of caution. Always make a copy of your working configuration before you make changes. Right. Heard that one before, have you?

! ***Warning:*** *Always make a copy of* any *configuration file before you change it. Don't say we didn't warn you. Not that we always follow our own advice.*

Copy the default Motif resource file to your home directory. This makes a good starting place to try things. So first, before you do anything else:

```
cp /usr/lib/X11/system.mwmrc ~/.mwmrc
cp ~/.mwmrc ~/.mwmrc.original
```

There. Now we have an immaculate copy of the current resource file stashed away for safekeeping, and we have a nice starting point for mucking around. Open it up with your favorite text editor (**vi**, of course) and you should see something like Figure 8-8. Depending on your version of Motif and X, the comment character may well be a "#" instead of the "!" you see here.

? **How can I use the Motif resource file to get help?**

Let's add the **Xman** program to our **.mwmrc** file. Of course, if you don't have Xman on your system, try the same thing with something else, like Xcalc or even **xeyes**!

The resource command to execute a program, whatever it is, is **f.exec**, so let's add the necessary line to our **.mwmrc** file. The syntax is **"label" f.command "options"**, so what we want to do is move down to the first section after something that reads like "Menu RootMenu" or some such. Shouldn't be

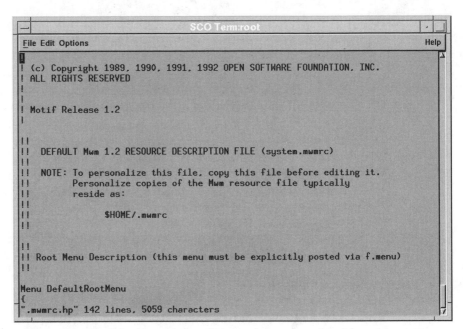

Figure 8-8 The Motif resource file can be customized to add many additional features

too hard to find. Then add the following line, somewhere in the middle of this section:

```
"Xman"      f.exec "xman"
```

Save the file and use the built-in restart command for Motif. Click the mouse in a blank area of the desktop and then select "Restart" from the menu. Confirm that you really want to do this, and Motif will restart. In the process, it will read your changed **.mwmrc** file, and you should now see an option for running Xman on the menu.

Is there a way I can add lines to my root menu?

Yes, by using **f.separator**. Add a line with a label of **no-label** and an **f.separator** as the resource command to put a line in the menu. If you include a label of quoted white space and a command of **f.noop**, you will get a blank line in the menu. Figure 8-9 shows a simple set of Motif menu

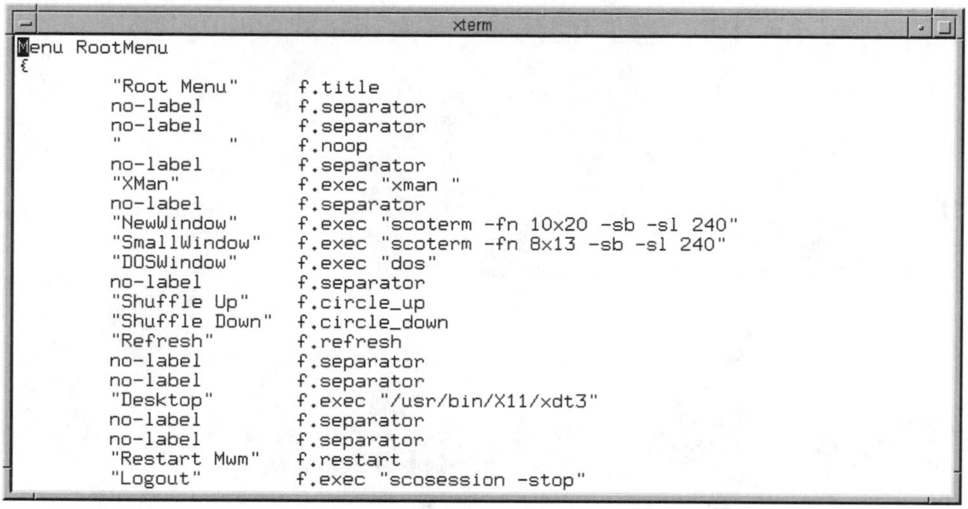

```
─                              xterm                          ◢ ⬚
Menu RootMenu
{
        "Root Menu"      f.title
        no-label         f.separator
        no-label         f.separator
        "         "      f.noop
        no-label         f.separator
        "XMan"           f.exec "xman "
        no-label         f.separator
        "NewWindow"      f.exec "scoterm -fn 10x20 -sb -sl 240"
        "SmallWindow"    f.exec "scoterm -fn 8x13 -sb -sl 240"
        "DOSWindow"      f.exec "dos"
        no-label         f.separator
        "Shuffle Up"     f.circle_up
        "Shuffle Down"   f.circle_down
        "Refresh"        f.refresh
        no-label         f.separator
        no-label         f.separator
        "Desktop"        f.exec "/usr/bin/X11/xdt3"
        no-label         f.separator
        no-label         f.separator
        "Restart Mwm"    f.restart
        "Logout"         f.exec "scosession -stop"
```

Figure 8-9   Adding lines to the root menu with **f.separator**

commands, enough to get you started. The possibilities are
nearly endless, with menus calling other menus, and so on.
So have fun.

Chapter 9

The UNIX Toolbox

Answer Topics!

The Unix Toolbox @ a Glance

- UNIX provides you with a veritable arsenal of tools for comparing both text and binary files, so here's where you'll learn all you need to know about so-called regular expressions and how to use the **UNIX comparison tools**.

- **Text manipulation tools** can help make your life a lot easier by letting you page through a file, see just the beginning or end of a file, and much more. You can even spell check your text files, create a custom dictionary to use while spell checking, sort a file, or clean up a mixed-case text file.

- In the section about **miscellaneous tools**, you'll learn how to compress a file, how to encrypt a file, and how to use the calendar program to perform a couple of handy functions.

Note: *Because of its origins as an operating system running on tiny little computers where RAM was at a premium, UNIX is composed of hundreds of little programs, each one designed to do one or two specific jobs very well and then pass its results on to another program so something else can be done to that data. This explains why the UNIX toolbox contains as many tools as it does, each of which is intended for a specific purpose.*

COMPARISON TOOLS

What is grep and what can it do for me?

Grep and its variants are probably the most useful commands in UNIX for comparing and finding text strings.

Grep is short for "Get Regular ExPression," and in most versions of UNIX it comes in three slightly different versions. The first is the regular **grep**, which lets you search for text that matches some string of text that can include wildcards, character sets, and metacharacters. The second is **fgrep** (short for Fast grep, but it's actually slower), and the third is **egrep** (short for Extended grep), which extends the regular expression matching ability of **grep** and also lets you create logical OR expressions to search for. There are also some public-domain versions of **grep** that each have their own peculiarities and advocates, but we'll stick with the standard ones here. And for the most part, we'll stick with plain old **grep**, not the others.

? So how do I go about using grep?

In its basic form, the syntax of **grep** is:

```
grep [-options] regexpr [filename(s)]
```

where the options are

- **-b** Returns the block number as well as the matching line
- **-c** Returns only a count of the number of matching lines
- **-h** Returns only the matching lines, but not the filenames they were in
- **-i** Ignores case when matching
- **-l** Returns the filenames where there are matches, but not the matching lines
- **-n** Returns the line numbers in addition to the matching line
- **-s** Suppresses error messages
- **-v** Returns only lines that don't match the regular expression
- **-w** Matches only whole words (not available in all versions of **grep**)

Of these, the most useful are the **-i** option to ignore case and the **-v** option to reverse the search and return nonmatching lines.

? Can I use grep -v **to find files that don't belong to me?**

Yes. Here is a quick way to find out if anyone has written files in your home directory that don't belong to you:

```
ls -lA | grep -v "$LOGNAME"
```

This will return a list of only the files in the current directory that are not owned by you. There's one exception: it would miss a file that included your login name in the filename even if the file belonged to someone else.

? Is it possible to use grep -i **for case-insensitive searching?**

Certainly. In fact, this can be quite handy for making sure that you use something consistently. For example, in this book we use "system administrator" as the form for that ultimate of UNIX gods, the superuser. But we found that sometimes we had the capitalization wrong and we weren't consistent between "system" and "systems". So, we used the following to find all of these instances, complete with their line numbers in the file:

```
grep -in "system.* administrator" chp[1-8].txt
```

This translates into "search chp1.txt through chp8.txt for the string "system administrator" where the string may be upper or lowercase, or any mixture thereof, and where there may or may not be a single character after the "m" in system.

! ***Warning:*** *The "." wildcard by itself will fool you! If we had neglected to put an asterisk after the "t" in the above* ***grep*** *expression, it would have missed the times we spelled system administrator without the "s" at the end. But the asterisk said to match zero or more instances of the previous metacharacter.*

+   ***Tip:*** *If your version of **grep** supports the **-w** option, take advantage of it! It's an option to match whole words only. You could, for example, look for all instances of "good" that were used as a whole word by using the regular expression "good", but this has a problem. What about a sentence that ends with the word "good"? It wouldn't match. We can't use the ".*" trick, since that would match "goody", and even "goodness". But if your version of **grep** will support the **-w** option, you can use*

```
grep -iw "good" files
```

*which will find all instances of the word "good" but not other words that have "good" buried within them. If your version of **grep** doesn't support this option, by the way, it gets much harder. The following should catch virtually all instances, but we suspect that we will have missed something:*

```
grep -i "[\'\"\{\([]good[] \'\",.?!\)\}]"
```

*Whew. That seems like just a bit too much work for the result. If your version of **grep** doesn't support the **-w** option, you might want to ask your system administrator to get a copy of the GNU version of **grep** that does include this useful option.*

? **What is a "regular expression"?**

We've tossed around the term "regular expression" fairly often throughout this book, and you will continue to see it in any additional reading you do about UNIX, including in the **man** pages. A *regular expression* is a string of characters, which may include wildcards and metacharacters, used by one of the text utilities as a search pattern. It looks much like the wildcards used by file utilities, and includes many of the same special characters, but is not quite the same.

A regular expression describes the pattern you are looking for. It can include sets of characters like **[aA]**, which would match both upper and lowercase instances of "A"; or wildcards like "*****", which matches any number of characters (including zero) but not special characters; or "**.**", which matches any single character. Two other useful metacharacters are **^** and **$**, which match the beginning and end of the line, respectively. A complete description of regular expressions is way beyond the scope of this book. You can find highly specialized books on UNIX tools, but most UNIX manuals also include good descriptions.

What command should I use to compare two text files?

Try **diff**. This is the one you will probably use most often. Its syntax is simple, but reading its output can be a bit annoying. The syntax is

```
diff [options] file1 file2
```

with the following options:

- **-b** Ignores repeating white space
- **-e** Creates a command script that can be fed to the **ed** editor to re-create file2 from file1
- **-f** Creates a script to re-create file1 from file2
- **-h** Disables **-e** and **-f** options; fast but less rigorous

If the two files are pretty similar, this can be a useful way to check to see what has changed. Redirect the output from **diff -e** to a log file, and you can see what was changed in the file and decide if that change was appropriate.

Is there a way I can compare three similar files to find differences among them?

Yes, use **diff3**. The resulting output lets you see what has changed, and in which file it has changed. You can actually do a pretty decent version control system based on this command.

What's the best way to compare binary files?

Use the **cmp** command. This lets you see if two apparently identical files actually are the same. For example, this is useful if the file sizes are the same but you think someone has accidentally changed one. When used with the **-s** option, you get back simply an exit code—0 if they are the same, 1 if they are different, and 2 if one or both of the files were inaccessible.

TEXT MANIPULATION TOOLS

? **What can the** more **command do for me?**

The **more** command lets you look through a file a page at a time by pressing the space bar. Press the "b" key to go back a page at a time. You can use **/regexp** to jump ahead in the file by searching for the regular expression, but you can't search backwards. There are other, more flexible paging programs around, however, so if you find yourself frustrated by the limitation of **more**, ask your system administrator to get a copy of **less** for your system. This little program lets you page back and forth through the file, and is quite a bit handier than **more**. Or get in the habit of using **vi** in its read-only form, **view**, as a substitute.

? **Can I pipe the output of long directory listings to** more **to prevent them from scrolling off the screen?**

Absolutely. Once you get in the habit of using **ls -lAF** as your directory listing command, it's hard to give up all that extra information, which is why we suggested you make a simple alias out of it to **ll** (for Long Listing). But the downside is that it is much more likely to scroll off the screen than a simple **ls** will. So, pipe the result to **more**, and you will be able to see your listing a page at a time—**ll | more**.

? **How can I see just the beginning of a file?**

Use **head**. Most versions of UNIX come with a program called **head** that will show you just the first few lines of a file (or of standard input if you are piping something to it). You can control the number of lines shown by using the **-nn** option on the command line, where *nn* is the number of lines to show. The default is usually ten. This command is extremely useful if you are looking for a particular file, for example, but can't remember its exact name. But you *do* remember that you had a particular phrase in the header of the file. If it's one of several files that end in **.ksh**, then try this command to find the file you want.

```
head *.ksh | more
```

This will show you the first ten lines of each file, complete with a one-line header to give you the filename. Figure 9-1 shows a typical result.

❓ Is there a way I can use head to find the files that have changed recently?

You know that the file you want is in the directory somewhere, and you just worked on it yesterday, so it should be one of the first files in the list if you sort your listing by date. Try

```
ls -tlA | head -20
```

to see just the last 20 files that have been modified.

❓ How can I see just the end of a file?

Use **tail**. The **tail** command works exactly like the **head** command, except that it shows you the end of the file, not the beginning. This makes it extremely useful for looking at things like **log** files, which grow over time. You don't want to have to read through the whole file to see what's happened; you just want to check the last few lines for recent changes.

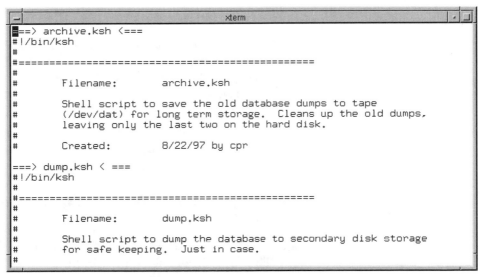

Figure 9-1   Use **head** to find the file you need

Since all the changes will be at the end of the file, **tail** is perfect for this purpose.

❓ Is it possible to send output to both a file and my terminal?

Yes, with the **tee** command. We use this one all the time when running full backups, for example. The output goes to a log file, just in case we want to check later, but it's nice to have the output going to the screen as well. That way, you can do something else and just glance over to the screen periodically to see how the process is doing. For example, you might do a backup with a command like this:

```
tar -cvf /dev/dat / | tee -a /tmp/bkup.log
```

The **-a** in the command tells **tee** to append its output to the file, not overwrite it.

❓ Can UNIX spell check my files for me?

Yes. UNIX comes with its own built-in spell checker, **spell**. Just take any text file and run the **spell** command on it, and UNIX will tell you which words it thinks are misspelled. The syntax is

```
spell [options] [files]
```

The most useful of the options is **+wordlist**, where *wordlist* is a file containing a user dictionary of words not included in the main dictionary. A useful way to set this up is to create a special dictionary for a given project that might have some specialized words or jargon that is used with it. Then keep that word list in the home directory of the project. You can even have an environment variable point to it so that it's easy to change or update your scripts.

❓ Is there a way to get spell to create a custom dictionary for me?

Here's an easy way to create that custom dictionary. Run **spell** twice. The first time, use something like this:

```
spell project.doc > words.special
```

The document you're checking is *project.doc,* and the output of the spell check is being directed to your own custom directory, called *words.special* in this example. After you run the **spell** program, edit the file **words.special** to remove any misspelled words, but leave in the jargon or other specialized terms you're using in your project. Now you have a custom dictionary for the project. Run the rest of your project files through **spell** to search for misspelled words as follows:

```
spell +words.special proj*.doc > words.wrong
```

Now you have the *actual* misspellings (that don't include your specialized terms) in the file **words.wrong**. You can use your editor (**vi**, we hope) to search files for words that are in **words.wrong**. You'll be able to find and correct actual misspellings without being continually asked about your specialized words.

❓ How can I create a sorted file?

UNIX comes with its own **sort** command. By default, it is case-sensitive, but you can easily turn that off with the **-f** option. **sort** can be used to sort output by the beginning of each line (the default) or by any field within the line, where fields are separated by either white space (tab or space, the default) or some other specified character. To sort the **/etc/password** file by group, you would use

```
sort +3n -t: /etc/passwd > /tmp/sorted.passwd
```

This says to sort the file by the fourth field (skip three fields and start sorting with the first digit of the fourth field), use a delimiter between fields of ":", and send the output to the file **/tmp/sorted.passwd**.

❓ Is it possible to clean up mixed-case files?

Yes. The translate utility, **tr**, is a handy little command that takes input and converts all the characters that are in one set of characters to the corresponding set in a second set. Probably its most common use is to convert a file or command to all upper or all lowercase characters. For example, to convert a file that is mixed upper and lowercase to all uppercase, try the following:

```
cat mixed.case | tr "[a-z]" "[A-Z]" > /tmp/upper.case
```

This takes every instance of a letter in the first set of characters ("[a-z]") and converts them to the corresponding character in the second set ("[A-Z]"). Note that this command is no smarter than you might expect, and knows absolutely nothing about the two strings you give it, except that they are the same length. So here is an easy way to do a *very* simple encryption of a file:

```
cat file | tr "[a-z]" "[A-Z]" | tr "[A-Z]" "[B-Z]A" > file.shifted
```

Of course, it wouldn't take a cryptographer longer than a few minutes to figure out that you'd shifted each letter one position. But it's probably not professional cryptographers who are peering at your files when they shouldn't. It's easy to do, and even easier to undo when you want to read the file.

```
cat file.shifted | tr "[B-Z]A" "[A-Z]" > file.unshifted
```

But if your needs for security are more serious than just keeping nosy eyes away from a sensitive file, you'll want to use the **crypt** command discussed below under "Miscellaneous Tools."

MISCELLANEOUS TOOLS

? How can I compress a file?

Use **compress**. This gem can save you tons of disk space for files that you really need to keep available on disk but you don't have to use very often. Just compress them, and when you need them for something, use the **uncompress** option. Compressed files have a filename that ends in **.Z** and they can take up significantly less space, depending on the type of file. For example, the TIFF graphic files will compress to about 5 percent of their original size, and our daily database exports compress to about 25 percent of their original bulk.

The amount of compression for other files will vary widely. Text files compress nicely; program files compress hardly at all. To compress a file or files, use **compress filenames**. To uncompress a file, use **uncompress filenames** or **compress -d filenames**. Both are the same, and both assume that the file to be uncompressed ends in **.Z**, so you don't need to add that to the command line.

? What's the easiest way to encrypt an important file?

Use the **crypt** command. This command is based on the famous Enigma encoding machine developed in Germany, but with a 256-element "wheel." As such, it can be broken, but not easily and not without a substantial amount of computing time and power, especially if the password used is not short. The **crypt** command is not available on versions of UNIX shipped outside the U.S. due to export restrictions, and may not be on the shipped version you receive even in the U.S. unless you specifically request it. If you have it, it'll provide a high level of security. The **crypt** command has the syntax **crypt [password] < infile > outfile**.

? Is there a way I can use the cal program to print a quick calendar?

Yes. This little prize produces, with no options, either a three-month calendar across your screen or a one-month or one-year calendar depending on what you ask for. The result of **cal** and **cal september** are shown in Figure 9-2.

? Can I use the calendar program to create a tickler file?

Certainly. Actually, you create the tickler file with **vi** or your favorite editor, and it should have the format **date event-description,** where each event is on a single line, and the dates are in some sort of reasonable form that **calendar** can interpret. Then add the command to your **.profile file** so that you get reminded every time you log in

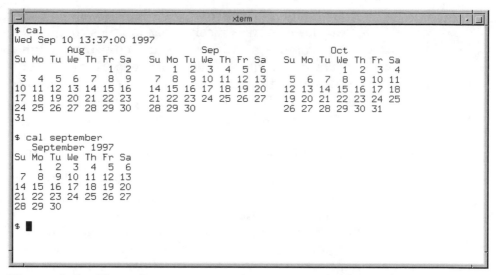

```
$ cal
Wed Sep 10 13:37:00 1997
        Aug                    Sep                    Oct
Su Mo Tu We Th Fr Sa   Su Mo Tu We Th Fr Sa   Su Mo Tu We Th Fr Sa
                1  2       1  2  3  4  5  6             1  2  3  4
 3  4  5  6  7  8  9    7  8  9 10 11 12 13    5  6  7  8  9 10 11
10 11 12 13 14 15 16   14 15 16 17 18 19 20   12 13 14 15 16 17 18
17 18 19 20 21 22 23   21 22 23 24 25 26 27   19 20 21 22 23 24 25
24 25 26 27 28 29 30   28 29 30               26 27 28 29 30 31
31

$ cal september
    September 1997
Su Mo Tu We Th Fr Sa
    1  2  3  4  5  6
 7  8  9 10 11 12 13
14 15 16 17 18 19 20
21 22 23 24 25 26 27
28 29 30

$ █
```

Figure 9-2   The **cal** program can give you a useful little calendar when you need it

of the event schedule for today and tomorrow. You can even add it to your **crontab** or as an **at** command if you wish. Then you get reminded periodically of the things you need to do today. The result looks like Figure 9-3.

```
9/15    Meet w/Dale about progress of new program. Must be completed by 10/15
9/15    3pm - New Model Meeting - ALL HANDS!
September 11    Call FedEx for pickup
9/21    Call Harry - see if he has any free basketball tickets!
/users/charlie
```

Figure 9-3   Use **calendar** to remind you of important events

Chapter 10

Connecting to the World

Answer Topics!

Connecting @ a Glance

Working on your single workstation or terminal is nice, but it isn't really what UNIX is all about. UNIX has been and will continue to be primarily a networked operating system, and this means some changes in thinking and behavior for those of us brought up in the DOS or MS Windows world. In this chapter we will explore some of the features and foibles of **UNIX workgroups and workgroup relations**.

Next we'll get into some of the tools that are primarily for bigger and more diverse networks, including the big bold world of the Internet. **Connecting to the larger world** is becoming more crucial every day, so here's what you need to know to get started.

WORKGROUPS AND WORKGROUP RELATIONS

UNIX and Workgroups

When you work in a local network, there are lots of ways you can take advantage of the distributed nature of the UNIX networking environment. Some UNIX systems have one large central server, much like a PC network, but others use multiple, smaller workstations. Both work, and if set up properly, will look very much the same to the users. But there are some important differences. If you have, for example, a large central server, and only terminals located at each desk, then the concept of copying files from machine to machine makes little sense, since they're all stored on a central machine. But if you are working in a distributed environment with multiple workstations, each of which may be the server for a different program or function, then the time will come when you need to copy files around to get them on the machine you need them on. But even here, much of this should be handled transparently, usually with a common $HOME directory structure.

We'll look at this local situation as if it were a distributed workstation environment—that is, multiple workstations, each with their own hard disks and processors, as well as some workstations that might not have a hard disk, or that might even be simple terminals or Xterminals. But don't worry if you are in a situation with one big central server and only terminals or Xterminals. Most of this will still apply to you, and if it doesn't, just skip over the irrelevant part(s).

❓ What is the single most common need in a local network environment?

Without a doubt, the need to share files with others in your workgroup. UNIX makes this simple, and we've actually already touched on some of the tricks to do this, but here we want to pull all that together. For some of this, you may well need the help of your system administrator to set up the initial group and directory structure, but once you get it all set up, you should be able to handle your files comfortably within your own group.

❓ What's the best way to handle file sharing?

Designate one person in your workgroup as a local system administrator. To distinguish this person from the main system administrator, let's call him or her the project manager. And, by the way, usually the best person for this position is the actual project manager or team leader for the group. Usually this person won't have all the powers of the main system administrator, but will serve many of the same functions. The project manager will be the owner of the main files and directories that the group will use, and will be the contact point between the workgroup and the system administrator. This makes it easier on the system administrator, who won't have to be constantly tweaking permissions, ownerships, and other such stuff for the group. This tends to make the system administrator more likely to be willing to help when you do need something. More important, it means that most of the time the workgroup can handle its own day-to-day operations, doing things in a way that makes it easier for everyone in the group, who will not have to wait to get something taken care of until the system administrator's priority queue finally gets around to the request.

The idea here is that the project manager will own all of the directories and "core" files for the group. Then everyone in the group will share a special group id. As you develop templates and standards for the group's work, you create those templates as read-only for the members of the group, and read/write for the project manager. If changes need to be made in a core file, the project manager makes the change, and it becomes available for all the others in the group. This is an excellent way to maintain standard forms throughout the group.

The other set of files that the project manager will have to worry about are resource files. These could be X or Motif resources to ensure the presence of standard buttons and styles (including fonts and colors) that are used in a programming project, a standard set of **vi** macros that everyone uses, or just the environment variables that control locations of files and inclusions.

? How can I make my workgroup's directory local?

Use **NFS** mounting. This will require the initial intervention of the system administrator to set everything up, but once established, it will allow the members of the workgroup to be working on different machines without having to be logged in to one single machine. This has several hidden benefits. Since everyone in the workgroup is working at his or her own workstation, each person has things arranged according to personal preference; yet files, scripts, and so forth that are common to the group all appear in the same relative place for everyone in the group. A second benefit is that the processing load is spread across multiple machines so the system won't tend to load down unduly when you are all working on a project at the same time. The catch to this, of course, is that you may need multiple versions of specialized software that you are using. If it's all located on one machine, that machine still ends up doing all the processing.

? What tools does UNIX offer me that can facilitate workgroup communication?

The UNIX tools range from the simple **ping** that lets you know if a machine is even connected, to commands like **talk** that let you carry on a conversation with another user on the network, to the various electronic mail programs that let you send email to your workgroup and beyond.

? What can ping do for me?

It can tell you which machines are currently available. The **ping** program is probably the most basic UNIX networking command. It simply sends a tiny little packet to the address you give it, and then listens to see if the other machine "echos" back the packet. You can use the machine's Internet address, which looks something like **192.78.222.81**, or you can use the machine's *name* as in:

```
ping rci1
```

The name will be either the one in your local **hosts** file or as resolved by the network nameserver, but in any case will be the name the network expects to use to find a particular machine. The result of **ping** will look something like that in Figure 10-1. If a machine doesn't respond to **ping**, it won't respond to anything else, because the network simply can't see it. Time to make an offering to the system administrator, unless the reason is simple and obvious, like the machine is turned off for some reason. In which case the system administrator is probably already involved, because rebooting a UNIX machine is not as simple as it is with a DOS machine.

? What's the best way to send a quick message to another user logged in to my machine?

Use **write**. **write** is perfect for sending a quick message to another user who is either on a terminal connected to your workstation or remotely logged in to it. For example, you can easily send a message to the project manager who is remotely logged in to your workstation with

```
write yasminek
```

```
-                                    xterm                              · _
$ ping -c 5 speedyg
PING speedyg (195.4.5.95): 56 data bytes
64 bytes from speedyg (195.4.5.95): icmp_seq=0 ttl=64 time=0 ms
64 bytes from speedyg (195.4.5.95): icmp_seq=1 ttl=64 time=0 ms
64 bytes from speedyg (195.4.5.95): icmp_seq=2 ttl=64 time=0 ms
64 bytes from speedyg (195.4.5.95): icmp_seq=3 ttl=64 time=0 ms
64 bytes from speedyg (195.4.5.95): icmp_seq=4 ttl=64 time=0 ms

--- speedyg ping statistics ---
5 packets transmitted, 5 packets received, 0% packet loss
round-trip min/avg/max = 0/0/0 ms
$ █
```

Figure 10-1   The **ping** program is used to find out if a machine is on the network

She would then answer back by responding with a similar **write** command to you. You could then suggest a meeting, or whatever, and when you were done, the command would terminate when you send an End Of File (EOF) character, usually a CTRL-D.

! *Warning: The **write** command writes directly to the terminal. This can cause some programs, such as **vi**, to go quietly (or not so quietly) nuts. Before you get in the habit of using **write** or any command that writes directly to someone else's display, you should have a clear agreement that this is acceptable behavior.*

? **Is there a way I can turn off write permission to my terminal?**

Use **mesg n**. This will protect you from the problems that come from people sending messages to you while you are working with an editor like **vi**, which is not very compatible with **write**. To reenable message writing to your terminal, use **mesg y**, and others will again be able to write to your terminal.

? **Is it possible to allow others to** write **messages to me without interfering with my work?**

Yes. If you are using X Windows, keep one Xterm window just for **write** conversations. When you're in a workgroup and you want to be able to send messages back and forth without causing each other problems, designate a specific window for "chatting" with each other. We like to use **ttyp1** as our chat window, and we keep it open but in the background. When a message comes in to that window, we get a beep and we just click on the window to pop it up to the top.

? How can I chat with another user who is on a different machine?

Use the **talk** command. **talk** also writes directly to your screen, but it will split the screen into two separate halves, one for what you are writing and one for what is being sent to you by the other user. Even more than with the **write** command, you need to be sure that the person receiving the request to talk isn't in the middle of something else. However, you can talk to a person on another machine in your workgroup just as easily as if that person were simply on another terminal attached to your machine. To chat with another user, the syntax is

```
talk username@hostname
```

where *username* is their login name, and *hostname* is their machine's name as defined in the **hosts** table.

? Can I send a message to everyone who is logged in to my computer?

Yes, with the **wall** command. Be aware, however, that it won't cross over to other machines, so you can't really use it to send a message to everyone on the network. In a traditional UNIX environment with a single large server and lots of terminals connected to it, this works perfectly. But in today's more modern distributed workstation environment, you'll have to use one of the mail commands to reach everyone in your workgroup.

? **My workstation has suddenly slowed down and I suspect that someone is chewing up more than his or her share of memory and CPU time. How can I find out who the culprit is?**

Use the **who** command to see who is logged in to your workstation. This command, which has lots of other options, is the ideal way to see who is logged in to your computer when used in its simplest form. The result looks like Figure 10-2.

The **who** command has lots of other options, mostly of interest to system administrators, but one option you might find useful is **-a** (for *all*). The output from this command may give you a bit more information than you really want, but if you combine it with **-H** (so you get headings to tell you what column is what), you can pick out the information you want. Figure 10-3 shows the output of the **who -aH** command.

? **How can I solve an identity crisis?**

Use the **who am i** command. If you have more than one account on a system, or are using a shared account for a project, you can find out who the system thinks you are, and which terminal or pseudo terminal you are logged in on with this command. And yes, you really do type it as three separate words. This is probably the only such command in the entire UNIX command set. Some systems support a

```
$ who
crussel     tty02          Sep 10 13:36
crussel     ttyp0          Sep 10 13:36
crussel     ttyp1          Sep 10 13:48
crussel     ttyp2          Sep 10 13:48
crussel     ttyp3          Sep 10 13:37
$ ■
```

Figure 10-2   Use **who** to see who is logged in to your computer

```
xterm
```

```
NAME       LINE          TIME          IDLE    PID  COMMENTS
   .       system boot   Sep 10 12:47
   .       run-level 2   Sep 10 12:47    2      0   S
asktimer      .          Sep 10 12:47   1:02    87  id=ck term=0   exit=1
scologin      .          Sep 10 12:47   1:02    91  id=sclb term=0   exit=0
authckrc      .          Sep 10 12:47   1:02   100  id=ack term=0   exit=2
rc2           .          Sep 10 12:49   1:02   140  id=r2 term=0   exit=0
crussel   - tty02        Sep 10 13:36   1:02  1116
LOGIN     - tty01        Sep 10 12:49   1:01   681
LOGIN     - tty03        Sep 10 12:49   1:01   682
LOGIN     - tty04        Sep 10 12:49   1:01   683
LOGIN     - tty05        Sep 10 12:49   1:01   684
LOGIN     - tty06        Sep 10 12:49   1:01   685
LOGIN     - tty07        Sep 10 12:49   1:01   686
LOGIN     - tty08        Sep 10 12:49   1:01   687
stdin
LOGIN     - tty10        Sep 10 12:49   1:01   689
LOGIN     - tty11        Sep 10 12:49   1:01   699
sdd       -             Sep 10 12:49   1:02   704  id=sdd
LOGIN     - tty12        Sep 10 12:49   1:01   703
crussel   + ttyp0        Sep 10 13:36  23:02  1124
crussel   + ttyp1        Sep 10 13:48   0:02  1287
crussel   + ttyp2        Sep 10 13:48    .    1291
```

Figure 10-3 The **who -aH** command tells you who's on the system and what's going on

different version of this command—**whoami** as a single word. If yours does, it can help you find out what account you are actually logged in to right now.

? Is there a command I can use to get just the real logins of people using my machine?

Try **who -f**. This option strips out any pseudo terminals that would be included in the command, giving you just a list of actual logins. If you are running the X Window System, this can be a more meaningful result.

? How can I find out more about the people on my machine?

Use **finger**. This command, which isn't supported on all versions of UNIX, tells you about not only the people who are logged in to your machine, but how long they have been active on your system, what their real names are, and all sorts of other stuff as well. You can also use this in a network to get information about other people *not* currently logged in.

? How can I find out where I am?

Use the **hostname** command. If you work in a distributed environment and you often have to log in to other machines, it can be a nuisance to keep track of which machine you're on at any point. This is especially true if you're working in X Windows and have several different terminal windows open. Use this command to find out where you are. If you find yourself doing this a lot, add it to your prompt by putting a pair of lines like this in your **.profile**:

```
host=$(hostname)
PS1='${host%%.*}:$PWD \$ '
```

You will then get a prompt like this:

```
rci:/users/charlie $
```

which gives you a constant reminder of who and where you are. If you like multiple-line prompts, just insert a **^J** into the string in front of the **\$** and you will get a nice two-line version of the prompt.

? What's the best way to communicate with my workgroup?

Use **mail** or one of the many improved versions of it. Actually, **mail** makes it almost as easy to communicate with your friends across the world as with your coworker in the next office. There are almost as many different improved versions of the basic **mail** program as there are versions of UNIX, but one that is widely available, easy to use, supports both text modes and graphics modes, and works on virtually any system is the **elm** package. Written by Dave Taylor, this program is available in the public domain (in other words, you don't have to pay for it or license it in any way). If you don't have it on your system, and the mail package you do have is hard to use, ask your system administrator to get a copy of **elm**. Everyone will be happier. It's available from a variety of anonymous ftp sites (more on what that means shortly), including **tut.cis.ohio-state.edu**.

What are the r commands and what can they do for me?

The **r** commands are a group of remote commands that make life much easier on a local network. Plus, they provide some useful tricks on your own local machine since they have some options that the more traditional commands lack. The commands in this group are:

- **rcp** The remote version of the **cp** command
- **rlogin** Logs in to another machine
- **rcmd** Executes a command remotely
- **rsh** Same as **rcmd** on systems where it exists

These commands make it simple to move around, execute programs, and manipulate files in a distributed environment. On many systems, the **rsh** command is reserved for a restricted form of the Bourne shell, and on these systems the command is called **rcmd**. But in either case, they allow you to open a shell on a remote system and execute a series of commands that are then displayed on your system. The **rlogin** command allows you to log in to the remote machine and execute commands just as if you were sitting at a terminal connected to it. And the **rcp** command allows you to copy files or whole directory structures between machines.

Can you give me an example of how to use rlogin?

Let's try using **rlogin** to work interactively on another machine. This command is perfect when you want to work on the other machine just as if it were your own workstation. The syntax is

```
rlogin remotehost [-l username]
```

Depending on how the system administrator has set up permissions, you may not even need to give a password on the remote machine. And if you have to do this often, and have accounts on both machines, you can—and should— create a **.rhosts** file on both machines that allows you to log in without a password. Your account on the remote machine doesn't even have to have the same username, as long as the

.rhosts file is set correctly. This file should have lines of the form

```
hostname username
```

where the **hostname** is the actual hostname as given in **/etc/hosts**, not an alias, and the **username** field is the actual user's login name on the remote machine.

? Are there other clever uses of rlogin?

Yes. Use it to log in to your own machine as a safety check when you make changes to your configuration. This single trick will save you a lot of time and aggravation if you just remember to do it *before* you log off. By doing (or attempting to do) a remote login to your own machine, you will force a new read of your configuration files, allowing you to test those changes you just put in without logging all the way out. That way, if you did something really fatal, you can just back out and restore the saved version you made first. You did make a copy before you started, didn't you?

? What is rcmd or rsh really good for?

Use **rcmd** or **rsh**, whichever is on your system, to run a single program on another machine. This command is the one to use when you want to launch a program or script on another machine, but don't need to actually work with multiple programs on that machine. Here you must have an equivalency set up using **.rhosts** on the remote machine, since you can't be prompted for a password. This command has the syntax

```
rcmd [-l username] hostname command
```

If this program is known as **rsh** or **remsh** on your system, substitute the appropriate command. In any case, they all work essentially the same, and all have the same pitfalls. Because they don't prompt for a password, they can constitute a potential security problem if the program they are running on the remote machine allows the user to shell out from the program. Furthermore, it can be tricky to set up these commands since in some cases, errors are not necessarily passed back through to you, but are eaten by the spawned shell on the remote machine. But they do have the undoubted advantage of simplicity once they are set up. You can include the commands inside a shell script, and then make that shell script available to all the users in your workgroup. They don't have to know anything about the nitty-gritty details of how it works, only that when they type **wp** they will start WordPerfect to edit the documents they are working on—even though the WordPerfect server isn't their machine at all.

? How should I use the rcp command?

Use the **rcp** command to copy files and directories from one machine to another. Within a local network, this is by far the easiest way to move files around. The syntax is similar to the familiar **cp** command, but now you need to add a machine name for the remote machine. So the command will have the syntax

```
rcp [options] remotehost:sourcefile localfile
rcp [options] remotehost:sourcefiles localdirectory
```

where the remote and local side of the command can be reversed. The options available are **-p**, which preserves the times and permissions of the remote files, and **-r**, which copies recursively down the directory structure below the starting remote directory. This last is a powerful addition that not all versions of the regular **cp** command support, but that allows you to copy entire directory structures with a single command.

? Can rcp still help me even if my version of cp doesn't support recursive copies?

Yes. You can still use **rcp -rp** to copy an entire directory structure on your local machine. Some versions of UNIX *still* don't support a smarter and more powerful version of the **cp** command that will handle recursive copies, but even these support it for remote copying, so cheat! Use **rcp** within your own machine, but treat one side of the command as if your local machine were in fact a remote one. To copy the **/tmp/local/bin** directory and all the directories under it to **/usr/local/bin** on your own machine, use this coding:

```
rcp -rp localhost:/tmp/local/bin /usr/local/bin
```

Voilá! Maybe someday soon your UNIX vendor will get with the program and make this workaround unnecessary, but in the meantime you have a way to get **mv** across filesystems.

CONNECTING TO THE LARGER WORLD

? What is ftp and how do I go about using it?

ftp is short for file transfer protocol. If you have to transfer files between different machines running different operating systems, such as from a UNIX machine to a DOS or MS Windows PC, your best bet is probably **ftp** because it is supported on a broad range of platforms and operating systems. We won't go into all the different commands that **ftp** supports, or all the ways that it can be used, but a typical **ftp** session might go something like this.

1. Start **ftp** by typing **ftp** on the command line. At this point, you can add the hostname of the machine you want to initially connect to. The available options are

   - **-d** Enables debugging mode
   - **-g** Disables filename globbing
   - **-i** Disables interactive prompting
   - **-n** Doesn't automatically log in upon initial connection
   - **-v verbose** Shows additional information about what is happening
   - **-t** Turns on packet tracing

2. Next you will connect to the remote site using **open host**, where host may be a simple local hostname, or a fully qualified hostname if you are attempting to connect to a remote machine.

3. You will be prompted for an account and a password on the remote system. If you are out on the Internet, and are trying to get a file that someone told you about but you don't have an account on the remote machine, use **anonymous** as the user, and when prompted for the password, answer with your email address.

4. Find the files you are looking for, using **cd** to change directories and **ls** to list the contents of the directory.

5. Set the mode of transfer to either ASCII or binary. The default is ASCII, so if you need to transfer a file that isn't ASCII, issue the **binary** command.

6. Transfer the files. Use **get** to copy the files to your local machine, or **put** to transfer a file from your machine to the remote machine.

7. Disconnect from the remote machine with the **close** command.

8. Exit out of **ftp** with either **quit** or **bye**. Both do the same thing.

There are far more commands available for **ftp**, but these are the basic steps to get you started. Print a copy of the **man** page for **ftp** before you start, and keep it next to your terminal and you should have no problems. Most of the commands are either the same as their UNIX equivalents or very similar.

? How can I use telnet to connect to a remote computer?

The **telnet** command is similar to the **ftp** command in one important way. It's designed to work across a broad range of platforms and types of terminals or displays. And like **ftp**, **telnet** has its good and bad points. If it's pretty and mouse button aware you want, **telnet** is not the tool for you, but if you have to connect to a remote computer with something reliable, **telnet** will usually do the job. To open a **telnet** session, use the syntax

```
telnet [options] [hostname]
```

where the options include

- **-a** Automatic login

- **-l** *user* Sends the username if the remote system can accept it

- **-r** Uses a similar interface to **rlogin**, with the escape character set to ~

There are other options covered in the **man** pages, but these are the most common ones. Once connected to the remote machine, you can execute commands in a subshell with the **!** command, get help with the **?** command, or basically type in any command you would normally type in if you were remotely logged in to that machine. There are, however, a vast and hopelessly confusing set of options and toggles you can set inside **telnet** that allow you to configure and manipulate it so that it can handle almost any kind of system on the other end that will let you connect in the first place. If you really need this kind of complexity, nothing else will do. Start with the **man** pages and an intimate knowledge of the quirks and foibles of the remote system and your system, and you should be able to get it all to work. But for most people, if you just treat **telnet** as if you had a simple, text-based login to the remote machine, you will be fine.

Chapter 11

Windows NT and UNIX Interoperability

Answer Topics!

NT and UNIX Interoperability @ a Glance

The basic TCP/IP utilities that come with both UNIX and Windows NT provide for an easy-to-use, minimal level of connectivity that will answer for many purposes.

For more demanding purposes, there are both NT and UNIX simulations of the other's networking and behavior so you can easily make your UNIX server look like an NT server, and vice versa.

Windows NT has a built-in Posix layer that provides minimal UNIX-like behavior, but you'll probably want a more comprehensive set of utilities from a third party if you spend a lot of time going back and forth between the two.

The Korn shell provides the ability to mimic many of the command-line utilities and behavior of the Windows NT command line.

BASIC TCP/IP CONNECTIVITY

? How can I copy files from my UNIX server to a Windows NT machine?

The simplest way to copy files from any UNIX machine is to use Microsoft's built-in ftp client. This is a basic, command-line ftp client that handles all the essential ftp commands and even does command-line redirection to do automatic downloads.

? Can I use ftp to copy files from my Windows NT machine to a UNIX or Linux machine?

Yes. You have two choices here. You can use the same Microsoft command-line ftp client to copy the files, letting

167

the UNIX machine be the server, using ftp's **put** command. An example session in Figure 11-1 shows the process of connecting to the UNIX server "xena" and copying a file from the **C:\MyFiles** directory to the home directory of user "charlie" on the UNIX server.

The second alternative, if you're at the UNIX machine's console, requires that you have the Microsoft ftp server running on Windows NT. With NT 3.51 and prior versions, this was an additional networking service that you could add to your NT networking. However, in version 4 and later of Windows NT, the ftp service is part of the Internet Information Server and requires that you install IIS in order to be able to service ftp requests.

? Is there an easier-to-use ftp client for Windows NT than the included command-line version?

Yes, there are a number of them. Virtually every TCP/IP add-on, including most NFS clients, XServers, and various other tools, includes a GUI version of ftp, so if you're using any of these, you're likely to have at least one alternative. If you don't have any of these, and don't really want to add one of them, you can use one of the shareware or freeware ftp clients. One of the best we've seen is "ws_ftp" from Ipswitch. A quite adequate "Limited Edition" is available as

```
Command Prompt                                              _ □ ×

C:\>cd MyFiles

C:\MYFILES>ftp xena
Connected to xena.
220 xena FTP server (Version 1.7.212.1 Sat Feb  1 01:30:15 GMT 1997) ready.
User (xena:(none)): charlie
331 Password required for charlie.
Password:
230 User charlie logged in.
ftp> binary
200 Type set to I.
ftp> put linux-chapter.doc
200 PORT command successful.
150 Opening BINARY mode data connection for linux-chapter.doc.
226 Transfer complete.
78005 bytes sent in 9.79 seconds (7.96 Kbytes/sec)
ftp> bye
221 Goodbye.

C:\MYFILES>
```

Figure 11-1   A basic ftp session to transfer a file from Windows NT to a UNIX server

shareware, or they have a fuller-featured "Pro" version for a very reasonable cost. The limited edition version is available from a wide variety of sources, and both are available direct from their web site, http://www.ipswitch.com. An example of the Pro version of ws_ftp performing the same transfer shown in Figure 11-1 appears in Figure 11-2.

? Can I run UNIX programs from my Windows NT machine?

You can use the built-in, graphical **telnet** client that comes with Windows NT to log onto the UNIX machine and run any character-based program on the UNIX machine. Any UNIX programs you run under this type of connection are run solely on the server. Your machine is serving as a dumb terminal. The Microsoft telnet emulation is, however, very basic and only suitable for simple character-based applications that can function successfully with only a simple vt-100 emulation. A simple session is shown in Figure 11-3.

? How do I launch the Microsoft telnet application?

You can start the Windows NT telnet application either from the NT command line, by typing **telnet**, or by selecting Start→Run and typing **telnet** into the box and clicking OK.

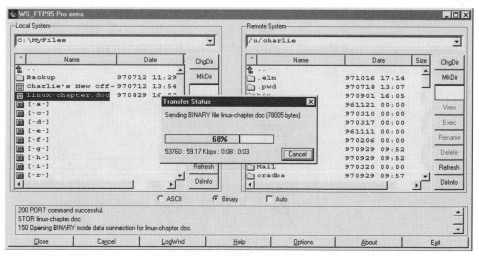

Figure 11-2   Using a graphical ftp client to transfer files from NT to UNIX

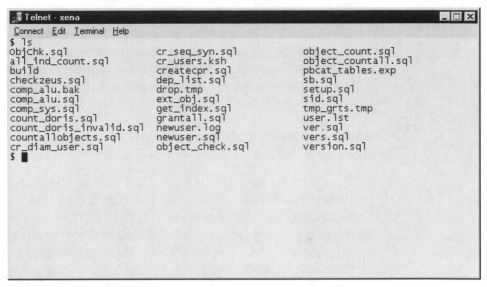

Figure 11-3 Using Microsoft's telnet to run a UNIX program from Windows NT

You can add the name of the machine (or its IP address) to the command, as shown in Figure 11-4.

? Are there better terminal emulators than the basic Microsoft one?

Emphatically, yes! There are a wide variety of choices available, from the simple, such as Century's TinyTerm, to the highly sophisticated. One we've used and found

Figure 11-4 Starting telnet from the Run menu

reasonably effective is FacetTerm (http://www.facetcorp.com). Another is vt320w from the same Ipswitch folks whose ftp client we use. Almost all of the third-party terminal emulators have either limited or timed versions available for download so that you can evaluate their applicability to your particular terminal emulation needs. We strongly recommend you try the emulator you are considering before plunking down good money. While most are good products, and far better than the built-in Microsoft telnet, terminal emulation for a particular application can be a tricky business and each emulator has its own strengths and weaknesses.

One feature that the better emulators provide is multiple window support. This lets you have multiple sessions open on the host from a single client—a real plus when you've got a lot of work to do on the UNIX host and some of it will be stuff that you can fire off and ignore for a while as you do something else.

Can I telnet from UNIX to Windows NT?

Yes and no. You *can* do it, but not without doing some work on the Windows NT machine first. Windows NT doesn't include a telnet *daemon* or server, only a simple client. But there are several third-party telnet daemons available for Windows NT, and even one from Microsoft. The NT Resource Kit has a beta version of a telnet server that you can install into Windows NT as a service.

What about graphical applications?

You can use virtually all X Windows applications from your Windows NT machine by installing an X Windows server onto the Windows NT machine. This will let you run both character mode and graphical applications from the UNIX server onto your Windows NT desktop without impacting your ability to also run Windows applications. There are many X Windows servers available for Windows NT and Windows 95 machines, and the general quality of them has improved remarkably over the last several years. Our personal favorite is XVision Eclipse from SCO (http://www.sco.com), but there are lots of others as well.

Can I use a web browser to access UNIX from a Windows NT machine?

Yes, assuming the UNIX machine is running a web server. One of the virtues of web technology is that it is, in large part, platform independent. So whether you are running a Netscape browser from your UNIX machine to get to your Windows NT machine, or Microsoft's Internet Explorer from Windows NT to your UNIX machine, the results are pretty much the same. The available options for web servers and browsers will, however, be somewhat different.

ADVANCED NETWORKING EMULATIONS

What is SMB and why should I care?

SMB is short for server message blocks; it is the underlying technology that Microsoft networking uses. UNIX servers can also use SMB, allowing them to talk to machines running Windows NT (or any other Microsoft networking stack). There are both freeware and commercial implementations of SMB available for a wide variety of UNIX and Linux versions, allowing you to add Windows connectivity to your UNIX network easily and essentially transparently to the Windows users.

What is NFS?

NFS is short for Network File System. Originally developed by Sun Microsystems, it is a pure TCP/IP method of providing file and printer sharing on a network. Since its origins are in the UNIX community, it tends to be the method of choice for sharing filesystems across UNIX networks. Implementations are available for Windows and Windows NT as well, but with some limitations.

How can I make my UNIX server visible to my Windows and Windows NT users?

You can use either an SMB server on the UNIX box, or an NFS client on the Windows machines. Both ways will work, and the choice of technology will depend in large part on where the primary emphasis is on your network and exactly what you're trying to accomplish. We tend to favor adding SMB to the UNIX boxes over adding NFS to the Windows side of the equation, but both can work successfully.

What are the advantages of SMB over NFS?

Server message blocks provide the most transparent access to the UNIX server *from the Windows user's perspective*. They see the UNIX server as simply another member of the Windows workgroup or NT domain. Printer and filesystem shares look and behave exactly like they were on a Windows NT or Windows 95 machine, and are used in exactly the same way. Plus, nothing extra has to be added to the Windows networking stack, which reduces the resource load on the Windows machine, an important consideration in many environments.

NFS can be nearly as transparent, but requires that the NFS client be loaded on every single Windows or Windows NT machine that will need access to the UNIX server. And the additional resource hit and occasional incompatibilities caused by adding another networking client can be a definite problem.

What are the advantages of NFS?

NFS is a good choice for networks where the primary work is done on the UNIX or Linux servers, and there are relatively few Windows clients that will need access to the UNIX resources, especially where there is a substantial UNIX expertise available. NFS can also be a viable choice to provide connectivity in the reverse direction, from Windows NT to UNIX if you use an NFS server on the Windows NT side. However, in our experience, the available NFS servers for Windows NT are suitable only for light duty work.

Can I have my UNIX servers function as part of an NT domain?

Yes. AT&T has ported the Advanced Server portion of Windows NT to UNIX under license from Microsoft. This product has then been integrated by several of the major UNIX vendors into their product offerings, providing full Windows NT domain-level connectivity and support on

UNIX servers. These offerings include Advanced File and Print Server, from The Santa Cruz Operation (SCO) and Advanced Server for UNIX from Hewlett-Packard. With these products and similar ones from other vendors, your UNIX server can be either a primary domain controller or backup domain controller for a Windows NT Server network—with or without any Windows NT Servers present on the network.

Can UNIX servers function as part of a Windows workgroup?

Yes. There are several products that allow a variety of UNIX versions to function as part of a Windows workgroup. Examples include VisionFS from SCO (http://www.vision.sco.com), FacetWin from FacetCorp (http://www.facetcorp.com), and samba (ftp://samba.anu.edu.au). All of these function as workgroup servers, though not as NT domain controllers.

What are the advantages of using NT domains?

The biggest advantage to using one of the Advanced Server on UNIX (ASU) solutions is the increased security and central administration that comes as part of a Microsoft domain environment. You use the exact same tools to administer ASU as you do to administer a Windows NT domain. Hardly surprising, since they are the same underlying source code. Plus, all users, shares, and security can be centrally administered, making it much easier to deal with large numbers of machines and users. Workgroup solutions tend to top out at somewhere around ten users/workstations. You *can* go farther, but the administrative load becomes excessive.

What are the advantages of a workgroup solution?

Workgroup solutions have the undoubted advantage of being easier to set up and configure, especially with relatively smaller numbers of workstations and users. While the tools you use will be different from the native Windows tools, they are usually flexible and easy to figure out. You don't need to make complicated decisions about the number of domains or worry about having backup domain controllers on the network to protect against failure, since the level of security is low enough that you can simply rebuild a server and go on about your business.

? Is there a free way to share UNIX filesystems with Windows clients?

Yes. There is a freely available source code included, a product called samba that you can download to your UNIX system and compile. It provides a high degree of interoperability between UNIX systems and windows clients. It is actively being developed and updated and can be a good solution in an environment where there are sufficient UNIX skills to compile and administer it. For more information on samba, including a comprehensive FAQ and the latest versions, point your browser at http://samba.anu.edu.au/samba.

? Are there precompiled versions of samba available?

Depending on your system, the answer may be yes. Several ports of recent versions of samba can be found either at the http://samba.anu.edu.au/samba site or as links off of it. In addition, a compiled version for SCO that is usually quite up-to-date can be found at ftp://ftp.celestial.com, an overall outstanding source for ports of popular packages to SCO maintained by Bill Campbell. (Our personal thanks to him for the stuff we've scored off his site over the years!)

? How do I let my UNIX users share a Windows NT filesystem?

Some versions of UNIX, such as SCO OpenServer, provide native connectivity to Windows NT filesystem shares, but many do not. For those that do not, your options are a bit limited. Essentially the only choice is to use one of the NFS servers on Windows NT. If you need this option, however, we'd advise you to consider the load you intend to put on the system. If your primary users are on the Windows NT side, with only an occasional UNIX user of the filesystem, then this can be a valid option. However, if your users are primarily or even significantly UNIX users, we suggest you stick to storing the files on a UNIX machine and use either an NFS client on the Windows NT machine or an SMB server on the UNIX side to manage the connectivity. Frankly, we've tried the two most popular NFS servers for Windows NT and found them not up to the task for more than occasional use.

? Can I use an NFS exported filesystem on Windows NT without loading an NFS client package?

Yes, but the caveat is that you won't want to subject it to regular or heavy use. If you have an SMB server somewhere on the UNIX network, you can use it as an NFS gateway, mounting the NFS filesystem on it and then sharing it out to the Windows clients via SMB. It works, but you're doubling your network traffic and encouraging problems. This is recommended only in an emergency or as a temporary kludge while you get a better solution.

? What about printing? Can I share printers between UNIX and Windows NT?

Absolutely. There are a number of ways to manage the process, but in general all the SMB and NFS options discussed for filesystems above will also share out printers. Additionally, Windows NT provides a native lpr client that lets you use any TCP/IP or UNIX printer on the network. The best option overall is to place the printers directly on the network, using TCP/IP to control them. Most laser printers have either a built-in network card or the ability to add one. And for those that don't there are a variety of TCP/IP-based network print servers available from a variety of vendors. We've used both the H-P JetDirect-EX (http://www.hp.com) and Milan FastPort (http://www.milan.com) print servers with good success.

? How do I add the TCP/IP printing service to Windows NT?

You'll need to be logged in with administrative privilege to the Windows machine. Then open the Control Panel, and double-click on the Network icon. Click on the Services tab and select Add. Highlight the **Microsoft TCP/IP Printing** option and click OK.

❓ How do I add a TCP/IP printer to Windows NT?

Click on the Printers options of the Control Panel and then double-click on Add Printer Icon to open the Add Printer Wizard. Select My Computer and then click Next to get to the port selector as shown in Figure 11-5.

Select the Add Port button to add an LPR port, then highlight the LPR Port option, as shown in Figure 11-6, to connect to either a native TCP/IP printer or a UNIX printer with remote printing enabled. Then click New Port.

In the resulting dialog box, type in the name or IP address of the print server or UNIX machine that controls the printer, and then the name of the printer or print queue. If it's an H-P JetDirect printer, you'll use RAW as the printer name as shown in Figure 11-7.

Follow the rest of the prompts to complete the process, telling Windows NT what type of printer is being printed to and other details. Don't forget to print a test page, just in case.

❓ How can I let my UNIX users use my Windows NT printers?

Unfortunately, Windows NT doesn't include an lpd (lp daemon), which means it can't act as a remote printer for

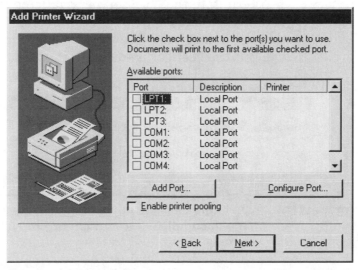

Figure 11-5   You'll need to add a new port to connect to a TCP/IP printer

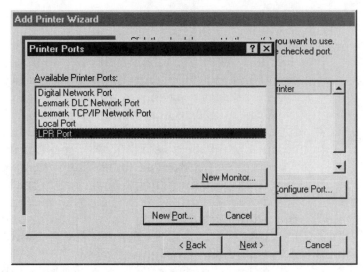

Figure 11-6 You'll need to add an LPR Port to your Windows NT printing system to connect to a remote lpr printer

UNIX machines. However, if you're using one of the SMB products, many will allow you to add a Windows or Windows NT shared printer into the native UNIX print spooler. These printers will use a simple passthrough interface script that sends the entire job, unmanipulated, to the Windows NT spooling system to manage.

Alternately, the NFS servers available for Windows NT generally include support for NFS printers, and there are other third-party and freeware lpd solutions available as well. But the best bet is to let UNIX manage the printers—it

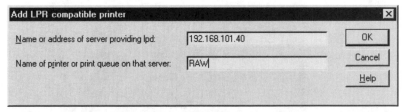

Figure 11-7 Type in the machine name or IP address and the printer name to complete the addition of a remote lp printer to Windows NT

generally does a *much* better job at it than NT. Microsoft never could manage print spooling well.

SHELL EMULATIONS: MAKING NT FEEL LIKE UNIX, AND UNIX FEEL LIKE NT

❓ What is the "standard" UNIX shell?

There is no standard UNIX shell. The most common alternatives are the Korn shell (our personal favorite), the Posix shell (the default shell on most new UNIX versions, and a close relative to the Korn shell), the Bourne shell (generally the lowest common denominator), and the C shell. There are also alternative freeware shells, such as the Bourne Again Shell (bash), that have gained a lot of adherents since they're generally available on a wide variety of platforms including Linux. Versions of most of the available shells are available on whatever UNIX you find yourself working on, and you should choose the shell you use based on the needs of the environment you're in, or the amount of scripting you expect to have to do. Interactive users tend to find the C shell or the Korn shell the most comfortable alternatives, while intense scripting should be done on the Bourne, Posix, or Korn shell, but should generally be written to Bourne shell limitations to prevent cross-platform problems.

❓ How can I make NT behave like UNIX?

There are a couple of products on the market that let you mimic the rich command-line power of UNIX even on Windows NT. Probably the most prevalent is the MKS ToolKit from Mortice-Kerns (http://www.mks.com). If you spend your time jumping back and forth between UNIX and Windows NT or Windows 95, we *highly* recommend this package. It's not perfect and it has a couple of things we really, really wish it did better. Still, it's a remarkably good Posix or Korn shell emulation running on Windows NT, and it includes all the most common UNIX command-line utilities that we'd be lost without. It even includes a quite satisfactory port of Perl to Windows NT for adding additional functionality to your command line.

? How can I make NT behave like UNIX without spending any money?

Your options here are bit more limited. You can certainly add many of your familiar UNIX commands, such as **ls** instead of **dir**, by using **doskey** macros. But most of the functionality simply isn't available without adding a third-party utility. Even the built-in Posix subsystem is no longer certified, and the limited functionality of the shell makes it difficult to completely mimic the behavior. If you really have to do this all the time, get a copy of the MKS ToolKit. If your only need is to occasionally use Windows NT, and you hate having to remember that your **cp** has to be typed out all the way to **copy**, then use a series of **doskey** macros to do the job. Load them into a batch file you can call from the command line. An example that handles **cp** would look like:

```
doskey cp=copy $*
```

? Can I make UNIX behave like the NT command line?

Well, yes, we suppose you can, if you really want to. Though why you would want to do this escapes us at the moment. But for those whose primary interface is the DOS, Windows 95, or Windows NT command line, and who only occasionally need to use the UNIX command line, we suppose it might make sense. The trick is to use the built-in ability of the Korn and Posix shells to create aliases that mimic the behavior of the Microsoft-centric command line. This is fairly straightforward for the simpler commands, but some are a bit trickier and may require you to write a shell script or two.

The one thing you won't be able to easily change is the direction of the "slash" key. As we saw earlier in Chapter 3, UNIX uses a standard forward slash to separate directory levels while the Microsoft-centric operating systems, including Windows NT, use a backslash for the same purpose. The backslash is normally, of course, the UNIX escape character. Getting the functions of the two keys to switch in UNIX is probably possible, but we've never seen it done, and we're afraid you'll just have to get used to the difference. You can make Windows NT switch the characters around to behave like they do in UNIX, using the MKS ToolKit, as we discussed above, so if this really drives you nuts, that may be your only solution. Actually it's not a bad solution, since you also get an extremely useful set of utilities and commands that Microsoft should have given the Windows NT user in any case, along with a full Posix shell implementation.

But what about the commands you're used to from your good old DOS days? No problem. Just add a series of aliases to your .kshrc file for the commands you miss the most. We've included a sampling of our favorites in Table 11-1.

DOS command	Korn or Posix shell alias	Comment
dir	ls -oA	Shows owner of file and most hidden files.
cls	clear	
type	cat	Try substituting your favorite pager here for the simple cat. We use **less**.
md	mkdir	
deltree	rm –r	Remember, this command is irrevocable and won't ask you to confirm!
del	rm	
copy	cp	No wildcard substitution.
move	mv	No wildcard substitution.
ren	mv	No wildcard substitution.

Table 11-1   Korn Shell Aliases for Common DOS and Windows NT Commands

Chapter 12

Disaster Avoidance and Recovery

Answer Topics!

Disaster Avoidance and Recovery @ a Glance

- **Preventing disaster** is always the best way to go, so here's how to think ahead a little and take a few relatively simple precautionary measures.

- The single most important thing you can do to protect yourself in UNIX (or any other operating system, we might add) is to do regular **backups**. We'll talk about specific backup strategies below, but right here we want to emphasize that there's no way to recover a deleted file other than by having a copy of it. So either don't delete the file or have a backup copy of it you can recover.

Note: *But wait, you say. Your system administrator does backups every day / week / whatever. Why should you have to worry about such things? After all, that's what she gets paid the big bucks for, right? It's true, but even in the best of all possible worlds where your system is completely backed up every night and there are never problems with the tape, this still isn't going to solve your problems. First, do you really want to lose an entire day's worth of work? Furthermore, restoring a single file from a system backup tape is not the sort of task that is likely to make your system administrator happy. Yes, it can be done, and in the event of ultimate emergency this may be your only hope. But far better to have taken the necessary steps to protect yourself.*

RISK AVOIDANCE

Preventing Disaster

It's always easier to not make a mistake than to recover from it once the mistake is made. And wouldn't we all be better off if we ran our lives on that principle? So the question is how to not make that mistake. Probably the first rule is to avoid certain irrevocable commands. UNIX makes it remarkably easy to simply remove entire directory structures without even a warning. This power is nice, if you're sure that's what you want to do, but if not, then going "oops" isn't likely to be adequate.

Warning: *Don't use the **rm -rf** command. This is one of those commands that is just too powerful for its own good. Actually, the ordinary **rm -r** command is also too powerful, but at least it will warn you before it starts deleting read-only files. When you add the **-f** (for force) switch, you have really left yourself no chance.*

Is it wise to create an alias for the rm command?

This is a touchy one. Some purists feel strongly that you shouldn't alias any of UNIX's built-in commands, while others do it all the time. We tend to think it's a bad practice if carried to the extreme, but in some cases it can be a lifesaver. For example, if you want to add an additional layer of protection, this is one way to do it. Try adding the following to your **.kshrc** file:

```
alias rm='rm -i'
```

Now, whenever you go to remove a file, you will be prompted for confirmation. The problem with this approach is that it can get pretty annoying if you have a bunch of files to remove and you're really sure you want to remove them. Under those conditions, you can get careless about the removal, answering "y" to the prompt without really reading it. A better solution is to move the files out of the way temporarily, and only remove them when they are old enough that you are sure you want to get rid of them.

How can I create an alias for rm that moves my files someplace safe?

This is the UNIX equivalent of some of the utilities available for DOS that move your files into a special holding directory. We have two simple little scripts we use. Both depend on your having a **tmp** directory under your $HOME directory, which is usually a good idea anyway. First, create the script **safe_rm.ksh** shown in Figure 12-1 and store it in your personal **bin** directory. Don't forget to make it executable with **chmod**. Now, create your alias for it:

```
alias rm='$HOME/bin/safe_rm.ksh'
```

and add that to your **.kshrc** file. To make this immediately available, re-source your **.kshrc** file with

```
. ~/.kshrc
```

```
xterm
I/bin/ksh
####################################################################
#
# A script to move files to a temporary directory rather than
# remove them.
# Use as an alias for the rm command.
#
if (mv $* ~/tmp)
then
        print "\nFiles have been moved to the ~/tmp directory.
        print "To remove them, use the purge command. \n \n"
else
        print "Error occurred, files not moved"
fi
~
~
~
~
~
~
~
~
~
~
"safe_rm.ksh" 14 lines, 374 characters
```

Figure 12-1 A safer way to remove files

Now, every time you issue the **rm** command, what you are really doing is running the **safe_rm.ksh** script and moving the files to your **tmp** directory.

? What's the best way to purge my tmp **directory of older files?**

If you're going to be stuffing all these files into your **tmp** directory, it's going to get crowded with all sorts of junk over time. So you'll need to have a way to purge the older files and send them off to oblivion. Create a script to do this automatically, again with an alias. The script, **purge.ksh**, which is shown in Figure 12-2, looks for all files in your **tmp** directory that haven't been changed in more than seven days, and then asks you if it's okay to delete them.

Now, create an alias for this so you don't have to add that annoying **.ksh** to the end of the command each time.

```
alias purge='$HOME/bin/purge.ksh'
```

Notice that we were kind of conservative with this script. Even though it's only deleting the files that haven't been modified or changed in the last seven days, you'll still have to

```
                                    xterm
#!/bin/ksh
###################################################################
#
# A script to purge files that have been copied to the ~/tmp
# directory using the aliased rm command.  Checks for files
# not changed in the last week and removes them.
#
cd ~/tmp
if (find . -ctime +7 -ok rm {} \; )
then
        print "\nFiles older than 7 days in ~/tmp have been removed."
else
        print "Error occurred, files not removed"
fi

~
~
~
~
~
~
~
~
"purge.ksh" 15 lines, 413 characters
```

Figure 12-2   A safe way to purge unneeded files in your **tmp** directory

confirm each and every deletion. If you want a more forceful version, try the **purge!.ksh** shown in Figure 12-3.

Of course, you will probably want to alias this one as well. So we have this alias:

```
alias purge!='$HOME/bin/purge!.ksh'
```

Now, anytime we want to clean up the directory of older files and we're sure there's nothing in there we actually care about, we just use **purge!** to remove all the files at least seven days old from the **tmp** directory.

❓ Can I add purge! to my crontab?

We're not generally in favor of doing this sort of absolute cleanup automatically, but if you're a lazy sort or absolutely sure that files in your **tmp** directory can be deleted, you might consider adding this to your **crontab** if you have permission to use the **cron** process. One way to do this is to run it only every Sunday night. That way, you know that no file in the directory is older than two weeks old, but that nothing from last week has yet been removed. The **crontab** entry for this would be

```
0 1 * * 0 $HOME/bin/purge!.sh
```

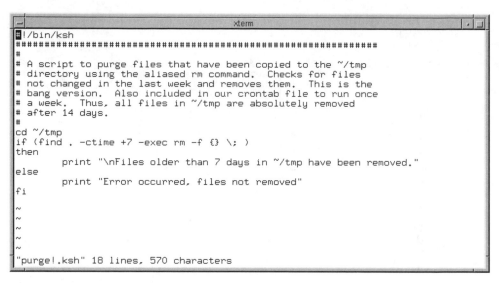

```
#!/bin/ksh
##################################################################
#
# A script to purge files that have been copied to the ~/tmp
# directory using the aliased rm command.  Checks for files
# not changed in the last week and removes them.  This is the
# bang version.  Also included in our crontab file to run once
# a week.  Thus, all files in ~/tmp are absolutely removed
# after 14 days.
#
cd ~/tmp
if (find . -ctime +7 -exec rm -f {} \; )
then
        print "\nFiles older than 7 days in ~/tmp have been removed."
else
        print "Error occurred, files not removed"
fi

~
~
~
~
~
"purge!.ksh" 18 lines, 570 characters
```

Figure 12-3   The purge-bang script is for when you are really sure

Hmm, perhaps you notice a change? The name has gone from **purge!.ksh** to **purge!.sh**. This is, of course, on purpose. When **cron** runs your **crontab** file, it only uses the basic Bourne shell to do so. Therefore, we modified the script accordingly, as shown in Figure 12-4.

Note: *New releases of some flavors of UNIX are using the Posix shell for **cron**. The Korn shell is compliant with Posix, so your **crontab** scripts must be either Korn shell or Posix shell. The **man** pages for **cron** will tell you which shell is used.*

However, you don't want to leave yourself without a way to run the real **rm** command for those times when you really, really want to remove a file. So use yet another alias, this time to **rm!** in keeping with the convention we've been using.

```
alias rm!='/bin/rm'
```

This uses the absolute path to the **rm** command, which will get around any stray scripts someone may have out there, and go straight to the source.

```
-                                 xterm                                  . 
#################################################################
#
# A script to purge files that have been copied to the $HOME/tmp
# directory using the aliased rm command.  Checks for files
# not changed in the last week and removes them.  This is the
# bang version.  Also included in our crontab file to run once
# a week.  Thus, all files in $HOME/tmp are absolutely removed
# after 14 days.
#
cd $HOME/tmp
find . -ctime +7 -exec rm -f {} \;


~
~
~
~
~
~
~
~
~
"purge.sh" 13 lines, 447 characters
```

Figure 12-4   When you run a script from your **crontab**, you have to use
the Bourne shell

? What's the very best way to protect crucial files against accidental erasure?

One important way to protect your files from inadvertent
removal, or even worse, deliberate mischief, is to use the
protection mechanisms built into UNIX.

Step one is to make really important files read-only. This
is easy to do and can save you plenty of trouble. If you have
files that you don't need to change, but do need to access
regularly, change their permissions to not allow
anyone—even yourself—to write to them.

```
chmod a-w filename
```

Now the file cannot be changed without taking extra
steps, even by you, the owner. Of course, you can get around
this by changing the permissions before you change the file.
But you have made the process awkward enough that you
are unlikely to do it by accident.

! *Warning:*   *The superuser can delete your file no matter what
you do. This is one of those sad but true facts. No matter how
much protection you put on a file, the superuser can blithely
delete the file or change it, with barely a moment's thought. Yet
another reason to stay on friendly terms with this person.*

? Can I create a special script to edit read-only files?

Certainly. If you want to make sure that some files are protected from casual change, it's quite easy to make a simple little script that modifies the permissions of the file, opens **vi** to edit it, and then changes the permissions back when you are done. We'll call it **vi!** for an alias:

```
alias vi!='$HOME/bin/vi!.ksh'
```

and we'll use the script shown in Figure 12-5 for this.

The nice part about this script is that it returns your permissions to their previous condition when you are done. This makes it relatively easy to edit a read-only file and yet maintain the protection from casual changes. This is usually a good compromise: somewhere between paranoia and carelessness.

? How can I put sensitive or critical files in directories that are inaccessible to others?

Change the permissions on these directories using the **chmod** command to deny access to anyone except you and the superuser.

```
chmod 700 dirname
```

This will make it impossible for anyone to accidentally or intentionally delete, change, or even read the files in these

```
#!/bin/ksh
###################################################################
#
# A script to edit files that are read only, and then return
# them to read only status when you are done.
#
if (chmod u+w $*)
then
        vi $*
        chmod u-w $*
else
        print "Error occurred -- unable to change permission"
        print "to +w."
fi


~
~
~
~
~
~
~
"vi!.ksh" 16 lines, 310 characters
```

Figure 12-5   A simple script to edit read-only files

directories—unless someone has access to your password. Another good reason to keep your password safe.

> **!** ***Warning:*** *Don't forget to change your $HOME directory as well. It's easy enough to protect your own directories, but also easy to forget to change the home directory itself.*
>
> ```
> chmod 700 $HOME
> ```
>
> *will change just your home directory so that no one can come snooping around.*

BACKUP, BACKUP, BACKUP!

UNIX and Backups

All these nice tips for ways to protect against accidentally deleting files or changing them when you don't mean to are great, and we strongly encourage you to use some combination of them. But nothing beats a verified backup when disaster strikes. The person with the primary responsibility for backups is the system administrator, but everyone who works with computers needs to take responsibility for backups of his or her own critical files. This isn't hard, it need not be onerous, and it can be a lifesaver.

The beauty of UNIX is that you don't usually have to worry about backing up programs or huge data files, because these are generally the domain of the system administrator. But you do need to think about your own local data files. The method you use will vary depending on the capabilities of your system, the amount of hard disk space available, and exactly what programs and media are available to individual users on your system. But most systems have enough hard disk space for you to maintain at least a copy of your most recent work on the hard disk, and if you have access and permissions, it's fairly easy to make copies of these files onto a floppy disk, too. The key to making this painless is to only back up what you need to, and then do it *often*. Personally, we prefer to do backups of current working files about twice a day, but you will need to decide what works for you. Many users like to automate the process as part of their logout routine, and the C shell even has a special file for this purpose—**.logout**. But if you use the Korn shell, you'll need to create your own equivalent. Before we get into the particulars of how to automate backups, however, let's look at the kinds of backup you can, and should, do.

? Why might I consider making a hard disk backup?

The modern hard disk is remarkably safe and stable, and almost never crashes. Hard disks bought today have an average "Mean Time Between Failure" (MTBF) of 100,000 to 300,000 and even 500,000 hours of continuous service, depending on the brand and model. That translates into 11-56 *years* between failures, which is certainly longer than you need to worry about, because computers bought today won't be in service in 11—much less 56—years. They'll be technologically obsolete long before then. Of course, it's still possible to get a lemon, which is why the system administrator faithfully does backups. So a backup to your hard disk may well be sufficient for your files. This will protect you against accidental erasure, and the stray corruption of a critical file that may be caused by circumstances beyond your control.

? What's the easiest way to make a hard disk backup?

Keep copies of your working files in a backup directory. This is probably the simplest way to handle your backup chores, and will suffice for most users. We call ours **.backup** and have the permissions set to 700 (that's full permission for the owner, but no permission whatsoever for anyone else). This should be enough to protect you from casual (or even not-so-casual) mischief, since the only other person who can get into this directory is the superuser. Then we keep current versions of our working files in that directory. For simple chores, where you don't need or want to keep different versions of your files, we have a simple alias we call whenever we are going to log out. It copies the files that have changed today into the **.backup** directory.

```
alias savwrk='find $HOME/* -mtime -1 -exec cp {} $HOME/.backup \;'
```

This alias works pretty well, but it isn't perfect. It won't, for example, copy files or directories that start with a dot. The alternative is to add into this any special directories or files that you want to make sure are copied. Or write a script that builds a smarter directory tree.

? When should I consider making tape or floppy backups?

Hard disk backups are nice, and they provide adequate protection for many purposes, especially considering that your system administrator is undoubtedly doing periodic complete tape backups. But there are circumstances where hard disk backups just aren't appropriate. If you are doing extremely sensitive work and can't leave copies of what you do on the hard disk, for example, you'll need to take the work off the hard disk when you aren't present. And if you would be totally devastated if you lost certain files, you probably want to do your own backups above and beyond what the system administrator is doing, especially if you are in an environment where the system-wide backups are done only weekly, for example.

? What's the easiest way to make a tape or floppy backup?

The most common mechanism for backing up files to an external storage medium such as tape or floppy is the UNIX **tar** (tape archive and restore) command. This command, which is available on virtually all UNIX systems and can be obtained for other systems such as DOS, is a simple and fairly efficient way to handle most of a user's backup chores. The system administrator may well have more powerful tools, which can easily span multiple machines and filesystems on the network, but fortunately you aren't likely to need those.

The syntax for the **tar** command is

```
tar key files
```

where **key** is one of the following basic actions:

- **c** Creates a new archive
- **r** Appends to an existing archive
- **t** Lists the contents of the archive
- **u** Updates the archive, adding files that aren't present or are newer
- **x** Extracts the files from the archive

and one or more of the following modifiers:

- **A**   Suppresses absolute filenames
- **l**   Gives an error message if a link can't be resolved
- **L**   Follows symbolic as well as hard links
- **m**   Doesn't restore modification times (everything gets current date/time)
- **p**   Extracts using the original permissions
- **v**   verbose-tar is quiet by default
- **w**   Waits for confirmation before each action
- **f**   The next argument is the device name to use

These are the most important of the **tar** options, and they behave pretty much consistently across a variety of platforms. There may well be specific options appropriate to your particular situation or implementation of **tar**, so check with your system administrator if in doubt.

The final argument for **tar** is the files to be archived. This can be specific files or directories, or **tar** can be part of a piped command line if the device is "-" for standard input or output.

? Can I use tar to copy files to a different machine or filesystem?

Since **tar** follows subdirectories, it is easy to use for transferring complete directory structures to a different place. If, for example, you wanted to copy files to a new place, keeping everything intact, you could use

```
cd sourcedir;tar cf - . | (cd targetdir;tar xf -)
```

which would copy everything from the source directory to the target directory. It's important that you use the dot for the source directory here so that the archive is created with relative path names. Use absolute path names for *sourcedir* and *targetdir* to avoid copying files to the wrong location.

❓ Can I use tar to back up my files to a floppy or tape drive?

If you have a floppy drive in your workstation, you probably already know what the device file name for it is, but if in doubt, ask your system administrator and then write it down where you won't lose it. One possible place is right on the front of the floppy drive in permanent marker. A typical device might be **/dev/fd0** for the first floppy, so the **tar** command to save your entire home directory and all the files in it would be

```
tar cvf /dev/fd0 $HOME
```

If you want to save the files with relative path names, not the absolute ones that this would give you, change to your home directory first, substitute a simple dot for the **$HOME**, and you're in business.

Chapter 13

The Korn Shell

Answer Topics!

The Korn Shell @ a Glance

- **Variables and parameters** are an important part of any programming language, and the Korn shell is no exception. Here we'll show you what you need to know in order to use them intelligently.

- In case you get confused, it's nice to know ahead of time exactly how the **Korn shell** does **math**.

- Although the Korn shell's math capabilities are somewhat limited, its capabilities with **string operators** are impressive, as you'll soon see.

- You'll save yourself some trouble if you are aware of the **predefined variables** that the Korn shell offers you.

- Finally, **flow control** is one of the most important capabilities of any programming language or environment. The Korn shell provides a wide array of flow control structures, so here's what you'll need to know in order to make the best possible use of them.

VARIABLES AND PARAMETERS

? What kind of use does the Korn shell make of variables and parameters?

Like any programming tool, the Korn shell lets you define variables and accepts input parameters. Parameters are anything that appears on the command line (or is piped into the command) after the command itself. The Korn shell separates or *parses* these parameters by looking for white space in between them, or, more properly, whatever characters are in the IFS (internal field separator) variable. By default, this is space, tab, and newline, but you can change this to make it easier to parse a set of options. But be sure to set it back when you get done. The positional parameters are automatically assigned by the shell as **$1**, **$2**, **$3**, and so forth. The value of **$0** is the name of the calling script. The variable **$*** holds all the values except **$0**, as a single string within which each value is separated by the first character of **$IFS**. The variable **$@** is equal to "$1", "$2", and so forth as separate parameters.

? How do I assign values to a variable?

Use the syntax

```
variable=value
```

For example, the following

```
wayne=harold
print "Wayne is now called $wayne"
```

results in

```
Wayne is now called harold
```

The Korn Shell and the POSIX Shell

The Korn shell was invented by David Korn in the 1980s at AT&T's Bell Labs. It's gone through several iterations, but the one most commonly available was written in 1988 and has been distributed on a wide range of UNIX platforms since that time—especially those known as System V Release 4 (SVR4)—though most flavors of UNIX based on the Berkeley System Distribution (BSD) also now support the Korn shell. The Korn shell continues to be developed, and new versions are likely to see the light of day over time. The Posix shell, however, seems to be replacing the Korn shell in many instances. Most of the features of the Korn shell have found their way into the common implementations of the Posix shell, and your Korn shell scripts should port to Posix shell with little or no changes.

Most of the examples we have used in this book have been written and tested under the Korn shell, and by this point in the book you've probably picked up quite a few things about it. But we felt that it would be useful to give you a reference for some of the basics of shell programming, as opposed to interactive use, that the Korn shell supports in a form less dense than the **man** pages.

KORN SHELL MATH

? **Is there anything in particular I should know about the way the Korn shell does math?**

You can do simple math within a Korn shell script, though if you want to do much of it, there are far better choices for programming languages than the Korn shell. But, for example, you can declare a variable, **i**, and assign a value to it in one of the following ways:

```
I=100
let I=100
(( i=100 ))
```

All three of these statements will assign the value of 100 to the variable "**i**". To perform arithmetic in the Korn shell, you may use the operators in Table 13-1 and the logical or relational operators shown in Table 13-2.

To tell the Korn shell to evaluate an arithmetic expression, enclose it in double parentheses: "(( ))". Even special characters lose their meaning inside these double parentheses, so you can use "*" without quoting or escaping it.

Operator	Action
+	Addition
-	Subtraction
*	Multiplication
/	Division (truncates to integer value)
%	Modulus
<<	Bit-shift left
>>	Bit-shift right
&	Bitwise AND
|	Bitwise OR
~	Bitwise NOT
^	Bitwise XOR

Table 13-1 Arithmetic Operators for the Korn Shell

Operator	Action
<	Less than
>	Greater than
<=	Less than or equal to
>=	Greater than or equal to
!=	Not equal to
==	Equal to
&&	Logical AND
||	Logical OR

Table 13-2   Logical or Relational Operators in the Korn Shell

!
■

Warning: *The Korn shell only does integer arithmetic.
You can use floating-point numbers, and it will accept
them without an error message, but it truncates them so
you may not get the answer you expect! For example, consider
the following:*

```
(( 7.2 / 1.8 ))
```

*This should, you would expect, evaluate to 4. But the answer
is actually 7 in the Korn shell, since it is really being
evaluated as "7 div 1".*

*Even though the entire expression is enclosed in double
parentheses, you still use additional parentheses inside the
expression to control the order of precedence. So, for example,
to multiply 7 times the result of adding 2+4 divided by 3, you
would use*

```
(( 7 * ( (2+4)/3) ))
```

*Note that the additional white space we've included in this
line is not significant. We find, however, that it makes the line
much easier to read.*

STRING OPERATORS

? **What's an example of a string operation that the Korn shell does especially well?**

Concatenation. To concatenate two strings in UNIX, simply stick them together without intervening white space. If you need to include white space, enclosing the whole thing in quotes gets around the problem. This is shown in Figure 13-1, where we made up some examples for demonstration purposes.

Most of the time, we refer to a string variable that we have created with a simple "$*strvar*" where the *strvar* is the variable. But this is actually a specific case of the more general syntax of "${*strvar*}," which works in all cases. So, for example, you can get away with referencing the ninth positional parameter you pass into your script with a **$9** and all is well, but you can't get away with **$10**. To reference the tenth (and later) positional parameter, you need to be more formal by using the **${10}** syntax.

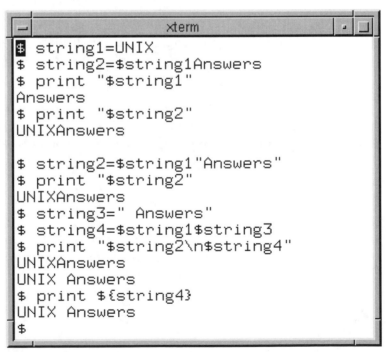

```
$ string1=UNIX
$ string2=$string1Answers
$ print "$string1"
Answers
$ print "$string2"
UNIXAnswers

$ string2=$string1"Answers"
$ print "$string2"
UNIXAnswers
$ string3=" Answers"
$ string4=$string1$string3
$ print "$string2\n$string4"
UNIXAnswers
UNIX Answers
$ print ${string4}
UNIX Answers
$
```

Figure 13-1 Concatenating strings in the Korn shell

? Does the Korn shell provide for useful string substitution operators?

Yes. These let you check to see what the value of a string is, and then substitute for the value, use a default, or exit out of the script. Table 13-3 shows the possibilities.

You can use these operators to check if a variable has been set, and then do something depending on the answer to that test.

! Warning: *You can't use the ${str:=expression} syntax to assign a value to a positional parameter. You'll have to use an intermediate local variable to get the job done. This is one nuisance in the Korn shell for which we have yet to see a good explanation or justification.*

Operator	Substitution
${str:=expression}	If *str* is unset or null, it returns *expression* and assigns *expression* to *str* as well. If *str* has a value, it returns that value.
${str:-expression}	If *str* is unset or null, it returns *expression* but doesn't change *str*. If *str* has a value, it returns that value.
${str:+expression}	If *str* is unset or null, it returns null. If *str* has a value, it returns *expression*.
${str:?expression}	If *str* is unset or null, it sends the value of *expression* to standard error and aborts the current command or script. If *str* has a value, it returns that value.
${str#pattern}	If *pattern* matches the beginning of *str*, it returns *str* with the smallest matching part deleted; otherwise it returns *str* unchanged.
${str##pattern}	If *pattern* matches the beginning of *str*, it returns *str* with the largest matching part deleted; otherwise it returns *str* unchanged.
${str%pattern}	If *pattern* matches the end of *str*, it returns *str* with the smallest matching part deleted; otherwise it returns *str* unchanged.
${str%%pattern}	If *pattern* matches the end of *str*, it returns *str* with the largest matching part deleted; otherwise it returns *str* unchanged.

Table 13-3 The Korn Shell's Substitution Operators

PREDEFINED VARIABLES IN THE KORN SHELL

? How can I redefine a predefined variable?

Actually, we showed you how to do this in Chapter 5 when we redefined the **PS1** variable to change our prompt. Table 13-4 shows the parameters and variables that are set by the Korn shell, and Table 13-5 shows the parameters and variables that are used by various aspects of the Korn shell.

Parameter	Meaning or Use
#	The number of positional parameters currently set
-	Flags passed to the shell on startup, or by the **set** command
?	The value returned, in decimal, of the last command
$	The process number of the current shell
_	Initially the fully qualified path name of the shell or script. Reassigned automatically to the last argument of the previous command
!	The process number of the last background command
ERRNO	The value of **errno** as set by the last failed system call
LINENO	The current line number of the script being executed
OLDPWD	The last working directory set by **cd**
OPTARG	The last option returned by the **getopts** command
OPTIND	The index (position) of the last option returned by the **getopts** command
PPID	The process ID of the parent of the shell
PWD	The current working directory
RANDOM	A psuedo-random integer between 0 and 32767 that changes each time the parameter is referenced, using the previous value as a seed
REPLY	Set by the **select** statement, or by **read** with no arguments
SECONDS	The number of seconds since the shell was started

Table 13-4   Parameters Set by the Korn Shell

Parameter	Meaning or Use
CDPATH	Search path for the **cd** command
COLUMNS	Number of columns in the current edit window
EDITOR	Default editor to be used for command-line editing
ENV	Path name of the script to execute when a shell is invoked
FCEDIT	Default editor for the **fc** command
HISTFILE	Path name of the command history file
HISTSIZE	Number of commands to keep in the history file. Default value is 128
HOME	The home directory. Default destination for **cd** command
IFS	Internal field separators, normally space, tab, and new line
LINES	Number of lines in the current display window
MAIL	Default mail file for the user
MAILCHECK	How often to check to see if new mail has arrived in the $MAIL or $MAILPATH file. Default is 10 minutes (600 seconds)
MAILPATH	List of possible mail destinations, delimited by colons
PATH	The command execution search path
PS1	The primary command-line prompt (default is "$ ")
PS2	The secondary command-line prompt (default is "> ")
PS3	The prompt string used within a select loop (default is "#? ")
PS4	The execution trace prompt (default is "+ ")
SHELL	The path name of the shell
TMOUT	If set to >0, the time until the shell will automatically terminate if no command is entered at the **PS1** prompt
VISUAL	The default command-line editor. Overrides EDITOR

Table 13-5 Korn Shell Variables and Parameters

FLOW CONTROL

? What flow control structures does the Korn shell offer me?

If you intend to get much accomplished with any programming language or environment, you must have some form of flow control. The Korn shell is no exception. It provides the following structures:

- **if/then/else**
- **for**
- **while**
- **until**
- **case**
- **select**

This is an adequate selection of flow control statements, but unfortunately the syntax is not exactly user-friendly. You'll probably find that it takes a certain amount of trial and error to get it all right.

? **What's tricky about using** if/then/else **statements in the Korn shell?**

These structures are the most basic and most commonly used form of flow control in a program. First you ask if something is true, and if it is, you do something. If it isn't, you may do something else, or you may just do nothing. The basic syntax is

```
if condition
then
statements
[elif condition2
then statements]
[else
statements]
fi
```

Each **if** is closed by a corresponding **fi** and within it can contain **else** and **elif** (else if) tests and statements. But the key to making the whole thing work is the *condition* part of the construct. And here the Korn shell gives us some power. The *condition* can be a simple test of the typical Boolean kind such as these:

```
if [[ $DISPLAY = "rci1:0.0" ]]
if (( n == 1 ))
if (( y >= 17 ))
```

Or it can be the result of running a program or even a series of programs. In this case the result or return code of the final program will be evaluated for the condition. An example might be something like

```
if echo $PATH | grep X11
```

which will test true if the path includes "X11" anywhere in it. This could also be a "multiple choice test":

```
if ( echo $PATH | grep interbase ) || whence gdml
```

This will test to see if the path contains "**interbase**" or if one of its programs, **gdml**, can be found. If either is true, then the condition will be true.

? Can you show me how to use for loops in the Korn shell?

The **for** construct lets you perform an operation a fixed number of times. This is useful when you need to perform an operation on a group of items, such as a list of filenames. This is a bit different from how a C or Pascal programmer might expect a **for** loop to behave. In that case, the syntax might be something like: **for i:=1 to 10 do**. Here we're passing a list of items to a variable, changing the value of the variable each time the loop is run. The syntax for this construct is

```
for name in [list]
do
statements that act on or use $name
done
```

Each time through the loop, the value of **$name** has a different value, as it goes through the items in **list** one at a time.

? What do I need to know about using while and until loops in the Korn shell?

The **while** loop combines a conditional test with a looping construct, and as long as the condition tests true, the loop will continue to run. Think about that for a moment. If you don't make absolutely sure that your **while** loop can eventually be false, you're never going to get out of it. The **until** loop is the exact opposite of a **while** loop. It will run until the condition is true. So the cardinal rule of **while** and **until** loops is to *first* make sure you define the exit condition. This will save you untold amounts of grief. The syntax for both is the same:

```
while condition
do
statements
done
```

Just substitute **until** in the above if you want to test for a false condition instead of a true one.

? What can case **statements do for me?**

The case statement is kind of like a multiple-choice version of the **if/then** clause. Its C counterpart is the **switch** statement, but the Korn shell version lets you test a string against patterns that can include wildcard characters and then, based on the pattern it matches, perform a series of statements. This is really nothing you can't do with a series of **if/then/elif** statements, but it's expressed in a more concise way. The syntax is

```
case expression in
pattern1)
statements;;
pattern2)
statements;;
...
patternN)
statements;;
esac
```

Notice the double semicolons (;;) after each set of statements. These must be used to finish each leg of the case statement.

Because the **case** statement lets us match against a pattern, it's especially useful for deciding what to do with a list of files. We can easily feed the **case** statement a file list, one at a time, by enclosing the whole in a **for** loop, and then, depending on what kind of file it is, do something different with the file. So you could take output from a **find** command, for example, that found every file that you hadn't changed in the last month to create a **filelist**, and then do something with those files, depending on what sorts of files they were. You could remove all of them with "**tmp**" in the name, move any with "**sav**" in the name to an archive directory, and so forth. Figure 13-2 shows a script to do just that.

❔ How should I use the select statement?

The Korn shell's **select** construct is a unique way to build a simple menu and branch based on the response to that menu. The **select** statement doesn't really line up with any corresponding statement in C or Pascal or any other language we know about. But it certainly makes it easy for you to do things that might otherwise be a nuisance. The basic syntax of **select** is

```
select var [in list]
do
statements that act on or use $var
done
```

```
$ cat clean
#!/bin/ksh
# File:clean
# Check for old files and clean up after yourself
#
for file in $(find $HOME -ctime +30 -print)
do
        case $file in
                *tmp)
                                rm -i $file;;
                *sav*)
                                mv $file $HOME/archive;;
                core)
                                rm $file;;
        esac
done
$
```

Figure 13-2   **Case** lets you do different things with different files, all in one easy to understand statement

This looks a lot like the syntax of a **for** loop, and it should because they are, in fact, the same. The difference is that with the **select** construct we don't pass everything in the *list* to the do...done part, only what the user selects from the menu that's displayed. Figure 13-3 shows an example of how this works.

```
$ cat pets
PS3='favorite pet? '
select var in Cats Dogs Birds Fish
do
        case $var in
                Cats)
                        print "Cats are my favorite pet";;
                Dogs)
                        print "Dogs make friendly pets";;
                Birds)
                        print "Birds are a cheerful addition to the house";;
                Fish)
                        print "Fish make for a quiet pet";;
        esac
        break
done
$ pets
1) Cats
2) Dogs
3) Birds
4) Fish
favorite pet? 1
Cats are my favorite pet
```

Figure 13-3 The Korn shell's **select** builds simple menus automatically

Chapter 14

Linux

Answer Topics!

Linux @ a Glance

- In order to begin using Linux, you need access to some **Linux basics**. Here's what you need to know about where to get Linux, different distributions of Linux, and more.

- Because **keyboard issues** crop up frequently when you're using UNIX, it's important to understand how to make your keyboard behave as you'd like it to. Under Linux, you can customize your keyboard to suit your tastes.

- One crucial difference between commercial versions of UNIX and Linux is **password security**. If you need to add security measures to your Linux system, here's how.

- The availability of popular **shells** determines how you'll interact with Linux. Luckily, a full range of shells is available on most Linux systems, so no matter which shell is your shell of choice, your needs can be accommodated.

- **Text editors** are another important tool for any UNIX user. Although plain old **vi** isn't a part of most Linux distributions, Linux provides enough alternatives to satisfy almost anyone.

- Even though it's available at little or no cost, Linux even comes with an **X Windows** system. We'll tell you what you'll need to know to customize your Linux X.

- Finally, there are the **other Linux tools**. Some of these may be familiar to you if you've used commercial UNIX systems, others not, so take a look and see what's available.

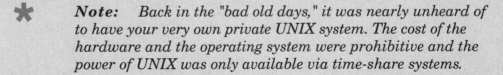 ***Note:*** *Back in the "bad old days," it was nearly unheard of to have your very own private UNIX system. The cost of the hardware and the operating system were prohibitive and the power of UNIX was only available via time-share systems.*

Thanks to the concerted efforts of a large group of programmers on the Internet, however, several variations of UNIX have been made available on cheaper, more accessible hardware. These versions of UNIX are just as powerful, just as useful, and just as marvelous as the big name commercial versions and they can be had for a fraction of the cost.

One of the most popular versions of these is Linux, which is available for free on the Internet or for a nominal cost from various vendors. This chapter is devoted to pointing out the differences between Linux and the big name commercial variants of UNIX.

LINUX BASICS

? Where can I get Linux?

Installing a UNIX operating system from scratch can be pretty painful for novices. Linux is designed to be a viable alternative operating system for novices, however, and different groups have put a lot of effort into making life a little easier for you. Basically, using one of the popular Linux distributions can save you a lot of time and pain.

There are many differences among the major distributions. Some provide smooth upgrade paths, some provide greater flexibility, and some are just fun to hack around with. As long as you use one of the common distributions you probably can't go wrong, and if you do have questions or problems you'll be able to find a large group of helpful people who can steer you back onto the path when you get lost in the wilderness.

You can get a complete copy of most of the distributions for free via anonymous FTP from various sites on the Internet. We recommend, however, that you purchase a copy on CD-ROM from a local vendor or via mail order in order to save yourself the time and agony of transferring that much data over the Internet.

? What's your favorite Linux distribution?

Redhat. It provides a solid and robust packaging system called **rpm** that allows you to install, upgrade, or remove entire packages of software with a single, simple command. Each release is thoroughly tested and contains the latest and greatest versions of a huge variety of software. In addition, many volunteers package up their favorite software packages that aren't included in the distribution and make them available using the **rpm** format.

Is Linux a "Real" UNIX?

Absolutely. Linux is a powerful and viable alternative to high priced commercial UNIX variants. Many hundreds of man hours have gone into making a system that is just as feature-rich and powerful as those being offered by the big name vendors. Don't let the fact that it's free (or freely available) lead you to believe that it's anything less. Linux is a real UNIX, not just a toy.

It is important, however, to adjust yourself to any environment. Linux, just like any other version of UNIX, has its own idiosyncrasies, its own gotchas, and its own things that it does better than others. Never sit blindly down at a system and think that it's going to operate exactly as any other system does. Take the time to explore and take advantage of the strengths of any individual system that you use, whether it's Linux, Solaris, HP/UX, or SCO.

Redhat also sells some popular commercial software packaged up and ready to drop into their systems. You can get more information about this distribution from http://www.redhat.com.

? What can you tell me about other Linux distributions?

Caldera is a high-quality commercial distribution that includes a lot of value-added features. It's built on an early version of Redhat but has diverged since then. It's not quite as open or as expandable as a stock Redhat distribution, but it has some additional commercial software that comes with it. Check it out at http://www.caldera.com.

The Debian folks have worked hard to put together a good, solid, and full-featured distribution that rivals Redhat in strength, diversity, and popularity. It's quite popular among the techie crowd and you really can't go wrong with it. It might be a little daunting for non-technical people, though, simply because of its scope. You can find out more about it at http://www.debian.org.

Slackware used to be one of the best distributions around and was extremely popular with most Linux people. It's still a strong distribution, but is waning in popularity due to the strengths of both Debian and Redhat. You can get more information about it from http://www.cdrom.com, which is the Walnut Creek CD-ROM archives.

Why Is Linux Free?

Linux systems owe a great deal of debt to the Free Software Foundation, which is the force behind the GNU project. These fine people have put together a complete suite of software for UNIX systems that are, for the most part, better, stronger, and faster than anything the commercial guys have been putting out. To top it all off, it's *free*. The fact is that if it weren't for the GNU tools, Linux could very well be nothing more than a kernel and some disk access code. Even the standard file utilities that you use (such as **ls**, **mv**, **cp**, and **rm**) are part of the GNU file utilities package.

Since you'll be hearing a lot about "free" software in the Linux community, let us take a few minutes to give you the standard spiel about it so that you won't end up embarrassing yourself. *Free* does not mean that it costs zero dollars, although that is often the case. *Free* means *freely available* and *freely redistributable*. It means that nobody can restrict you from having it. It also means that if you want the source code, you can get it with almost zero hassle. You can modify it, pick it apart to see how it works, improve it, customize it, basically do anything you want with it. The only thing you can't do is prevent someone else from having it too. If you sell it to someone (which you're allowed to do), you also have to provide them with the source code if they ask for it (you're allowed to charge a reasonable copying fee) and you cannot prevent them from walking around giving copies of that software (that they paid $4,500 for) to anyone they want for free.

This sounds kind of goofy, but only because everyone is conditioned to the licensing restrictions that have become so common. It actually works out very well because some of the best software in the world is distributed in this fashion. The GNU system includes *everything* you need to have a useful, working, UNIX system. In fact, it now even has its own kernel, although it's still in the experimental stages.

If you'd like more information about the Free Software Foundation, you can access their main FTP repository at ftp://prep.ai.mit.edu or you can write to the following address for more information: Free Software Foundation, Inc., 59 Temple Place, Suite 330, Boston, MA 02111-1307, USA.

They do a great service to the computing community as a whole and we encourage you to take a few minutes to familiarize yourself with them.

Don't be confused, though. Linux owes a great deal of debt to GNU, but GNU and Linux are different entities. A great many of the "under the hood" utilites are GNU, most of the code for the system is distributed under the GNU Public License, and the system would be quite different if it weren't standing on the backs of hundreds of GNU/FSF programmers. However, Linux is *Linux*, not GNU. Just because I use most of the GNU utilities on my Solaris system doesn't make my Sparc system a GNU box. It's the kernel that defines the core of the system, not the other way around.

What does all this have to do with you and why should you care? All this is important to know because the utilities that you'll be using on a day-to-day basis on your Linux system are GNU utilities, which means that they are, for the most part, feature-enhanced versions of the standard UNIX tools that you might already be used to. If you're comfortable at the command line typing in long strings of UNIX commands, you probably won't notice a difference, at least not immediately. We do encourage you, though, to take a look at the documentation and **man** pages for the things you use daily and explore some of their more advanced features. For most commands, you can get some basic help just by adding ' **--help** ' to the command name, and there are **info** pages (type **info** at the shell prompt) for even more documentation.

Even the lowly **ls** command has some spiffy features that you won't find elsewhere. Don't believe us? Try typing **ls --color** and you'll see exactly what we mean.

KEYBOARD ISSUES

? **What's wrong with my keyboard?**

UNIX was designed long before the first PC was even a dream. Consequently, it has some weird ideas about how keyboards work and what happens when various keys on them are pressed. PC keyboards are not like normal "big iron" keyboards and it may take a bit of fiddling in order to get your keyboard to behave as you'd like it to.

Most Linux keyboard behavior can be modified in the same way you'd modify keyboard behavior in any other version of UNIX. However, you can make permanent changes to your Linux keyboard mapping by editing the default keytables that are loaded on startup.

? What are keytables and how can I go about editing them?

Keystrokes are merely a set of events, much like anything else in life. You press a key on your keyboard. This generates a *key code* that gets sent to the kernel. The kernel then looks up that code in a *keytable* to determine what to do for that particular event.

You can't change the code that gets generated, but you can change the entries in the keytables using your favorite text editor. In fact, that is exactly what you do when you edit the keytable on your system, or when you edit an **xmodmap** file (more on that later). If you open the default keytable on your system, which is more than likely **/usr/lib/kbd/keytables/us.map**, you'll see the guts of the translation system, and it's not nearly as complex as you've been led to believe all this time. It's just a series of text entries.

Let's look at some easy ones:

```
keycode   16 = q
keycode   17 = w
keycode   18 = e
keycode   19 = r
keycode   20 = t
keycode   21 = y
keycode   22 = u
keycode   23 = i
keycode   24 = o
keycode   25 = p
```

Does this look familiar? It should, because it's the top row of letters on a standard keyboard, and this is the part of the table that applies to those keys. If you were to change one of those entries, you would change what was generated when you pressed the key in question. To change what a key does when pressed, just change the entry after the equal sign to whatever you want the new value to be. But before you make any changes, it's probably a good idea to make a copy of the original file. Just in case.

When you're finished making changes, reload the keyboard tables (**/usr/bin/loadkeys <your keyboard map name>**) and you now have a customized keyboard.

❓ Can you give me an example of how "power users" edit the default keytables?

A popular thing to do among "power users" is to swap the CAPS LOCK and CTRL modifiers around so that pressing the CAPS LOCK key gives you a control sequence. If you do a lot of switching back and forth between a "real" UNIX keyboard and a PC keyboard, you may find it useful to do this too.

❓ How do keytables really work?

OK, by now the smart ones among you are thinking "but wait, what about all those other weird entries I see in the table?" What you're referring to are entries that look a little more complicated, like this one:

```
            keycode    2 = one
shift       keycode    2 = exclam
alt         keycode    2 = Meta_one
alt shift   keycode    2 = Meta_exclam
```

Let's demystify these while we're at it. The extra fields here are just codes for when certain *modifier* keys are pressed with the key in question. For example, pressing the key labeled 1 on your keyboard doesn't really generate a "1." It generates a keycode of 2. Don't get confused, this is just the lookup code, remember? Now, if you pressed this key alone (without pressing SHIFT, CTRL, or ESC), the kernel would look up code number 2 in the list, map it to the "1" entry, and promptly spit out a "1" on your display. What happens when you press SHIFT-1 though? The kernel goes "Hmm... there's a SHIFT key with this one, so I need to use the SHIFT modifier, which is the second field" and you get a ! symbol (a "bang" in UNIX parlance). There are also other entries for other states that a key can be in. If you mess around with these, be careful, because you can really hose your keyboard—to the point that a reboot won't help at all.

❓ What are "meta" keys?

Another confusing point that often arises around UNIX keyboards is when people refer to "meta" keys. If you're an **emacs** user you are probably quite used to seeing meta sequences. Even if you're not an **emacs** user, you've probably heard the term before. Well, to make a long story short, there's really no magic involved with the meta key. It's just another modifier key like the CTRL key. However, most PC keyboards don't have a key labeled META. Most well-written UNIX applications take this into account and allow you to simulate a meta sequence by pressing and releasing the ESC key to simulate pressing a META key. If you want a real live permanent META key, though, you'll have to edit your keytables and swap around some key functions.

Personally, we find the CAPS LOCK key rather annoying, so we usually end up mapping it to CTRL and mapping the left-hand CTRL key to a META key. We do this in console mode by editing the keytables. We have to do it again in a different way when we're in graphical mode, since key mappings don't get carried over automatically. In graphical mode there's nothing magic about Linux, though, and you can use any of the standard UNIX hacks to map your keyboard around enough to confuse anyone in your workgroup. We'll revisit this issue again when we talk about X Windows, just to keep it fresh in your mind.

PASSWORD SECURITY

What can you tell me about Linux and password security?

One place where Linux differs noticeably from some of the commercial versions of UNIX is in the area of password security. Out of the box, Linux does not come configured with so-called shadow passwords. Shadow passwords are something you really shouldn't have to worry about unless you're a system administrator, but if you do happen to be your own system administrator and you want to increase the security of your system, you might want to consider upgrading. Most of the common FTP sites will have suites of precompiled programs to enable shadow passwords, and if you're a Redhat user you can download **rpm** packages and upgrade on the fly.

Even though most of the distributions don't come with shadow passwords enabled by default, the Redhat distribution has definitely beaten several of the commercial UNIX variants to the punch by including a little add-on called

PAM. PAM stands for "Pluggable Authentication Modules" and it's the newest rage in increasing the security of your system. What these little gems are is simply a set of common libraries of security modules. Each module is designed to do only a few things, such as get a password and authenticate it. Any program that needs to pay attention to security uses these modules to satisfy any security requirements. This prevents programmers from accidentally inserting security flaws into whatever program they're writing. Everyone can concentrate on making the small security modules as tight as possible instead of chasing down security holes in his or her programs.

We believe that PAM is the wave of the future. The newer versions of the commercial UNIX variants are starting to come out PAM-enabled. Once again, Linux is already there, waiting for the world to catch up.

SHELLS

? What shells does Linux offer me?

Most commercial UNIX vendors ship the Bourne shell as their default shell. Some of them also throw in the Berkeley C shell, and the Korn shell is also being shipped with newer versions of the operating systems.

Once again, Linux is just a little bit different and a little bit better. The default shell for a Linux operating system is the Bourne Again shell, referred to as "**bash**." This little beauty is another example of some of the really fine software to come out of the GNU project and is freely available for pretty much every version of UNIX and even Windows 95.

bash understands all Bourne shell syntax, so if you are a hardcore Bourne shell user, you'll be right at home. In fact, if **bash** is called as **/bin/sh** in a shell script, it will completely mimic the standard Bourne shell. **bash** also understands most Korn shell syntax and borrows a lot of features from nearly every popular shell. This includes filename completion, history recall, command line editing, and lots more.

Most versions of Linux currently ship with **bash** version 1.14 as the default shell. You can determine which version you're running by pressing CTRL-X, CTRL-V from a shell prompt or by typing **echo $BASH_VERSION**. Version 2.01 is available at all the popular FTP sites, and adds 100%

Posix compliance as well as nearly 100% Korn shell compatibility. It's worth your time to upgrade.

Linux doesn't leave other shell users in the cold, though. It uses **tcsh** as a value-added replacement for **csh** and usually includes some popular alternative shells such as **ash, zsh,** and **pdksh**. Each of these shells has a place and a purpose and you can spend a lot of time exploring the strengths and weaknesses of each of these.

However, we have to admit that our hands-down favorite shell for both programming and interactive use is **bash**, so let us share a few tricks that **bash** allows us to do.

What can you tell me about the bash startup files?

First off, you're probably used to having a **.login** and a **.cshrc** file if you're a **csh** user, or a **.profile** and **.kshrc** if you're a **ksh** user. **bash** uses similar files (**.profile** and **.bashrc**) and can also use a **.bash_login** instead of a **.profile** if you need to coexist with other shells. We recommend at least the following settings in your **.bashrc**:

```
export FIGNORE='.o:#:~'
set no_exit_on_failed_exec
```

The first entry causes filename completion to ignore anything ending in **.o**, **#**, or **~**. The second entry prevents your shell from dying unexpectedly if an **exec** call fails for some reason. **exec** is often used to start up new programs and replace the currently running program. If you don't know what it is now, don't worry about it too much. Just put it in your startup file and when the time comes for you to need it, you'll be glad you listened.

Can I display my current directory in my shell prompt?

The short answer is yes. It's much easier to display a customized shell prompt in **bash** than in most other popular shells. You might have seen some really weird gyrations that other people do in those inferior shells just to get their current directory or hostname into their shell prompt. Well, you'll be happy to know that you don't have to stand on your head if you're a **bash** user because the people who wrote **bash** were smart enough to include shell variables for such things.

Just as in some other shells, PS1 is the variable you need to play with to customize your prompt. Table 14-1 shows you the possible values for the PS1 shell variable.

All these allow you to do some pretty awesome things with your prompts. After you get done messing around with all the possibilities, though, you might like to simplify your life by using something like the following:

```
export PS1='\h:\w\$ '
```

This will give you a nice, clean, no-nonsense prompt containing your shortened hostname and your current

Value	Result
\a	an ascii "bell" character (to annoy your officemates)
\d	the date, formatted like "Sun Aug 24"
\h	the short hostname (up to the first "." character)
\H	the full hostname
\n	a newline character
\s	the name of the shell
\t	the current time in 24-hour, HH:MM:SS format
\T	the current time in 12-hour, HH:MM:SS format
\@	the current time in am/pm format
\u	the username of the current user
\v	the version of **bash**
\V	the release of **bash** (version plus patch level)
\w	the current working directory
\W	the basename of the current working directory
\!	the history number of this command
\#	the command number of this command
\$	inserts a "$" character if you're not the superuser, and a "#" if you are
\nnn	a character corresponding to the octal value of nnn
\\	a backslash character
\[	begins a sequence of non-printing characters (for putting in terminal control sequences)
\]	ends a sequence of non-printing characters

Table 14-1 Bash Values for the PS1 Shell Variable

working directory, with everything below your **$HOME** shortened to a "~" character. That's a lot easier than some of the ways you have to accomplish this in other shells.

We'll revisit this topic again in the X Windows section to show you a neat trick you can do with your terminal display windows and your shell prompt as well.

TEXT EDITORS

? What text editors does a standard Linux system offer me?

Linux does not ship with **vi**. What it has instead is a value-added replacement called **vim**. **vim** adds a lot to **vi** such as an optional graphical interface, multiple subwindows, multiple levels of undo, and lots of other nifty features. On most normal Linux installations, **vi** is just a symbolic link to **vim**, so typing **vi** will get you vim anyway.

You probably won't notice the difference unless you really push the limits of **vi**, in which case you'll probably really like the added capabilities of **vim**. Just in case you don't, you can lobotomize **vim** to operate in strict **vi** mode. Take a few minutes to explore **vim**'s online help by typing **:h** once you're in it.

Most Linux distributions also include **emacs**, and some even come with **Xemacs**. Both the GNU version of **emacs** and the graphically (and functionally) enhanced **Xemacs** are fully supported under Linux with little or no change in functionality.

LINUX AND X WINDOWS

? Can I have a graphical user interface on Linux?

Yes. As you've already seen, UNIX has its very own graphical interface, X Windows, which, while very powerful and very customizable, can also be very confusing. Some of the confusion arises because of the disconnection between the graphics subsystem and the window manager. PC-based graphical interfaces such as Windows95, the Macintosh OS, or IBM's OS/2 are usually smoothly integrated into the OS and the distinction between the program that does the graphics and the program that manages your mouse motions or keystrokes is not obvious. In fact, you'd be hard pressed to change the windowing system on a normal PC without changing the entire operating system. UNIX users do this all the time, though, because UNIX isn't a toy operating system.

X Windows is really nothing more than a display engine. It accesses the graphics capabilities of your system, puts the system into a graphic or "bitmapped" mode, provides a set of display hooks, and begins to manage your keyboard and mouse for you. However, it doesn't allow you to directly control, start up, or shut down programs. In fact, by itself it doesn't really do a whole lot at all. In order to really accomplish anything, you need to run a special type of program, called a window manager, once you're in X mode.

There are many different window managers, each with its own specific look and feel. Most commercial UNIX systems ship with a favorite window manager, usually one that includes some special customizations for the OS in question. Sun, for instance, used to ship OpenWindows as their primary graphical interface, while Silicon Graphics shipped a variation of Motif called 4Dwm. For the most part, commercial UNIX vendors are starting to converge on a common window manager called CDE, which stands for "Common Desktop Environment." This is an industry-standard initiative based primarily on the Motif libraries with a lot of stuff borrowed from Hewlett Packard's "VUE" window manager and some serious under-the-hood stuff from Sun Microsystems.

By and large, the most common interface in the UNIX world is a variation of the Motif Window Manager, or mwm. This is a *commercial* product, though, with few free alternatives. Since Linux is at heart a free system, it doesn't come bundled with Motif because as of yet, no one has completely cloned the Motif system and made it freely available.

Instead, Linux users usually find themselves experimenting with a wide variety of different window managers that are more stylistically suited to the way they work. Linux people are, by and large, a rather anarchist bunch that likes using things just because they are different.

This isn't meant to be a criticism at all. In fact, it's one of the greatest strengths of the Linux community. People aren't satisfied with using what someone crams down their throats. If they don't like something, they usually end up creating something that they like better and then everyone benefits from their efforts.

There is, though, a common window manager that most Linux systems end up using out of the box. FVWM (Feeble Virtual Window Manager) is the defacto standard window manager in use by most of the Linux community. There are offshoots of this window manager, such as FVWM95 (which is FVWM lobotomized to look like Windows95) or Bowman or a myriad of others. We'll concentrate on FVWM and I'll share some tricks for customizing it to look and act a lot like (but better than) that commercial hog, **mwm**.

? Where's my graphical login screen?

Many modern flavors of UNIX greet you with a nice friendly graphical login screen instead of the old boring character prompt—provided, of course, that you're working on a graphics-capable terminal. Linux is a little different, though. Out of the box, it still gives you that intimidating character-mode prompt. However, it's pretty easy to change your system to provide you with that warm and fuzzy graphical login, which is called XDM (for X Display Manager).

! ***Warning:*** *XDM only works if you've got X Windows up and running on your system.*

? How do I configure XDM?

First, check to make sure that Linux is configured correctly before enabling XDM permanently. You'll need root access to do this stuff, so if you don't have root access (it's not your own system perhaps), skip over all this.

Log in as **root** and type the following:

```
# init 5
```

The # sign is your prompt character, so don't type that. Now, your computer should go through a few wild gyrations, and when it finally stabilizes you should see a nice graphical box with password and login fields in it. When you log in, you'll be running in the graphical world of X Windows.

❓ How can I start up permanently in X Windows?

If you like X Windows and want to enable it permanently, you'll need to make some changes to your **/etc/inittab** file.

If you log in as **root** and open your **/etc/inittab** file with your favorite text editor, you should see something that looks approximately like the following:

```
# Default runlevel. The runlevels used by RHS are:
#    0 - halt (Do NOT set initdefault to this)
#    1 - Single user mode
#    2 - Multiuser, without NFS
#    3 - Full multiuser mode
#    4 - unused
#    5 - X11
#    6 - reboot (Do NOT set initdefault to this)
#
id:3:initdefault:
```

To enable X Windows, simply change **id:3:initdefault** to **id:5:initdefault**, and the next time you reboot your system it will come up graphical.

❓ What's a widget?

A widget is basically just a building block, like a tinker toy. Just as there are different basic objects in a set of tinker toys, there are also different basic objects in a widget set. Widgets include things like scrollbars, menus, and buttons. A widget set has a specific look and feel to it, and the widgets are the biggest contributor to how a window manager operates.

Don't be confused, though. There are also sets of widgets that have absolutely nothing to do with the window manager. These sets of widgets exists for the express purpose of giving programmers a common set of tools to use in writing graphical applications, and programs can be linked to specific widget sets and will look similar no matter what window manager they are running under. For now, we'll just confine ourselves to the window manager and leave the eggheads to worry about the other stuff.

? Why are widgets important?

One of the things that makes **mwm** look and feel the way it does is its widget set. This includes the buttons, popup menus, and the way the frames look around graphical programs. That's right, the program itself doesn't own those decorated frames. Those are part of the window manager and they provide you with a means for manipulating the program output on the display and interacting with it. FVWM has a widget set that looks very similar to the **mwm** widget set, which makes it similar in look and feel as well. There are also specific things coded into FVWM that are meant to emulate some of the more popular features of that other window manager.

? How do I customize FVWM?

The place to start customizing your window manager is your **.fvwmrc** file, which should be stored in your home directory. If you don't have one yet, you can copy a default one for your system. The system default configuration file, either for those who don't have a customized personal one or for those people who are looking for a place to start customizing one, is usually located in **/etc/X11/fvwm/system.fvwmrc**. Just copy this file to your home directory, rename it **.fvwmrc**, and fire up your favorite text editor.

It would take a whole book to detail all the customization possibilities for FVWM. You can spend many fun (or frustrating) hours adjusting all sorts of tiny little details. Instead of trying to teach you everything about FVWM, let's just settle for teaching you how to learn about it instead. As a great philospher once said, "If you hit a man over the head with a fish, he'll have a headache for a day. If you teach a man to hit *himself* over the head with a fish, he'll have a headache for the rest of his life."

? Just what is focus policy and can I change it?

Perhaps the single most important aspect of a window manager is something called "focus." How a window manager handles focus is something that can either make your life simple or drive you into fits of rage. Focus is simply which window currently owns the keyboard input. If you're typing something, you quite probably don't want what you type to be sent to every window that you have open. That would be pretty confusing. Instead, the window manager selects one window that receives your input. The most common configuration aspects around focus are:

Click to type	You select the active window by clicking on the frame or title bar.
Point to type	You select the active window by moving your mouse cursor into it.
Autoraise	Determines whether the active window automatically comes to the top of any overlapping windows.

Some window managers, such as Microsoft Windows, allow only one method of focus control. These usually default to "Click to type" and are probably what you're most familiar with. These window managers usually also have Autoraise set to true, so that when you click on the window it comes to the top of the stack.

Other window managers, such as FVWM, give you more control over your destiny and allow you to choose which method you want to run with. If you don't put any configuration settings into your **.fvwmrc**, FVWM will default to "Point to focus, no Autoraise" which is, in our opinion, the *only* acceptable way to run. However, if you add the following settings (and restart FVWM) to your configuration file, you can adjust it to suit your personal preferences:

```
AutoRaise 750
ClickToFocus
```

This sets your windows to autoraise 750 milliseconds after they receive the input focus. It also sets it so that you have to click on part of the window (the frame or the title bar or the corner widgets) in order to make the window active.

Probably the surest way to irritate an experienced UNIX person, and the most irritating way to configure your window manager, is to have PointToFocus active and AutoRaise set to a ridiculously small value. This will result in windows popping to the top every time you move your mouse cursor around. Since this is UNIX, after all, you are quite able to shoot yourself in the foot and set things up this way if you so choose.

❓ Can I make FVWM look like the motif window manager mwm?

Yes and no. You can make FVWM look a *lot* like **mwm** and you can even make it behave somewhat like it. You can also cause FVWM to obey some **mwm** stylistic guidelines and decoration hints. Add the following lines to your configuration file and, as always, restart your window manager:

```
MWMFunctionHints
MWMHintOverride
MWMDecorHints
MWMMenus
MWMBorders
MWMButtons
```

We've now set everything up to emulate the basic look of Motif. However, by default Motif has really wide borders. We find these quite ugly, so we trim our border sizes down with the following entry:

```
NoBoundaryWidth 0
BoundaryWidth 5
```

The first entry defines boundary width, in pixels, for windows that have no title bar and no borders. This defaults to 1 pixel. We set it to 0. The second entry is the width, in pixels, of the boundaries for the rest of the frames. The default **mwm** boundary width is 10 pixels, which are great big crayon-style borders. Ugly ugly ugly.

❓ How do I change the colors in FVWM?

Colors are also highly customizable, and any color configurations should appear first in your configuration file, before anything else. You can set the colors of the active window frames, inactive window frames, and popup menu colors with the following entries:

```
StdForeColor          Black
StdBackColor          LightSkyBlue
```

```
HiForeColor                Black
HiBackColor                DarkTurquoise
MenuForeColor              Yellow
MenuBackColor              Navy
```

Std color settings refer to the foreground (text) and background (window elements) of a window when it's *not* active. Hi settings are for when they *are* active. Menu color settings refer to the colors of the popup windows.

? What other useful settings should I know about for FVWM?

Other settings you might want to take a look at are the ones that control how new windows are placed and where windows go when they are iconified, how windows react when you resize them, and what happens when you move your cursor to the edge of the screen. Try out the following settings:

```
EdgeScroll 0 0
StubbornIconPlacement
RandomPlacement
SmartPlacement
StubbornPlacement
OpaqueMove 100
OpaqueResize 100
```

EdgeScroll basically says "Don't do anything when my cursor hits the edge of the screen." If you're not used to FVWM's virtual screen handling, it can be disconcerting (and annoying) to have it switch workspaces on you when you bump the edge of the screen with the mouse cursor. The placement directives basically tell FVWM to automatically place new windows when they are created and try to find a good place for them (i.e., not on top of other windows if at all possible) and to leave icons where you put them instead of arranging them for you. Finally, the Opaque directives tell FVWM how to display windows when you move or resize them. The number refers to a percentage of the total screen area, with 100 obviously meaning the entire screen. Anything that is below this percentage of the total screen area will be "simplified" when you either move or resize the window, and will only be displayed as a stylized frame of the correct dimensions. Anything at or above the percentage will be displayed as the actual frame with all the window contents intact. Set this to a small value if you have a slow graphics system, and leave it set to 100 if you have a reasonably fast one.

There are many additional configuration possibilities that you can explore. Read the documentation, explore the **man** pages, and have fun customizing. Figure 14-1 is an example of a customized FVWM window display after some basic customizations have been accomplished.

Are there any other window managers for Linux?

There are several other good window managers available for Linux, and some of them are probably already installed on your system. These include, but are not limited to, choices such as **twm**, **olwm**, **bowman**, or **afterstep**. In addition,

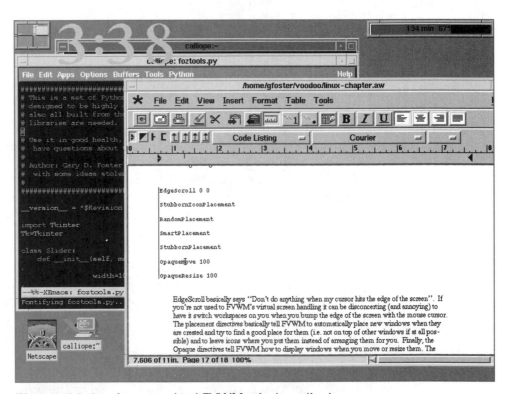

Figure 14-1　A customized FVWM window display

commercial versions of Motif (both the libraries and the window manager) and CDE are available. There is also a project currently underway to create a free, non-commercial Motif clone. This is known as "**lesstif**" and is included with some Linux distributions. It's also available from http://www.hungry.com or from most of the popular Linux FTP repositories. It includes both the libraries and an **mwm** clone.

❓ Can I customize my keyboard under X Windows like I did in console mode?

You can customize your keyboard to your heart's content, editing keytables and remapping keys, but when you start up X Windows, these changes won't be carried through. You'll have to redo the work that you did earlier, but in a slightly different fashion.

Luckily, you can apply everything you learned earlier about console keyboard remapping, albeit in a slightly different manner.

Running X Windows under Linux is nearly identical to running a commercial X release with a commercial version of UNIX. The same keyboard remapping tricks can be applied. In this case, though, the tool that you'll use to edit your keyboard tables is **xmodmap**.

Xmodmap can read any file. We recommend naming it **.xmodmaprc**, although you can name it whatever you choose. In that file, you'll need to insert commands that are similar to the ones that you inserted in the console keytable file. Here's a sample entry that remaps some keys to be a little saner:

```
clear lock
remove control = Control_L
keycode 37 = Alt_L
keycode 64 = Meta_L
keycode 66 = Control_L
add control = Control_L
add mod1 = Alt_L
add mod4 = Meta_L
```

Most of this should look pretty familiar by now. You can determine the keycode that is generated by a particular key by running **xev**, which will pop up a small window and display some text in the terminal window from which you started it. If you move the mouse cursor over the window and press a key, a lot of text will get spewed out. In this case, we're looking for the keycode entry so that we can assign a different keysystem. You may or may not have different keycodes than the ones above, since they generally vary from system to system. Be sure and check your own keycodes using **xev** before blindly typing in the entries above.

The things that might not look familiar to you are the clear and add entries. These remove or add modifier capabilities to various keys. In this case, we want the new ALT_L key to generate modifier bit 1 (which just happens to mean "alt"), the META_L key will generate a modifier bit 4, and the SCROLL_LOCK key will be a toggling or locking key.

If you end up doing anything even remotely fancy, I recommend getting and using a little gem of a program called **xkeycaps**, written by Jamie Zawinski. It might even be on your system already. This is a graphical interface to **xmodmap** that will take all the difficulty out of making your keyboard do anything you want it to do.

Once you have created an **xmodmap** file, you'll want to load it up automatically on startup. Insert the following command into the **.xinitrc** file in your home directory so that it will be executed automatically every time:

```
xmodmap $HOME/.xmodmaprc
```

❓ How can I change the title bar of my xterms?

Another handy thing you can do is change your shell prompt so that your current working directory is displayed in the title bar of your window. This will allow you to shorten your normal shell prompt so that you won't have a really long annoying prompt if you're buried deep in a directory somewhere. Try the following bit of code in your **.bashrc**. The results are displayed in Figure 14-2.

```
if [ "$TERM" = xterm ]; then
  PS1='\h:\$ \[\033]0;\h:\w\007\]'
else
  PS1='\h:\w\$ '
fi
```

```
calliope:/usr/local/lib/xemacs-20.3-b16/etc

LPF                emacskeys.sco      moriokam.xpm.Z     vladimir.xpm.Z
MACHINES           emacsstrs.sco      mrb.xpm.Z          vladimirm.xpm.Z
MAILINGLISTS       enriched.doc       mrbm.xpm.Z         vm/
MH-E-NEWS          eos/               ms-kermit          w3/
MORE.STUFF         etags.1            ms-kermit-7bit     wing.xpm.Z
MOTIVATION         frame-icon/        mule/              wingm.xpm.Z
MSDOS              gnats/             piper.xpm.Z        wmperry.xpm.Z
NEWS               gnu.xbm            piperm.xpm.Z       wmperrym.xpm.Z
ORDERS             gnu.xpm            recycle.xpm        xemacs-fe.sh*
ORDERS.EUROPE      gnuattach.1        recycle2.xpm       xemacs-icon.xpm
ORDERS.JAPAN       gnuclient.1        refcard.ps         xemacs-icon2.xbm
README             gnudoit.1          refcard.tex        xemacs-icon2.xpm
SERVICE            gnuserv.1          sample.Xdefaults   xemacs-icon3.xpm
TERMS              gnuserv.README     sample.emacs       xemacs-ja.1
TUTORIAL           gray1.xbm          sgml/              xemacs.1
XKeysymDB          hypb-mouse.txt     sink.xbm           xemacs.xbm
ajc.xpm.Z          ida-logo.xpm       slb.xpm.Z          xemacs.xpm
ajcm.xpm.Z         idd/               slbm.xpm.Z         yow.lines
altrasoft-logo.xpm jareth.xpm.Z       sounds/
app-defaults/      jarethm.xpm.Z      sparcworks/
baw.xpm.Z          jens.xpm.Z         sperber.xpm.Z
calliope:$ pwd
/usr/local/lib/xemacs-20.3-b16/etc
calliope:$ █
```

Figure 14-2 A clean and elegant shell prompt

OTHER TOOLS THAT ARE DIFFERENT UNDER LINUX

? **What are some tools that might be different under Linux?**

Other things you might encounter that are different from more conventional UNIX tools include, but aren't limited to:

less	A better pager than the standard **more**.
gzip	Better compression than the standard **compress**.
crypt	Usually not available, due to U.S. export restrictions. There are replacements available, though, which aren't subject to U.S. export control laws.
ispell	An internationalized version of the standard **spell** utility.
ncftp	A friendlier and more versatile command-line ftp client.
gcc/g++	C/C++ compilers, usually an expensive added option for commercial UNIX boxes.

control-panel	A graphical system management tool that is comparable to or better than nearly every commercial vendor's offering.
ghostview	Displays postscript files.
gv	Also displays postscript files, in addition to Adobe acrobat (.PDF) files. Sort of a ghostview on steroids.
samba	Allows you to share resources to and from Microsoft Windows machines.

Chapter 15

awk, perl, and sed

Answer Topics!

awk, perl, and sed @ a Glance

● In addition to a full-service toolbox, UNIX offers three programming languages intended to help you expand your toolbox to suit your particular needs. **awk** is a pattern-matching language that can be used for simple tasks or for complex text manipulations.

● **perl** is another pattern-matching language that may suit some of you better than awk, but this depends on your needs and inclinations.

● Finally, **sed** is a command-line, streaming editor that lets you feed a text file through it so that you can change a file entirely from within a script.

THE AWK PROGRAMMING LANGUAGE

awk Is the Product of Three Familiar UNIX Names

awk is named for its three codevelopers, Alfred Aho, Peter Weinberger, and Brian Kernighan. It's available as part of the standard UNIX distribution in its original form at least and usually also in a later version written in 1985 by the original authors called "new awk" or *nawk*. If you get serious about awk, you'll want to make sure your system has the nawk version, or you can obtain the GNU version, *gawk*, which adds most of the same enhancements to the original that nawk did. We'll use awk for this discussion.

? **How can I call awk and what are some of the options it offers me?**

The awk program is called with the command-line syntax:

```
awk [option] [script] [file]
```

The most common option is **-f scriptfile**, which reads in the script from a file instead of on the command line. An awk program consists of the form:

```
pattern {action}
```

where either the pattern-matching part or the action part is optional. If no pattern is specified, the action is performed on every line of the input; if no action is specified, the default action of **{ print $0 }** is performed on each line that matches the pattern. Since "$0" is a special parameter whose value is the entire line of input, the result is that the default action is to print the line that matches the input. This leads to one obvious use of awk as a somewhat more sophisticated version of **grep**. For example, the following will look for every line in a file that begins with a number and print out the entire line.

```
awk '/^[0-9]/ ' filename
```

Obviously, there are more powerful uses for awk than as a simple replacement for **grep**, but this does help point out a bit about the syntax of awk. Here we've used awk simply as a command-line program. The program we want to run is enclosed in single quotes to make sure that the shell doesn't try to interpret it, and we've used the same regular expression syntax we are accustomed to—except that the pattern is delimited by slashes ("/"). The pattern we're trying to match is the start of the line (the ^ part), followed immediately by a digit (the [0-9] part).

? Can you give me a slightly more useful example of how to use awk?

Suppose you want to count the number of lines in a file. You could use **wc** to do this, of course, but how are you going to find out anything about awk by using **wc**? Figure 15-1 shows two versions of the **linecount** script, as well as the results of running them and the results of running the **wc** program to count the lines.

The first version is intended to be run by an explicit call to awk with this as the script file for awk to use. It has a single-header comment line to keep it very small so it will all fit on the screen, but you would, of course, add additional information in your initial header. Then it has the reserved word "**END**" followed by an action enclosed in braces to print the message with the number of lines in the file. The word

```
$ cat linecount.awk
# awk script to count lines in a file
END     {
         print "The file \""FILENAME"\" has", lc, "lines."
        }
{  ++lc }
$ awk -f linecount.awk safe_rm.ksh
The file "safe_rm.ksh" has 14 lines.
$ cat linecount
#!/usr/bin/awk -f
# awk script to count lines in a file
END     {
         print "The file \""FILENAME"\" has", lc, "lines."
        }
{  ++lc }
$ linecount safe_rm.ksh
The file "safe_rm.ksh" has 14 lines.
$ wc -l safe_rm.ksh
     14 safe_rm.ksh
$
```

Figure 15-1 Three different ways to count the lines in a file

END tells awk to do this only once, after all other processing has been completed. There is an equivalent reserved word "**BEGIN**" that lets you do a set of actions before you start processing the file. Also notice the word "**FILENAME**" in the middle of the print statement. This is another reserved word that contains the filename of the file being processed. If the script is processing standard input, the variable will return "**-**". Included in this print statement is the variable "**lc,**" which is one we made up, and that we didn't have to initialize, declare, or do any of that other boring programming stuff to. Finally, we have the actual counting. Here, we have a very C-like expression—"**++lc**"— which is a shorthand way of writing out the more verbose "**lc = lc + 1**", which would be equally acceptable to awk. Notice that we didn't have to initialize lc to anything, it simply starts out life with a value of zero unless we give it some other. Since we want to start counting from one, not zero, we use the C construct of "**++lc**", which says to increment **lc** before we evaluate it, keeping us one ahead.

The second version of the line-counting program is what we like to think of as the stand-alone version. It uses the Korn shell's ability to execute a program directly by inserting that line that looks like a comment as the first line in the file. This line tells the Korn shell to process the rest of the file through the awk program using the -f option, which will feed it the rest of the file as an awk script. This is the minimalist version of what is known as a "shell wrapper"; it provides a handy way to run your favorite scripts without having to type in that more awkward command-line syntax. You can do far more sophisticated wrappers to parse for command-line options and so forth, but this is good enough for our purposes. Now we just type in **linecount filename** and we can count the number of lines in the file. Finally, a more interesting version of the program. Figure 15-2 shows how this would look if we modified it to count only the comment lines in the file.

Here we use the same basic program, but now we tell awk to only count the lines if they began with a leading "#". We even told it to ignore that initial line that we use on some of our scripts to make sure they're processed using a particular program or shell.

```
                                   xterm
$ cat comcnt
#!/usr/bin/awk -f
# awk script to count lines in a file
END     {
            print "The file \""FILENAME"\" has", cc, "comment lines."
        }
/^#/ && !/^#!/ { ++cc }
$ comcnt safe_rm.ksh
The file "safe_rm.ksh" has 5 comment lines.
$
```

Figure 15-2   Using awk to count the number of comments in a file

This is only the tiniest beginning of the ways you can use awk to handle tasks in your daily computer life. You can combine the powerful pattern-matching abilities with the capacity to act on only that part of the input that matches the pattern, to create useful, easy-to-read, formatted reports and documents. See Appendix D for sources of information about awk.

THE PERL PROGRAMMING LANGUAGE

perl Is an Eclectic Gem

Unlike awk, which was written by three people, perl was written essentially by a single person, Larry Wall. Others, inevitably, have influenced its growth and nature, but ultimately the blame rests with Larry, as does the credit, of course. perl is officially short for "Practical Extraction and Report Language," which is a good enough description as far as it goes. But consider that many believe it's actually short for "Pathologically Eclectic Rubbish Lister," and you'll begin to get a more accurate feel for the character of both the language and its creator. Most people who've tried perl seem to either adopt it for a wide variety of uses, or run screaming into the night. Whether awk or perl is a good choice for you, you'll have to decide on your own. But we do think that you should add one or the other to your everyday toolbox. We tend to think that the greater flexibility and power of the expanded regular expressions in perl give it a slight edge. Besides, as eclectic as its syntax is, it tends to grow on you.

? Can you point out some of the differences between awk and perl?

In this section we'll take the two scripts that we created for awk and "port" them to perl. The end results are the same of course, but you'll be able to see where the two programs differ.

We'll bypass the command-line version of the line-counting program and go straight to the version with the minimalist shell wrapper around it. Except now instead of running the awk program, this will run the perl program. Normally, you would have the line

```
#!/usr/bin/perl
```

as the first line of your perl scripts, but ours is in an unusual place, so our first line reads:

```
#!/work/bin/perl
```

The results are the same, however. This line tells the shell program that its sole job is to execute the perl program and just pass the statements in the file directly to perl to deal with. Figure 15-3 shows the two perl scripts for counting the number of lines in a file, and the number of comment lines in a file, the same two tasks we did with awk. But now the programs look a bit different.

awk uses an implicit while loop that automatically sends the entire contents of the files given on the command line to the pattern-matching and action part of the program. But in

```
                                    xterm
$ cat lc.p
#!/work/bin/perl
# perl script to count lines in a file
$filename = $ARGV[0];
while (<>) {
        ++$lc
        }
print ("The file \"$filename\" has $lc lines. \n ");
$ cat comcnt.p
#!/work/bin/perl
# perl script to count comment lines in a file
$filename = $ARGV[0]
while (<>) {
        if (/^#/ && !/^#!/) {
           ++lc;
           }
}
print ("The file \"$filename\" has $lc comment lines.\n ");
$
```

Figure 15-3   Our two scripts, rewritten for perl

the perl example, you see that we need to build the while loop explicitly, with the statement:

```
while (<>) {
++$lc;
}
```

That probably makes sense to you because most programming languages expect you to create your own **while** loops where you need them. But what's that "**(<>)**" supposed to mean? This is known as the "diamond operator" and it takes the file in the array **$ARGV[0]**, which was the file we passed to the program on the command line, and examines each line of that program until it reaches the end. Which is what the awk script did automatically.

The other thing that the awk program had that we have to do explicitly here is pass in the filename whose lines we're counting. Here we need to stick that filename into a variable that won't get mucked up during the while loop so we can reference it at the end after we've counted all the lines.

In the second program, which counts the comment lines in the file, we see again the differences and similarities between the two languages. In awk we simply added the pattern-matching criteria to the beginning of the line that did the counting, but here we need to add an explicit **if** clause. Again, some things that awk does automatically have to be explicitly called out in perl. We don't find this a hardship, and even think it makes the resultant code a bit easier to read, but others feel strongly that this is not as elegant.

It's important to notice the identical code describing the pattern match. While perl does add important new pattern-matching tools (our favorite is "**\b**" to define a word boundary), it still uses the same syntax as awk.

As you can see, there are substantial differences between perl and awk, even though both perform many of the same functions. In the broader sense, perl goes beyond where awk is or is likely to go, and is continuing to be actively developed. It is not, however, a part of the normal UNIX distribution, though it is freely available.

THE SED PROGRAMMING LANGUAGE

Automating Is Easier

Performing repetitive changes on a text file, or a series of text files, is a common computer task. While an interactive text editor such as **vi** or **emacs** might be your first choice for a tool, there are better (albeit less well known) alternatives. One of those alternatives is *sed*, a noninteractive stream editor.

? What is sed?

sed is a tool that allows you to perform scripted or repetitive edits on a file. Since it is noninteractive, you do not use the traditional editing interface. Instead, you issue a set of commands to perform a series of tasks on an input stream and the results are directed to an output stream. You can use standard shell redirection (pipes and such) to manipulate, create, or redirect these streams.

? Why learn yet another tool?

Traditional UNIX editors are great tools for the job they are designed for. They work well for interactive editing tasks involving generating new files or updating old ones. Some of them even have useful scripting capabilities that allow you to perform programmed or scripted editing tasks across a file or group of files.

Most of them, however, are serious overkill when you need to do large-scale repetition, small edits, or just need to get in and get out quickly. In addition, most editors don't allow you to insert them into the middle of UNIX's "piping" commands and even if they did, the overhead involved in starting them up would be horrendous.

UNIX power users have a long tradition of using the right tool for the right job and you can never have enough tricks in your bag. sed isn't the right tool for writing a résumé or even a letter to your Aunt Hortense. However, it simply can't be beat when you need to change every pipe character to a colon in a dozen different files and then send those files to another program for processing.

How does it work?

sed reads a set of characters, a stream, from stdin and writes to stdout. It can be given a series of operations to perform on the command line, if they are short, or it can read a set of instructions from a script file. A common invocation might look something like this:

sed -e '{some **sed** command}' input_file > output_file

or alternatively, if reading a set of commands from a script file, it might look similar to this:

sed -f {script file} input_file > output_file

Unless you specify otherwise, sed will apply the commands you enter to every line in the input stream. You can limit the lines that get affected in various ways such as specifying beginning and ending line numbers or even start or end blocks by pattern matches. These affected lines are normally referred to as *addresses*, and these addresses can be specified as either zero, one, or two addresses. Addresses can be any combination of either patterns (which are enclosed in slashes), line numbers, or line specifier symbols.

Commands are extensive and varied. Some of these include:

- **=** Print the line number of the line to stdout
- **s** Perform a substitution on the address
- **d** Delete the addressed lines
- **w** Write the addressed lines to a file
- **q** Quit when the address is encountered

There are many more commands available, but this list should give you a small taste of what sed can do.

❓ Can you give me some examples of how to use sed?

By combining both addresses and commands, you form a complete **sed** command, which might look something like this:

```
sed -e '/foo/d' myfile
```

This sed invocation would delete every line that contains the word "foo" and print the results to standard out. This is an example of using zero addresses, which results in attempting the match on every single line. Another example would be:

```
sed -e '50d' myfile
```

which would result in deleting line 50 of myfile, while

```
sed -e '50,$d' myfile
```

would delete everything from line 50 to the end ($ refers to the last line in the stream). Another common task involves replacing one pattern of text with another. This is done using the **s** command, instead of the **d** above, and might look similar to the following:

```
sed -e 's/foo/bar/' myfile
```

This example would substitute the *first* occurrence of the word "foo" with the word "bar" on each line. If you wanted to replace multiple occurrences on the same *line,* you would need to append a *g* after the command, as in the following:

```
sed -e 's/foo/bar/g' myfile
```

Regular expression patterns can be used in the search space above (instead of "foo", for example), which can add more power to your editing. If you wanted to place a series of asterisks in front of specific lines, for example, you might use:

```
sed -e '/foo/s/^/***/' myfile
```

This would find every line with the word "foo" in it, and replace the beginning of the line (^ is a special symbol that refers to the beginning of the line) with three asterisks.

A final word of warning is in order. Since sed is stream-oriented, it does *not* read the entire input file into memory before it opens the output stream. This means that if you try to edit a file in place with something like this:

```
sed -e 's/foo/bar/' myfile > myfile     # THIS IS WRONG
```

you will end up with a zero byte file and a very silly look on your face.

Appendix A

Command Reference

Of course you know that there are hundreds of commands in the various versions of UNIX, so you won't find all of them here. But you will find a lot of very useful ones—especially the ones used for the tricks in this book. We'll show you the syntax and available options and a little on how each command works.

Because there are variations among the flavors of UNIX, your version may have slightly different syntax and/or options than the ones shown here. If you see a command that looks like it might do what you want to do but you don't see exactly the right option or you get a syntax error upon execution, check your documentation for possible variations.

alias *[options] name[='cmd']*

OBJECTIVE:
Assigns a shorthand name to substitute for *cmd*. If *='cmd'* is omitted, it prints the alias for *name*. Korn shell only.

OPTIONS AND VARIABLES

-t	Creates a tracked alias for a UNIX command. The shell will remember the full path name of the command, making it easier to find.
-x	Exports the alias so it can be used in shell scripts.

at *options time [date] [+increment]*

OBJECTIVE:
Lets you schedule jobs to be executed later.

OPTIONS AND VARIABLES

-l *[jobID]*	Lists your currently scheduled jobs. Include a *jobID* if you want information on just one job.
-r *[jobID]*	Removes specified job from the queue. You can remove only your own jobs unless you're the superuser.
time	Specifies the time the job should start. The format is *hh:mm [modifiers]*. A 24-hour clock is assumed unless you add the modifier am or pm, in which case time is based on a 23-hour clock.

bg *[jobids]*

OBJECTIVE:
Put current job or specified *jobIDs* in the background. Korn shell only.

cal *month year*

OBJECTIVE:
Displays a calendar on the standard output.

OPTIONS AND VARIABLES

month   Use a number between 1 and 12 or enough letters to represent a unique month.

year   Any number between 1 and 9999. You have to include all four digits.

cancel *requestIDs* or cancel *printer*

OBJECTIVE:
Cancels a print request generated by the lp spooler.

OPTIONS AND VARIABLES

requestIDs   Cancels by *requestID* number. Use lpstat to see a list of *requestIDs*.

printer   Cancels the current print job for this printer.

cat *[options] filelist*

OBJECTIVE:
Concatenates (joins) files together. Use the > operator to combine several files into a new file or use >> to append files to an existing file.

OPTIONS AND VARIABLES

-e   Prints a $ to mark the end of each line. This option valid only with the -v option.

-v   Displays control characters and other nonprinting characters.

-s   Suppresses messages about unreadable files.

-t   Prints each tab as ^I and each form feed as ^L.

-u   Prints output as unbuffered.

filelist Optional list of files to be joined.

cd *directoryname*

OBJECTIVE:
Changes the current working directory.

OPTIONS AND VARIABLES
directoryname   The name of the directory you want to make current.

chmod *mode files*

OBJECTIVE:
Changes the mode of files. A file's mode controls the permissions for access associated with that file. Only the owner of a file (or the superuser) can change its mode.

OPTIONS AND VARIABLES

Who

u	User
g	Group
o	Others
a	All (default)

Opcode

+	Add permission
-	Remove permission
=	Set permission to be only what's specified

Permission

r	Read
w	Write
x	Execute
s	Set user (or group) ID

cp *[options] file1 file2*

OBJECTIVE:
Copies files.

OPTIONS AND VARIABLES
file1	The file to copy.
file2	The destination name.

date *MMDDhhmmyy* or date *+format*

OBJECTIVE:
Displays the system date and time.

OPTIONS AND VARIABLES
MMDDhhmmYY

MM	The month (01-12)
DD	The day (01-31)
hh	The hour (00-23)
mm	The minute (00-59)
YY	The year (00-99)—optional
+format	Consists of a % sign followed by:

n	Inserts a newline
t	Inserts a tab
m	Month (digits)
d	Day of month (digits)
y	Last two digits of year
D	Date as mm/dd/yy
i	Hour
M	Minute
S	Second
W	Day of Week (0-6, 0=Sunday)

diff *[options] oldfile newfile*

OBJECTIVE:
Compares two text files to find where they differ.

OPTIONS AND VARIABLES

-b	Ignore repeating blanks and end-of-line blanks.
-e	Generate a script for the editor ed.
-f	Produce a script to re-create *file1* from *file2*.

echo *-n string*

OBJECTIVE:

Writes the string to standard output. By default, echo follows all output with a newline. *-n* suppresses this. The special escape characters, preceded by \, will produce special output sequences:

Character	Meaning
\b	Backspace
\c	Don't print a newline at the end (same as *-n*)
\f	Form feed
\n	Newline
\r	Carriage return
\t	Tab character
\\	Backslash

fg *[jobIDs]*

OBJECTIVE:

Put current job or specified *jobIDs* in the foreground.

find *pathname condition*

OBJECTIVE:

Searches the specified directories generating a list of files that match the criteria specified.

OPTIONS AND VARIABLES

-name *file*	Matches the specified *file*. If enclosed in quotation marks (""), *file* can contain wildcards * and ?.

-perm *mode*	Matches all files whose mode matched the numeric value of *mode*. All modes must be matched—not just read, write, and execute. To match everything except this mode, use *-mode*.	
-type *x*	Matches all files whose type is *x*, in which *x* is the following:	
	c	Character device
	b	Block special
	d	Directory
	p	Named pipe
	f	Regular file (none of the preceding types)
-atime *days*	Matches all files last accessed *days* ago.	
-mtime *days*	Matches all files last modified *days* ago.	
-newer *file*	Matches all files modified more recently than *file*.	
-ctime *+n	-n	n*	Matches files that were changed more than *n* (*+n*), less than *n* (*-n*), or exactly *n* (*n*) days ago. Change refers to modification, permission, or ownership changes.	
-exec *command*	Run the UNIX *command* on each file matched by **find**.	
-ok *command*	Same as -exec but prompts for confirmation before the command is executed.	
-print	Prints the names of the files found.	
-user	Matches files belonging to a *user* name or ID.	

finger *[options] users*

OBJECTIVE:
Displays information about users on the system

OPTIONS AND VARIABLES

-b	Omit user's home directory and shell from the output.

-f	Suppresses header lines.
-l	Forces the long output.
-p	Doesn't print the **.plan** file.
-q	Displays a quick list of users.
-s	Displays a short format.
users	Specify either an exact login name or as a first or last name.

grep *[options] regexp [files]*

OBJECTIVE:
Searches for a pattern or regular expression [*regexp*] in files and reports when it finds it.

OPTIONS AND VARIABLES
-c	Prints only a count of matched lines.
-l	Displays only the names of files containing a match.
-i	Eliminates case sensitivity.
-v	Prints all lines that *don't* match.
-n	Prints matching lines and line numbers.
-s	Suppresses error messages for nonexistent or unreadable files.

head *[-lines files]*

OBJECTIVE:
Prints the first few lines of a file.

OPTIONS AND VARIABLES
-lines	Specified the number of lines to print. The default is 10.
files	A list, separated by spaces, of the files you want printed. The default is standard input.

jobs *[options] [jobIDs]*

OBJECTIVE:
Lists running or stopped jobs. Include *jobIDs* to check on specific jobs. Korn shell only.

OPTIONS AND VARIABLES

-l	List job IDs and process group IDs.
-n	List only the jobs with status changes since the last notification.
-p	List process group IDs only.

lp *[options]* *[files]*

OBJECTIVE:
Sends *files* to the printer.

OPTIONS AND VARIABLES

-c	Copies *files* to print spooler.
-d *dest*	Sends output to printer named *dest*.
-f *form-name* [-d any]	Spooler prints the request only when the specified *form-name* is mounted on the printer. With the -d any option set, the request goes to any printer with *form-name* mounted.
-L	Sends the print job to the printer attached to the terminal.
-n *number*	Specifies the *number* of copies to print.
-P *pages*	Prints on the page numbers specified in *pages*.
-R	Removes file after printing.
-t *title*	Use *title* on the printout's banner page.

lprint - *file*

OBJECTIVE:
Sends a *file* to a printer attached to the terminal.

OPTIONS AND VARIABLES

-	Print from standard input instead of *file*.

lpstat *[options]*

OBJECTIVE:
Shows the status of the lp spooler system and print requests.

OPTIONS AND VARIABLES

-a *list*	Shows whether the printers in *list* are accepting requests.

-c *list*	Shows the class names of the printers in *list*.
-p *list*	Shows the status of the printers in *list*. Normally used to make sure a printer is enabled.
-d	Shows the default printer destination.
-f *list*	Verifies that the *list* of forms is known to lp.
-r	Shows whether the print scheduler is on or off.
-s	Shows a status summary (almost everything).
-t	Shows all status information (reports everything).

ls *[options]* *[directories]*

OBJECTIVE:

Lists contents of directories. If no *directories* are given, lists the files in the current directory.

OPTIONS AND VARIABLES

-A	Shows all files, including hidden files (files that start with a period). Doesn't include the current directory or parent directory.
-a	Shows all files including the current directory (.) and the parent directory (..).
-C	Lists files in columns.
-x	Lists files in rows going across the screen.
-d	Lists only directory names, not their contents.
-l	Gives a long listing including permissions, owner, size, filename, date last modified, and so forth.

mail *[options]* *[usernames]*

OBJECTIVE:

Read or send mail to other users. You can type **?** for a summary of commands.

OPTIONS AND VARIABLES

-e	Checks for mail in your incoming mailbox.
-f *file*	Opens *file* to read mail. If no *file* is specified, the mbox file is used.
-F	Stores outgoing mail in a file with the same name as that of the first recipient of the message.
-H	Shows a header summary of the mailbox contents.

-s *subject*	Sets the subject line in the mail header to *subject*.
-u	Reads user's incoming mailbox.

make *[options] [targets] [macro definitions]*

OBJECTIVE:

Updates one or more targets according to dependency instructions in a description file in the current directory. This file is called **makefile** or **Makefile** by default. Options, targets, and macro definitions can appear in any order. Macros definitions are typed as *name=string*.

OPTIONS AND VARIABLES

-e	Overrides *makefile* assignments with environment variables.
-f *makefile*	Use *makefile* as the description file.
-i	Ignores command error codes.
-n	Prints commands but doesn't execute.
-p	Prints macro definitions and target description.
-q	Query. Returns 0 if the file is up-to-date, nonzero otherwise.
-r	Don't use default rules.
-s	Don't display command lines.
-t	Touch the target files. Causes them to be updated.

man *[options] [section] [title]*

OBJECTIVE:

Displays information from the online reference manuals.

OPTIONS AND VARIABLES

-a	Shows all pages matching *title*.
-b	Leave blank lines in output.
-d*dir*	Specifies the directory *dir* to be added to the search path for entries.

mesg *n y*

OBJECTIVE:
Controls whether or not others can send messages to your screen.

OPTIONS AND VARIABLES

n   Doesn't let users send messages to your terminal.

y   Allows messages (the default).

mkdir *[options] dirname*

OBJECTIVE:
Makes new directories.

OPTIONS AND VARIABLES

-m *mode*   Sets the access *mode* for all new directories.

-p   Creates all intervening parent directories if they don't already exist.

dirname   The name of the new directory.

more *[options] [files]*

OBJECTIVE:
Displays the named files one screen at a time. Press ENTER to get the next line or the spacebar to get the next screen.

OPTIONS AND VARIABLES

-c   Page through the file by clearing each window instead of scrolling. This is sometimes faster.

-f   Counts logical lines instead of screen lines.

-l   Ignore form-feed characters (^L).

-r   Force display of control characters in the form ^*x*.

-s   Display multiple blank lines as one.

mv *[option] source target*

OBJECTIVE:
Moves or renames files or directories.

OPTIONS AND VARIABLES
-f   Overwrites existing files, regardless of permissions settings

Source	Target	Result
File	*name*	Rename file as name.
File	Existing File	Overwrite existing file.
Directory	*name*	Rename directory as name.
Directory	Existing directory	Make directory a subdirectory of existing directory.
File(s)	Existing directory	Move files to directory

newgrp *group*

OBJECTIVE:
Changes a user's group identification. Only the group ID is changed; the user remains a member of all groups previously assigned. If you omit the *group* name, you're returned to the group you're in at login.

news *[options] [items]*

OBJECTIVE:
Reads news posted in the **/usr/news** directory. With no arguments, news prints all current items. This is not an interface for USENET news.

OPTIONS AND VARIABLES
-a   Shows all news items, whether current or not.
-n   Lists names of articles, not their contents.
-s   Reports the number of current items.

nice *[option] command*

OBJECTIVE:
Execute a command with lower priority. In other words, make nice with the other users.

OPTIONS AND VARIABLES

-n   Run the *command* with a niceness level of *n* (1-19). The default is 10. The higher the *n*, the nicer you're being.

openwin *[options]*

OBJECTIVE:
Sets up OpenWindows, the windowing environment based on the Open Look graphical user interface.

OPTIONS AND VARIABLES

-banner   Displays the OpenWindows banner screen at startup.

-noauth   Reverts to a lower security mode.

-includedemo   Includes the path to the demo directory in the user's search path.

pack *[option] files*

OBJECTIVE:
Compresses files so they take up less space.

OPTIONS AND VARIABLES

-     Print more statistical information such as the number of times each byte is used, relative frequency, and so forth.

files   A space-delimited list of the files to be packed.

passwd *[options]*

OBJECTIVE:
Lets you change your own password.

OPTIONS AND VARIABLES

-s   Displays password information such as username, password status, date last changed, and so forth.

pg *[options] files*

OBJECTIVE:
Lets you view text files one page at a time. Unlike more, lets

you move backward as well as forward. Pressing ^ while in **pg** places you in reverse search mode. Pressing / returns you to forward search mode.

OPTIONS AND VARIABLES

-e	No pause at the end of a file.
-f	Don't split long lines.
-n	Issues a **pg** command without waiting for a carriage return.
-s	Messages and prompts display in standout mode (reverse video).
+*number*	Begin display at line *number*.
+/*pattern*	Start display at the first line containing *pattern*.
files	A list of space-delimited filenames.

ping *[options] host*

OBJECTIVE:
Tells you if another machine on the network is operational. This command sends out an ECHO_REQUEST packet to the specified machine. If the packet is sent and received successfully, the connection is considered alive.

OPTIONS AND VARIABLES

-n	Displays network addresses as numbers.
-c *count*	Stop after sending *count* ECHO_RESPONSE packets.
-r	Bypass the normal routing tables and send directly to a *host* on an attached network.

pr *[options] files*

OBJECTIVE:
Lets you format a file while printing it to the standard output.

OPTIONS AND VARIABLES

+*page*	Begins printing at the page number *page*.
-*col*	Specifies *col* columns of output.
-a	Prints files in a multicolumn format.
-d	Double-spaces the output.
-f	Separates the pages with a single form-feed command.

-m	Merges the files, printing each file in a column. Overrides the *-col* option.
-t	Doesn't print the header or footer.

purge *[options] files*

OBJECTIVE:
Gets rid of files by overwriting them. These can be files on the command line or files listed in a special policy file maintained by the system administrator.

OPTIONS AND VARIABLES

-f	Don't warn about files that don't exist or are inaccessible.
-m *number*	Overwrites each file *number* times.
-r	Recursively purges directories.
-s	Overwrites files in the policy file that are designated as system files.
-u	Overwrites files in the policy file that are designated as user files.
-t *group*	Overwrites files in the policy file that are designated as the type *group*.
-v	Lists the name of each file as it's overwritten.
files	A space-delimited list of files to purge. May be regular files, directories, or special-character files.

pwd

OBJECTIVE:
Prints the full path name of the current working directory.

rcp *[options] hostname:file1 hostname:file2*

OBJECTIVE:
Copies files between two machines.

OPTIONS AND VARIABLES

-p	Preserves modification times and modes of the original files.
-r	If the source and target are both directories, copies each subtree rooted at that name.

rlogin [options] system

OBJECTIVE:
Lets you log into a remote computer.

OPTIONS AND VARIABLES

-8	Allows 8-bit-data transfers instead of 7-bit-data.
-e*c*	Specifies the escape character *c*.
-l *username*	Logs into the remote system using *username*. The default is the same as your local username.

rm *files*

OBJECTIVE:
Removes one or more files. To remove a file, you must have write permission for the directory that contains the file. If you don't have write permission for the file itself, you'll be prompted to confirm the deletion.

This can be a very dangerous command. *Be careful.*

OPTIONS AND VARIABLES

-f	Remove write-protected files without prompting.
-i	Prompts for each deletion.
-r	If *files* is a directory, remove the entire directory and its contents.

rmdir [options] directoryname

OBJECTIVE:
Removes directories. The directory has to be empty first.

OPTIONS AND VARIABLES

-p	Removes *directoryname* and any intervening parent directories that become empty as a result.
-s	Suppresses standard error messages that result from using -p.

sdiff [options] file1 file2

OBJECTIVE:
Produce a side-by-side comparison of *file1* with *file2*. Output is:

text text	Identical lines.
text <	Line exists only in *file1*.
> text	Line exists only in *file2*.
text ᛁtext	Lines are different.

OPTIONS AND VARIABLES

-w*width*	Specifies that the output line is to be *width* characters.
-l	Identical lines appear only on the left side of the output.
-s	Doesn't show identical lines.
file1	File in the left column of the output.
file2	File in the right column of the output.

set

OBJECTIVE:
Displays the values of all shell variables.

setcolor *[options] [argument]*

OBJECTIVE:
Set screen color and other attributes.

OPTIONS AND VARIABLES

-b *color*	Sets background color to *color*.
-g *color1 color2*	Sets foreground to *color1* and background to *color2*.
-n	Sets the screen to "normal," a white foreground and a black background.
-r *color1 color2*	Sets the screen's reverse-video foreground to *color1* and the screen's reverse-video background to *color2*.
-o *color*	Sets the border to *color*.

sleep *seconds*

OBJECTIVE:
Suspends execution of a process for the number of *seconds* specified.

sort *[options] [files]*

OBJECTIVE:
Sorts the lines of the named *files*.

OPTIONS AND VARIABLES

-b	Ignores leading spaces and tabs.
-c	Checks to see if the files are already sorted and if they are, produces no output.
-d	Sorts in dictionary order.
-f	Ignores uppercase and lowercase differences.
-i	Ignores nonprintable characters.
-m	Merges sorted input files.
-n	Sorts by numeric order.
-r	Reverses the order of the sort.
-u	Identical lines in the input appear only once in the output.

spell *[options] +userdict files*

OBJECTIVE:
Checks the spelling of a text file.

OPTIONS AND VARIABLES

-b	Uses British spelling.
-v	Displays all words not literally in the dictionary.
-x	Shows every possible word stem.
+userdict	Use the sorted *userdict* as a local dictionary to add to the system dictionary.

strings *[options] files*

OBJECTIVE:
Searches for ASCII characters in binary files.

OPTIONS AND VARIABLES

-	Search the entire file, not just the initialized data portion of object files.
-o	Shows the byte offset in the file where the string was found.
- *number*	Minimum string length is *number.* Default is 4.

stty *[options] [settings]*

OBJECTIVE:
Sets terminal I/O options for the current standard input device.

OPTIONS AND VARIABLES

-a	Shows current settings of the currently logged-in terminal.
-g	Reports current settings in hexadecimal.
settings	Settings can be either the output of a previous -g flag or a series of **stty** commands.

tail *[options] [file]*

OBJECTIVE:
Lets you view the last lines of a text file. The default is the last 10 lines.

OPTIONS AND VARIABLES

+n	Outputs *n* lines from the beginning of the input.
-n	Outputs *n* lines from the end of the input.
b	Refers to clocks when added after +n or -n.
c	Refers to characters when added after +n or -n.
r	Outputs the lines in reverse order.

tar *[options] [files]*

OBJECTIVE:
Copies *files* to or restores *files* from an archive medium. If any *files* are directories, the whole subtree is acted upon. Options don't need to be preceded by -.

OPTIONS AND VARIABLES

Function Options

c	Create a new archive.
r	Appends the *files* to an existing archive file.
t	Prints the names of *files* as they appear in the archive file.

**Function
Options**

u   Performs an update, appending files to the archive if they're not already present or if they've been modified since the last backup.

x   Extracts specified *files* from an archive.

Options

A   Suppresses absolute filenames.

f *archive*   Store *files* in or extract *files* from the specified *archive*.

l   Print error messages about links that aren't found.

m   Don't restore modification times; update them to the time of extraction.

v   Filenames are displayed as they're being processed.

w   Wait for user confirmation.

tee *[options] files*

OBJECTIVE:

Split the output into two files. Send one copy to standard output, the other to *files*.

OPTIONS AND VARIABLES

-a   Append output to *files* rather than overwriting them.

-i   Ignores all interrupts.

-u   Causes output to be unbuffered.

files   The space-separated list of files into which you want to capture the output.

time *command*

OBJECTIVE:

Prints the amount of execution time, process execution time, and system time for a process.

OPTIONS AND VARIABLES

command   The command you want to time.

tr [options] [string1] [string2]

OBJECTIVE:

Copies standard input to standard output, substituting characters from *string1* to *string2* or deleting characters in *string1*.

OPTIONS AND VARIABLES

-c   Restricts the output to the characters specified in *string1* and effectively appends those characters in *string2*.

-d   Delete characters in *string1* from the output.

-s   Strip out repeated output characters in *string2*.

unmask [value]

OBJECTIVE:

Displays or sets the file creation mode mask.

OPTIONS AND VARIABLES

value   A three-digit octal code specifying the read-write-execute permissions to be turned off.

unpack files

OBJECTIVE:

Expands one or more *files*, created with pack, to their original form.

unset [-f] names

OBJECTIVE:

Erases definitions of variables or functions listed in *names*. In the Korn shell, the functions must be stated explicitly with the -f option.

wall [file]

OBJECTIVE:

Sends a message to all logged-in users. If a *file* is indicated, input is taken from the file rather than standard input.

who [options]

OBJECTIVE:
Displays information about the current status of the system. With no options, you'll get a list of currently logged-in users.

OPTIONS AND VARIABLES
am i	Prints the name of the user invoking the command.
-A	Displays UNIX accounting information.
-a	Shows all available information.
-b	Reports information about the last reboot.
-H	Prints the header line.
-l	Reports inactive terminal lines.
-q	Displays only the usernames and a count.
-t	Reports the last change of the system clock.

whodo

OBJECTIVE:
Reports a list of who is on the system and what they're doing.

write user [tty]

OBJECTIVE:
Lets you send a message to another user's terminal (if they've allowed it through the use of the **mesg** command).

OPTIONS AND VARIABLES
user	The name of the person to whom you want to send the message.
tty	If the person happens to be logged into more than one terminal, you can specify the terminal you want the message to go to.

xsetroot [options]

OBJECTIVE:
Sets the appearance of the workspace's background.

OPTIONS AND VARIABLES

-help	Displays a summary of command line options.
-def	Resets unspecified attributes to their default settings.
-bitmap *file*	Uses the bitmap found in *file* to set the workspace background.
-mod *x y*	Makes a plaid background. The *x* and *y* are integers from 1 to 16.
-gray	Makes a gray background.
-solid *color*	Makes the workspace background a solid *color*.

xterm *[options]*

OBJECTIVE:
Lets you set the windows variables.

OPTIONS AND VARIABLES

-bg *color*	Sets the background color of the **xterm** window.
-fg *color*	Sets the foreground to *color.*
-fn *font*	Substitutes *font* for the default font.
-help	Displays a summary of available **xterm** options.
-RV	Reverses the foreground and background colors.
-sb or +sb	Displays a scroll bar for the **xterm** window and saves lines that are scrolled off the top so they can still be viewed.

zcat *file*

OBJECTIVE:
Displays uncompressed output for the contents of a compressed file (one ending with .z) while leaving the compressed file unchanged.

Appendix B

Error Messages

Most of the error messages in UNIX are pretty straightforward. In other words, if you ask to switch to a directory called WORKFIPES and UNIX reports that such a directory doesn't exist, it wouldn't take you long to figure out that you'd mistyped WORKFILES. But some messages are moderately or extremely cryptic, so we're including them in this appendix, in alphabetical order.

-c: bad option(s)	You invoked a shell with an option that the shell didn't understand.
at: bad date specification	The time at which the job is to be executed is stated incorrectly.
bad conversion	The **date** setting syntax is incorrect.
bad format character	You didn't use a valid format character. See the list under the **date** command in Appendix A.
bad string	When using the **tr** command, the two strings are not equal.
cannot open ...	Indicates a problem with the file system. Call the system administrator.
cannot open item	You've invoked the **news** command to read an article, but the specified article doesn't exist.
can't assign *device*	The device is not in the assignable device table.
cat: input *filename is output*	You used the same file as both an input and an output file.
cmp: EOF on *file*	In doing a compare, one of the files is shorter than the other. The system will substitute the name of the shorter file for *file*.
crontab: can't open your crontab file	Assuming you're authorized to use **cron**, you probably tried to list your **crontab** file using the **-l** flag or you gave a bad flag and **crontab** interpreted it as a filename.
ERROR: arg counter (bd1)	The wrong number of arguments have been supplied. Probably one of the filenames is incorrect.
find: bad option - *the_invalid_stuff*	When using the **find** command, you have to supply a matching specification for the files you want to find. Whatever you supplied isn't valid. ***the_invalid_stuff*** is replaced with what you specified.
find: incomplete statement	That fussy **find** command is saying that you didn't supply enough arguments.

INVALID OPTION (-*x*) - PROCESSING TERMINATED	This dire-looking message merely means that you gave the **nl** command with an option it doesn't recognize. The system substitutes the option letter you specified for -*x*.
line too long	You're trying to input a line using **cut** or output a line using **paste** that's longer than 511 characters.
ptar: directory checksum error	You may have specified the wrong media type for the floppy or tape drive, or the tape may need to be rewound.
Read error in ...	Indicates a problem with the filesystem. Call the system administrator.
rm: illegal option -- ?	You supplied **rm** with an option it doesn't recognize.
shutdown: not found	Means that **/etc** is not in your search PATH. It's only in the PATH for the superuser, so you can't use this command unless you are, in fact, that august personage.
Sorry	This brief statement of sympathy pops up when you try to change your password and you enter your old password incorrectly. You'll need to invoke **passwd** and try again.
sort: invalid use of command line options	Notification that you gave **sort** an option it doesn't recognize.
tar: directory checksum error	You may have specified the wrong media type for the floppy or tape drive, or the tape may need to be rewound.
too many files	You're trying to **paste** together more than 12 files.
unknown tab code	When using the **tabs** command with the -*list* option, you've tried to specify a tab stop that doesn't exist.

Appendix C

Glossary

absolute path name   The complete name of a file, including the total path of directories showing the file's location in the directory tree. An absolute path name starts with the root directory—/.

address   Either the name of a specific machine or the name of the entire UNIX system. Both meanings are used in discussions of email and communications.

AIX   A version of UNIX made by IBM Corporation.

anonymous ftp   A remote login that requires no password. You type in **anonymous** as the user name and your email address as the password, enabling you to copy files from another computer to your own.

archive   A file containing a collection of other files. Chiefly used for backup.

argument   On a command line, this is something that follows a command. For example, on a line that says **cp my.file your.file** the command is **cp**, **my.file** is the first argument, and **your.file** is the second argument.

ASCII   *A*merican *S*tandard *C*ode for *I*nformation *I*nterchange. Usually means a file that's in text, is therefore viewable and printable, and has no binary (non-ASCII) characters.

at   Command that lets you schedule tasks to be run in the future.

awk   A programming language geared toward text manipulation.

background   A program that runs behind the scenes with no input from you is running in the background. Commands can be run in the background by starting them with an ampersand (&) at the end of the command line.

backslash   The character \. In UNIX, it changes ("escapes") the interpretation of the next character.

bang   The character **!**. A shell escape character. Also used to indicate that the command should be carried out regardless.

Berkeley Software Distribution   The long name for BSD UNIX, a version of UNIX developed and distributed by the University of California at Berkeley. This version was notable for its advanced networking capabilities.

bin directory   A directory for storing executable files. Your home directory probably has a subdirectory named bin.

block size   The largest amount of data that a UNIX filesystem will always allocate contiguously. In other words, files that occupy less than the block size will always be contiguous. Larger files may be fragmented.

Bourne shell   The original shell. Created by Steven Bourne of Bell Labs. Its program name is **sh** and it prompts with **$**.

BSD   See **Berkeley Software Distribution**.

buffer   A temporary storage area such as a file or an area of the computer's memory. Lots of things have buffers, including printers and many text editors.

C, C++   C is the programming language in which virtually all UNIX programs are written. UNIX itself is written mostly in C. C and its enhanced relative, C++, were both developed at Bell Labs and are widely used by UNIX programmers.

C Shell   A shell written to look as much as possible like the C programming language. It prompts you with **%** and its program name is **csh**.

client   In the X Window System, an application, as opposed to the server that manages the resources and provides the display. In a distributed filesystem, a client is a terminal or workstation connected to a server.

command line   The text you type at a shell prompt. A command line can have more than one command separated by operators like semicolons (**;**), pipes (**|**), or double ampersands (**&&**).

command mode   When a program expects the input to consist of executable commands.

command substitution   Using the output of one command as input for another command.

compiler   A program that turns source code into an executable program. For example, C programming code must be run through a compiler before the computer can recognize the code as a program.

compression   A way to shrink files so they don't take up as much space. Programs that do this include **compress** and **pack**.

concatenate   To combine two or more sequences of characters into a single sequence.

control character   A character you make by holding down the CTRL key while pressing another key.

core dump   A quaint phrase describing a memory listing produced when a program terminates abnormally. The term originated decades ago when magnetic cores were used for memory storage.

current directory   The starting point for path names that don't begin with **/**. A filename by itself is assumed to refer to a file in the current directory. Also called the **working directory**.

current job   The job most recently started or stopped. When you use the **jobs** command to see a list of jobs, the current job will be marked with a plus sign (**+**).

daemon   (pronounced "demon") A program that's invisible to users but works in the background performing important housekeeping tasks. **Daemons** manage everything from networking to printing to notifying you of incoming mail.

default   A value or state assumed when no other is supplied.

dot (.) files   Files that are read when you log in. If you use the C shell, it will read **.cshrc** and **.login**. Bourne shell reads **.profile**. Korn shell uses **.profile** and **.kshrc.** Dot files set up your environment, and are "hidden" from the ordinary **ls** command.

double quote   The " character. This is used around a UNIX command to instruct the shell to do variable and command substitution but no other interpretation. See also **single quote**.

dumb terminal   A terminal that has no processing power of its own. It usually doesn't have any nice stuff like a mouse or a screen that can do graphics either.

end-of-file (EOF) character   The character that indicates the end of a file. In UNIX, it's the combination CTRL-D.

environment variable   A shell setting that makes up part of your environment. For example, one environment variable can be the designation of a particular directory as your **HOME** directory.

escape   A character, usually a backslash or a tilde, that gives a special meaning to the character or characters after it.

etc   Directory containing everything but device files and program files.

execute permission   A setting for an executable file that denotes who can run the program.

filesystem   A set of files stored on a disk or one partition of a disk. A system has one root filesystem containing files and subdirectories, and may have additional filesystems mounted on it. Each filesystem contains files and subdirectories and these subdirectories in turn may contain further subdirectories. Any directory can hold files.

filter   A type of UNIX program that takes input from one file and provides output to the display or another file. The **more** and **sort** commands are commonly used filters.

foreground   A program that has control of your terminal. In UNIX, the default is to run commands in the foreground.

fork   When UNIX starts a new process, it does so by creating a child process. This is called *forking*.

ftp   *F*ile *t*ransfer *p*rotocol. A protocol that defines how to transfer files from one computer to another, it's most often used to describe a program that moves files using the file transfer protocol.

gateway   A computer that connects two or more networks and relays messages and other communications from one network to another.

globbing   The Berkeley term for *file substitution*.

GNU   *G*nu's *N*ot *U*NIX. A freely available substitute for UNIX. See also **Linux**.

grave   The character ´. Also called a *prime,* it is used for command substitution. Not the same as a single quote (').

header   The first part of an email message that gives information about the message such as the sender's name and when it was delivered. Can also refer to a descriptive block of information at the beginning of an archive file.

hidden file   A file beginning with a dot (**.login**, for example) that's not normally returned by the **ls** command.

history   A record of previous commands maintained in the computer's memory. Only in the C and Korn shells.

home   The environment variable containing the full path name of your home directory.

home directory   The directory the user is deposited in after logging in. This is set with the **home=** command in the **.profile** file.

host   A computer that provides services to other computers.

hostname   The name of your UNIX system.

HP/UX   A version of UNIX made by Hewlett-Packard.

I/O   Input and output. Information going into or coming out of a computer or program.

inode   Pronounced "eye-node," it's short for information node. A data structure that describes a file—where the file is stored, how long it is, and so forth. In any filesystem, the number of inodes, and therefore the maximum number of files, is set when the filesystem is created.

input mode   The mode in which a text editor accepts input and includes it in the edited file. The opposite of **command mode**.

job   The contents of one command line, no matter how complex. For example,

```
cat perl.tar.Z | zcat | tar xvf -
```

is one command line, hence one job, even though it's formed from three processes. This is the definition used in most UNIX documentation, though real people tend to use the terms *job*, *process*, and *program* interchangeably.

job control   Changing the status of a job. This includes starting, stopping, killing, or moving between the foreground and the background.

job shell   A superset of the Bourne shell devoted to job control.

kernel   The core of the operating system that interacts directly with the computer. The *kernel* allocates resources, maintains the filesystem, and manages the computer's memory.

kill character The character that when typed causes the current line to be deleted.

kludge Rhymes with "huge." A program or a feature that doesn't work as well as it should or gives the impression of being jerry-rigged. Not something the programmer is especially proud of.

Korn shell An enhanced version of the Bourne shell written by David Korn. Its program name is **ksh** and it prompts with a **$**.

library A set of commonly used C-language functions.

link An entry in a directory, consisting of a file identifier that names a file in the directory and an *inode* number.

Linux A freely available version of UNIX.

logging in The process of making a connection to a UNIX machine.

.login file See **dot (.) files**.

login name The name you use when logging into a UNIX system.

login shell The shell that's called on your behalf when you log in.

mailbox A file where messages are stored by a mailer.

mailer A program for sending and receiving email.

man page A file of information about a UNIX command. The **man** command displays technically detailed information about all UNIX commands.

meta key A specified key used with other keys to create additional key combinations. On a PC keyboard, ALT is the *meta key*.

metacharacter A character used in a regular expression or in a shell command that has a special meaning rather than standing for itself. For example, > is a *metacharacter* in a shell command that stands for output redirection.

Motif A graphical user interface created by the Open Software Foundation and based on the X Window System.

mount Make a filesystem available to users either locally or remotely.

NFS *N*etwork *F*ile *S*ystem. Software that allows UNIX and many non-UNIX systems to share files and printers via a TCP/IP network in a way that makes them appear local to the user.

named pipe A kind of file that behaves like a *pipe* and exists independently of any process. Many different processes can read from it and write to it.

newline The character that marks the end of a line in most UNIX files. You can usually produce a *newline* at your terminal by pressing either the ENTER key or CTRL-J.

null character The character whose binary representation is all zeros. By convention, it's used to mark the end of a string.

option An indicator that can be attached to a command to modify what the command does. Options usually begin with a dash (-). The terms *option* and *switch* are more or less interchangeable. An option can have several settings while a switch usually has two: on or off, enabled or disabled.

ordinary file A text or data file with no special characteristics. The most common type of file in the UNIX system.

orphan A process that keeps running even when its parent process has been killed.

packet A portion of a message that's transmitted as a unit over a network.

pager   A program that breaks its input into screen-size chunks and sends these pieces to your terminal, waiting for confirmation after each one.

parameter   A variable in the shell script that corresponds to an argument passed to the script.

parent process   A process that generates another process.

parse   To split into pieces to interpret.

perl   Another programming language geared toward text manipulation.

permissions   A security tool that controls who can access or change a file.

pipe   A connection between two processes that passes the output of the first to the input of the second. Signified by the pipe (|) character.

pipeline   A sequence of processes connected by *pipes*.

prime   Another name for the accent *grave*.

process   A single stream of computer instructions. One *job* may be built from several different *processes*.

.profile   See **dot (.) files**.

prompt   A character used by the shell to show that it's waiting for input. In addition, some programs provide their own unique prompts.

queue   A waiting line, the most common variety of which is the printing *queue*.

quote   See **double quote, grave, single quote**.

real-time   Right now as opposed to whenever the computer gets around to it.

recursive   A program or routine that repeats an action over and over. For example, the **find** program moves through a directory tree *recursively*, doing something in every directory.

redirection   Taking the output of a command and sending it somewhere other than the default location.

regular expression   An expression used to specify a set of *strings* being searched for. Regular expressions use *metacharacters* to specify variables.

reset string   A *string* that can be sent to a crazy mixed-up terminal to restore it to sanity.

root   Another name for the superuser.

root directory   The main, top-level directory of a filesystem. All the files in the system are either in the *root directory* or in a subdirectory of the root directory (or a subdirectory of a subdirectory and so on).

SCO   A version of UNIX made by The Santa Cruz Operation.

sed   Yet another programming language geared toward text manipulation.

server   In a distributed filesystem, a computer that supplies files and services to other computers.

shell   A program that reads and interprets commands from the user into instructions the computer can understand. Popular shells include the Bourne, Korn, and C shells.

shell script   A file that contains a list of UNIX shell commands. When you run a shell script, you're telling UNIX to execute every command in the list.

single quote   The ' character. This is not the same as the **grave** (`). The single quote is used around the part of the command line where the shell should do no interpretation.

slash   The / character. It separates elements in a path name. See also **backslash**.

Solaris   A version of UNIX made by Sun Microsystems.

string   A sequence of characters.

superuser   The person logged in under the name **root** who has permission to access any file and carry out other operations not permitted to mere mortals.

swapping   Using the hard disk as temporary storage when RAM is at a premium.

switch   See **option**.

system administrator   The person responsible for keeping the UNIX system running smoothly and securely.

TCP/IP   *T*ransport *C*ontrol *P*rotocol/*I*nternet *P*rotocol. A network protocol used to link UNIX and non-UNIX computers worldwide over a wide variety of media from high-speed optical network cabling to regular phone lines.

terminal   A screen and keyboard connected to a computer somewhere else.

terminal emulator   A program that enables a big powerful computer to act like a small, dumb one. Typically, a PC can run a terminal emulator so you can use another computer running UNIX.

timestamp   UNIX stores the time when a file was last modified, accessed, or had a change to its *inode*. These times—especially the time of modification—are called *timestamps*.

toggle   Turning features on or off.

truncate   To cut or shorten. For example, the instruction to truncate a file after line 20 means to remove all lines after line 20.

UUCP (UNIX-to-UNIX System Copy)   Program that copies files from one system to another over ordinary phone lines.

vi   A very powerful text editor that's packaged with most UNIX systems.

window manager   X Window program that defines how other programs appear and behave onscreen.

Windows 95   A popular 32-bit graphical operating system for PCs, made by Microsoft.

Windows NT   A cousin of Windows 95, with enhanced networking capabilities.

working directory   The directory you're currently in. The **pwd** command tells you your working directory.

X server   A program that draws the screen display if you use the X Window System or one of its relatives.

X terminal   A terminal that can act as an X server but relies on a machine elsewhere on the network for most of its computing power.

X Window System   Graphical windowing system developed by MIT that's the basis for fuller interfaces such as Motif or Open Look.

Xterm   A popular X Window program that provides a command-line interface to the UNIX operating system.

Appendix D

Resource Guide

BOOKS

UNIX Primers

These books are not about one particular feature or flavor of UNIX, but about the subject in general. We have seen many others, but these are the ones we liked best.

Abrahams, Paul W. and Bruce R. Larson. *UNIX for the Impatient, Second Edition.* Reading, MA: Addison-Wesley, 1996.

An excellent starting place if you already know a little UNIX and want to learn a lot more. Dense at times, irreverent at others, but covers almost everything at least a little, and many things quite well. One of our favorite references.

Christian, Kaare and Susan Richter. *The UNIX Operating System, Third Edition.* New York, NY: John Wiley & Sons, Inc., 1994.

A widely available introduction to UNIX concepts and techniques that includes history, basic concepts, and sections on topics of major interest (shells, shell scripts, text editors, **sed** and **awk**, etc.).

Gilley, Daniel. *UNIX in a Nutshell: A Desktop Quick Reference for System V & Solaris 2.0, Second Edition.* Cambridge, MA: O'Reilly & Associates, 1992.

Dense but comprehensive. Covers almost everything with good examples. A valuable reference to have on your desktop.

Glass, Graham. *UNIX for Programmers and Users: A Complete Guide.* Englewood Cliffs, NJ: Prentice Hall, 1993.

Another good overview of UNIX topics with sections on various shells, utilities, networking, and programming tips.

Nutshell Handbook Editors & Jerry Peek. *UNIX Power Tools*. New York, NY: Bantam, 1993.

Includes a CD-ROM with all sorts of goodies on it. An excellent book for those who are beyond the beginner stage. The organization is a bit difficult to get used to, but it seems to work in the end.

The Waite Group. *UNIX Papers for UNIX Developers & Power Users*. Carmel, IN: Sams, 1987.

This collection of papers by various authors is a bit uneven, but contains some excellent materials that you may want to consult someday. The paper on shells is particularly noteworthy.

Vendor-Specific UNIX Books

Many of the books written and oriented toward a specific vendor's implementation of UNIX are nonetheless good general references. Here are some we use:

Cutler, Ellie. *SCO UNIX in a Nutshell*. Cambridge, MA: O'Reilly & Associates, 1994.

The SCO version of the *UNIX in a Nutshell* book. Just as comprehensive, just as dense, still a good book to have on your desk and one of the first we pull out if the **man** page wasn't quite enough.

Heslop, Brent D. and David Angell. *Mastering Solaris 2*. Alameda, CA: Sybex, 1993.

Interesting mostly as an operating system moving from BSD to AT&T style, but has a useful command reference.

Russel, Charlie and Linda L. Gaus. *SCO OpenServer: The Windows Network Solution*. Upper Saddle River, NJ: Prentice Hall PTR, 1997.

A nuts-and-bolts guide to setting up and maintaining a completely functional SCO-based network. Humorous, accessible, and generally a valuable reference to have on hand.

Spicer, Peter. *Inside SCO UNIX, Second Edition*. Carmel, IN: New Riders Publishing, 1993.

Has an excellent and easily understood command reference. Generally pretty accessible.

UNIX Architecture/Design/History/Culture

Andleigh, Prabat K. *UNIX System Architecture*. Englewood Cliffs, NJ: Prentice Hall, 1990.

A good reference on UNIX subsystems and internals. Well-organized and useful for those knotty UNIX-specific questions that you hope will never haunt you.

Bach, Maurice J. *The Design of the UNIX Operating System*. Englewood Cliffs, NJ: Prentice Hall, 1986.

Another indispensable reference covering topics that include the UNIX buffer cache, internal representation of files, process scheduling, memory management, and the I/O subsystem. Not as well organized as the book above, but more comprehensive.

Gancarz, Mike. *The UNIX Philosophy*. Boston, MA: Digital Press, 1995.

One man's attempt to distill a "philosophy of UNIX." Interesting if and when you should find yourself in a philosophical frame of mind.

Libes, Don and Sandy Ressler. *Life with UNIX. A Guide for Everyone*. Englewood Cliffs, NJ: Prentice Hall, 1989.

An excellent source for material on the history and culture of UNIX. Includes a lot of information about Usenet.

Salus, Peter. *A Quarter Century of UNIX*. Reading, MA: Addison-Wesley, 1994.

A valuable source of information on the history of UNIX as told to the author by its "mothers and fathers." Contains transcripts of fascinating interviews.

The Korn Shell

Always one of our favorite topics, and a source of both satisfaction and frustration.

Korn, David G. and Morris I. Bolsky. *The Korn Shell Command & Programming Language*. New York, NY: Prentice Hall, 1989.

Written by the guys who should know, this is a good book, though not for beginners.

Rosenberg, Barry. *Korn Shell Programming Tutorial*. Reading, MA: Addison-Wesley, 1991.

Good coverage of a number of topics. Stronger as a tutorial than as a reference.

Rosenblatt, Bill. *Learning the Korn Shell*. Cambridge, MA: O'Reilly & Associates, 1993.

A good intermediate-level book, with clear explanations. Covers interactive command-line use as well as shell programming.

Valley, John. *UNIX Desktop Guide to the Korn Shell*. Carmel, IN: Sams, 1991.

Seems to be more about the Bourne shell than the Korn shell in places, and covers more general UNIX topics than one would expect in a shell-specific book.

UNIX Text Editors

Another favorite subject, and an area where we are constantly looking for new resources.

Cameron, Deb and Bill Rosenblatt. *Learning GNU Emacs*. Cambridge, MA: O'Reilly & Associates, 1991.

A good book for beginning-to-intermediate Emacs users, compared to most of the books out there which seem to be much too dense.

Dougherty, Dale and Tim O'Reilly. *UNIX Text Processing*. Cambridge, MA: O'Reilly & Associates, 1987.

Yet another valuable contribution from O'Reilly & Associates. This tutorial on UNIX editors and formatters includes coverage of **nroff**, **troff**, **tbl**, **eqn**, **pic**, **vi**, **ex**, **sed**, and **awk**.

Hewlett-Packard Company Staff. *The Ultimate Guide to the VI and EX*. Redwood City, CA: Benjamin-Cummings Publishing Co., 1990.

Perhaps not the ultimate guide, but certainly a good one. Covers **vi** thoroughly and well.

Lamb, Linda. *Learning the vi Editor*. Cambridge, MA: O'Reilly & Associates, 1991.

A comprehensive and useful volume. It includes an invaluable pull-out quick reference card that's dog-eared from overuse.

X Window System

Cutler, Ellie and Daniel Gilley, et al. *The Xwindow System in a Nutshell*. Cambridge, MA: O'Reilly & Associates, 1992.

"In a nutshell" is perhaps a little optimistic for this tome, but it's a handy book all the same.

Quercia, Valerie and Tim O'Reilly. *X Window System Users Guide, Fourth Edition*. Vol. 3. Cambridge, MA: O'Reilly & Associates, 1993.

This is a huge volume and it's just one of the many books oriented toward the programmer of X. Its principal virtue is that it provides a good reference for users. Doesn't cover Motif or OpenLook at all, but does cover the **twm** window manager that comes with X.

Southerton, Alan. *The Shell Hacker's Guide to X & Motif: Custom Power Tools & Window Manager Tricks*. New York, NY: John Wiley & Sons, Inc., 1993.

Not as much about X as about how to make Motif jump through some interesting hoops.

Miscellaneous Useful Books

Aho, Alfred V., et al. *The AWK Programming Language*. Reading, MA: Addison-Wesley, 1988.

Written by the authors of the language, it is comprehensive but not always comprehensible. But an essential reference.

Dougherty, Dale. *sed & awk*. Cambridge, MA: O'Reilly & Associates, 1990.

Dense but excellent coverage that ties these two important resources together.

DuBois, Paul. *Using csh & tcsh*. Cambridge, MA: O'Reilly & Associates, 1995.

The essential guide for those of you who prefer the cshell.

Farrow, Rik. *UNIX System Security: How to Protect Your Data and Prevent Intruders*. Reading, MA: Addison-Wesley, 1991.

Clear explanations of UNIX system security issues and potential solutions.

Garfinkel, Simson and Gene Spafford. *Practical UNIX Security*. Cambridge, MA: O'Reilly & Associates, 1991.

A good overview of system security issues and solutions.

Schwartz, Randal. *Learning Perl*. Cambridge, MA: O'Reilly & Associates, 1993.

An excellent tutorial coverage of perl for the person new to the language.

Wall, Larry and Randal Schwartz. *Programming Perl*.
Cambridge, MA: O'Reilly & Associates, 1991.

Too dense by far for the beginner, but an excellent reference once you get going.

Other Books

Probably the single best resource, when you just want a quick answer to something, is the **man** page on that particular program. Nine times out of ten, this will be all the information you need. If you prefer hard-copy books, however, the UNIX manuals that come with your system are the same **man** pages, all pulled together into a book. The only problem is, they are probably taking up several feet of space on your system administrator's desk.

However, if you ask nicely, there are frequently additional copies floating around that you can use. Or you can even order a whole set if you want to be ostentatious about it. But be warned that anyone with official manuals on his or her desk is likely to end up becoming the next system administrator. Don't say we didn't warn you.

ONLINE RESOURCES

The vast world of the Internet offers an almost unlimited resource for the UNIX user. But it can be an intimidating place, especially for the person moving to UNIX from a PC. In the commercial online world, there is CompuServe which has several UNIX-related forums. For general UNIX stuff, the UNIX Forum (GO UNIXFORUM at any ! prompt) is excellent, with lots of help and tips. For those using SCO, the SCO Forum (GO SCOFORUM) is outstanding. We found this to be among the very best of the CompuServe forums, and the Libraries have all the latest updates for SCO users, as well as precompiled versions of many popular programs.

For obtaining programs in source code, we were able to find much of what we wanted available for anonymous ftp from **ftp.uu.net**. Another good source is **archive.cis.ohio-state-edu**, and for precompiled SCO versions of many programs we're indebted to Bill Campbell and **ftp.celestial.com**.

Index

! (bang), 47
" (double quotes), 75-76
(pound sign), 46
(pound sign) pattern-matching
   operator, 76
$ (dollar sign)
     changing prompt from, 73-75
     identifying shells and, 14
$str:=expression operator, 203
% (percent sign), 14
' (single quotes)
     changing prompts and, 73-74
     defined, 75
* (asterisk), 139
. (dot) command, 53
. (dot) directories, 33
. (dot) files, 22-23
.. (dot-dot) directories, 33
' (grave quotes), 76
~ (tilde) shortcut, 40

A

About
     sed programming language,
      245-246
     this book, 7
Add LPR compatible printer dialog
   box (Windows NT), 178
Add Printer Wizard dialog box
   (Windows NT), 177
Advanced network emulations,
   172-178
     adding TCP/IP printing to
      Windows NT, 176-177
     advatages
       of NT domains, 174
       of workgroups, 174-175
     filesystems
       NFS exported, 176
       NT with UNIX users,
        175-176
       UNIX with Windows
        clients, 175
     NFS technology, 172, 173, 176
     printers
       sharing between
        UNIX and Windows
        NT, 176

       using Windows NT
        printers from
        UNIX, 177-178
     SMB technology, 172, 173
     UNIX servers
       available to Windows
        users, 172-173
       as part of NT domain,
        173-174
       as part of Windows
        workgroups, 174
alias command, 251
Aliases
     creating for rm command, 4-5,
      185-186
     for DOS and Windows NT
      commands in Korn shell,
      181
     setting permissions with, 31
     tips for using, 77
     for using DOS commands in
      UNIX, 80-82
ANSI escape sequences for
   changing colors, 79
:args command, 47
Arithmetic operators for Korn
   shell, 200
ash shell, 222
Asterisk (*), as wildcard, 139
at command, 111-112, 251
Autoindent, 60
Automating repetitive tasks, 245
awk programming language,
   239-242
     books about, 298
     example of using, 240-242
     origin of name, 239
     perl and, 243-244
     syntax for invoking, 239-240

B

Background jobs, 101, 106-108
     checking status of, 106
     moving to foreground, 107
     redirecting output and error
      messages to a file, 108-109
     sending jobs to background,
      106, 108

     using tee command with, 109
BACKSPACE key, 12
Backups, 183-184, 191-195
     of configuration files, 133
     file, 5
     of hard disk, 192
     tape or floppy, 193-194
     tar command for, 193-195
     UNIX and, 191
Banner pages, 88
bash (Bourne Again) shell, 221-224
     displaying current directory
      in, 222-224
     startup files for, 222
     values for PS1 shell variable,
      223
bg command, 252
Books about UNIX, 293-299
     architecture, design, history,
      and culture, 295
     Korn shell, 296
     miscellaneous, 298
     UNIX manuals, 299
     UNIX primers, 293-294
     UNIX text editors, 296-297
     vendor-specific, 294-295
     X Window system, 297-298
Bourne Again Shell. *See* bash shell
Bourne shell, 13, 14
     emulating on Windows NT,
      179
     running crontab script from,
      189
     using at command with, 112
Buffers
     named, 57
     paste, 56

C

c (change) command, 52
C shell, 13, 14
     changing prompts, 76-77
     customizing start-up scripts
      for, 72-73
     emulating on Windows NT,
      179
cal command, 252
Caldera Linux, 215-216